FRIDA

Art, and One Woman's Triumph Over PTSD

Eli N. Weintraub

Lotus Flower
B O O K S

Advance Praise for Frida and Me

"I cried when I read this book. Eli Weintraub grabs you with a memoir that reads like a fast-paced novel, and just doesn't let go. What an amazing journey, and what fortitude this young woman called upon, to find her life again after she nearly lost it. This is a powerful true story!" – Connie Shelton, *USA Today* bestselling author

"A must-read! Eli reveals her early life, months in Mexico studying art, and then the trauma of near death after a horrible bus accident and the physical and emotional damage that resulted. She is courageous in revealing her deep soul searching experiences and years of healing, ultimately with the help of her compassionate counselor and art therapist." – Judy Wright, MS, Program Manager of the University of New Mexico's Employee Health Promotion Program (retired)

"*Frida and Me* movingly describes the process Eli and her therapist undertook in their work together, using art to enable Eli to assemble the pieces of her shattered self that were beyond words. The art Eli created during her healing journey is beautifully displayed in the book, helping readers better understand her inner experience as she processed her traumas. Eli poignantly describes the confusion, disorientation and disconnection from self a person with PTSD lives with, and how lost they feel when they don't understand what has happened to them. I found this personal and inspiring account beautifully written and hard to put down [and] will recommend *Frida and Me* to clients, their families and therapists." —Laurel Parnell, Ph.D., director, Parnell Institute for EMDR, and author of *Rewiring the Addicted Brain*

"An astonishing story of art's abilities to heal physical and psychic trauma. The artwork and accompanying narrative of Frida and Me carry the reader through the artist/author's difficult journey following a horrific bus accident. The account courageously highlights the witness of art in service of the soul." – Linney Wix, Ph.D., ATR-BC, Professor Emerita

"I was moved by Eli Weintraub Maurx's story and the courageous healing work that she undertook, using art. She was able to trust the honesty and depth of her powerful images, and my hope is that her story will inspire others to use creative expression in their healing journeys." —Deborah Schroder, ATR-BC, LPAT

FRIDA AND ME

Art, and One Woman's Triumph Over PTSD

Eli N. Weintraub

Lotus Flower
BOOKS

Frida and Me
Published by Lotus Flower Books, an imprint of
Columbine Publishing Group LLC
PO Box 416, Angel Fire, NM 87710

Book layout and design by Secret Staircase Books
Cover illustrations © Ceuzo, Rostislav Dubina, Photowitch, and
Roberto Atzeni
Interior illustrations © Nancy Eli Weintraub Maurx

First trade paperback edition: September, 2019
First e-book editions: September, 2019

Publisher's Cataloging-in-Publication Data

Weintraub, Eli N.
Frida and Me / by Eli N. Weintraub
p. cm.
ISBN 978-1945422690 (paperback)
978-1945422706 (e-book)

1. Memoir. 2. Memoirs, Jewish. 3. Memoirs, Women.
4. Mental Health--Depression. 5. Post traumatic stress disorder. 6. Art
therapy. 7. Trauma and healing. I. Title

Weintraub, Eli N., Memoir.

For Mom and Dad
Thank you for all your blessings and courage. I carry you forward within, and hope this book helps the road be a little less bumpy for those in crisis.

Acknowledgements

There have been many in my past that touched my life and made me who I am today.

I want to thank my family for hanging in there during the significant trials and tribulations resulting from my accident and continuing to be a steady, loving force in my life.

Barbara Sturgill, who passed shortly after my therapy work with her, remains a daily blessing in my heart.

Thank you to the Stratton family for all the supportive love of my youth.

Thank you to my husband for the great years we've had together building, living and loving. You grounded me and taught me that 'I can'. Thanks to my publishing team at Lotus Flower Books, who helped me fulfill this goal of writing my story. Your compassionate support and encouragement allowed me to dream bigger and believe in myself.

A big shout out to all the nurses, doctors, therapists and medical workers who give life every single day. Take care of yourselves too!

To all my friends who have encouraged me to walk another step forward even when I thought I was going backwards, you have been the threads of my life tapestry. Thank you for being a part of my life.

Author's note: My birth name was Nancy, and that is how I refer to myself as this story opens.

View from Los Alamos, New Mexico -- The Mesa

Prologue

Like many people, I had a vision for my life's journey. I would get an education, pursue a profession, meet my soul mate, have two or three babies, be surrounded by loving family and friends, travel, help my community, grow old with my husband, and pass our legacy to our grandchildren. Of course there would be trials and tribulations, alterations to plans and gloomy days included. That's life.

Little did I realize how differently it would all turn out.

I grew up in Los Alamos, New Mexico, and had a great childhood, tagging along after three older brothers. They helped to instill a fearless tomboy spirit in me, as I had a tendency to rebel against the confines put on girls. I wanted freedom, like the freedom my brothers enjoyed. This resulted in rebellion based in reaction instead of choice.

As soon as I was out of high school, I went against my parents' orders and traveled to Mexico to attend a language and art school in San Miguel de Allende. Other than the terrible state of my relationship with the parents, the experience was more amazing than I could have dreamed.

I was immersed in the Mexican culture—creating art, learning Spanish, and developing character and maturity. Horizons felt unlimited and my potential soared. A final whirlwind round of travel and I would be on the way home to finish university.

Then the bus crashed.

The doctors worked to save me as I came within a few hours of dying. I survived five surgeries in a three month hospital stay. Pain, infection, loss, unconsciousness, medication—all laid a new foundation of who I have become. I still struggle with many triggers and body alterations from that era. Nothing has ever been the same.

I tried for months to do as I was advised, but nothing fit anymore and I just wanted to flee. During the next ten years, I lived in thirteen homes across different states, lost in a muddle of undiagnosed PTSD. I fell in and out of friendships, stayed distant from the family and sought peace. There was self-abuse, bad choices, risky people and behaviors. Oftentimes, the peace of death seemed more inviting than the difficulties of living.

When I encountered the story and the art of Mexican artist Frida Kahlo, I knew I had met a kindred spirit. Then, by complete serendipity, I met Barbara Sturgill, a counselor who used art therapy in her sessions. We began working on my trauma and, over a five year period, art helped put me back together so that I could be a functional part of society.

I began writing about this process in 2014, contacting some of the people from the past, unable to connect with others. I've used real names when permission was granted, others have been fictionalized to protect their privacy. All the events are true and are told as they happened. During portions of the story where I was unconscious or not present, I have recounted exactly what was told to me by the people who shared the journey with me. This book is about that journey and my proven experience using art as a tool to help overcome the overwhelming patterns of PTSD. I literally have art and art therapy to thank for saving my life.

I wrote this book for all the people who could benefit from the knowledge that art can help heal trauma. It is for survivors of trauma, their families, friends, caretakers, therapists and professionals. My wish is that it will help prevent such lengthy dysfunctional outcomes as I suffered. Read my story and please share it with anyone who is hurting.

With blessings,
Eli Nancy Weintraub

Chapter 1

The Rebel

Austin, Texas, 1992

As I stood offstage in the wings waiting to present my artwork at the Psychology Symposium, amazed that this group of professionals would want to hear what I had to say, I couldn't help but reflect upon what had brought me here. After five years of art therapy and the intuitive direction of the artist Frida Kahlo, I had found peace after many years of distress. I remembered back to the innocent young girl I had been and her amazing journey.

Los Alamos, New Mexico, August 1976

I clamped my arms across my chest and sent my parents a steady glare. "Melinda's parents are letting her go. It's a language and art school, Dad, and the chance to experience a different culture. San Miguel de Allende is a beautiful Mexican town. I'm nineteen and I'm going."

"Nan, you will not trot off to some art school in another country, a third world country at that. I don't care if the President says it's okay; it's not okay with us." My father waved his finger in my face. "You will continue your education at UNM and do as we say. We are providing the funds for you to make something of yourself, you owe us respect. End of conversation." With that, he turned and walked away, ordering my mother to follow.

Mom turned to me. "Listen to us. We love you and only want the best for you. You have so much potential. Mind your father; it's in your best interest. You can do what you want after you graduate." Her eyes were intense and sad; she'd known something like this was going to happen.

Dad was hard on me, probably because I was so like him. We fought all the time, much more than my three older brothers ever dared to. Mom was tired of being caught in the middle and trying to keep the peace, but she loved us both dearly.

I didn't want to hear Mom's words of reason. "I will learn Spanish, along with the arts, and that will help me find work here in New Mexico. I'm going. I will find a way. Dad hates me, he hates that I'm a girl, he hates that I have a mind of my own, unlike my brothers." My temper rose at the unfairness of it.

"Nan, don't bring your brothers into this; this is your battle only." Mom's voice became angry. "You think you know everything. If only you'd gone through what we and your grandparents have, you'd stop acting ugly and appreciate all that has been done for you."

Sarcastically I replied, "Yeah, if I ever even knew any of them, or if you or Dad would talk about your families. How am I supposed to know any of that, being raised on this isolated mesa where people ask if a Jew is a kind of Indian? Dad thinks the only good person is a scientist. Personally, I think they're all devoid of soul and need the arts to give them perspective on humanity, instead of figuring out how to blow everyone up with nuclear bombs."

Dad overheard and stormed in, grabbing me by the arm and yelling, "You snot-nosed kid, who do you think you are! I have worked my whole life to care for my family, past and present. You are grounded until further notice and won't be going anywhere for a long time. School starts in a few weeks, so no holidays for you this year." His grip was tightening, and I started crying as I silently vowed to be in Mexico by the first of the year.

Mom pleaded with Dad to let go of my arm and when he finally did, he gave me a deadly stare before leaving the room. I knew I'd dealt a serious blow to my father. He was a proud chemical engineer. From family lore, I knew he had a rough life and moved from the East Coast in 1945— to follow an opportunity with the labs and to escape his family.

But this was now, and I had my own life to lead.

Hot with anger, I ran outside to my favorite canyon overlook, stared into the distant Española valley, and contemplated what had just transpired with my father. I had no idea that my decision would change my life forever.

Chapter 2

Where I'm Comin' From

My paternal grandparents, David and Minnie Weintraub, immigrated to America in 1909 to avoid being persecuted by the Russians. Anti-Semitism was running rampant, forcing families to flee for their lives. Much of my family history is unknown from this period as towns were burned, wiping out records of entire populations. Those who did successfully arrive in America had their names changed, since no one could pronounce their given names. The trail of ancestry was lost and memories of that period were so horrible, many survivors didn't even want to remember.

David and Minnie settled in New Jersey, where my dad Lazarus (Larry) was born. Grandpa Weintraub started a jewelry business and eventually a clock shop, where Larry was expected to work to help support his mother and four sisters.

Grandpa Weintraub was strict and relentless with Larry in following his Jewish heritage through hours of Talmudic studies and Torah teachings. On one level, Larry loved the focused solitary time to learn and nurture his spiritual self, but he also felt the stirrings of youth. He knew he did not want to be a tradesman like his father, so he applied to Cooper Union, one of the best and most difficult universities, to pursue chemical engineering. He did it against his father's wishes.

Grandpa Weintraub thought the sciences were works of the devil. "One should apply his spiritual self to life, not let the mind lead," was his response. At sixteen, Larry was admitted with a scholarship as one of the youngest students and began his university studies with diligence, while continuing his religious studies at the synagogue. Life was hard during the years of the Great Depression, but he was a frugal man and was very determined. His frugality remained with him for life, and it taught me a skill which helped me survive with little.

* * *

Annette Goldberg (my mother) was the firstborn descendent of her family from Poland. "I was the special one. I was the first to be born on this continent in 1922 to carry the family lineage." Mom smiled as she fondly told me of her status. Little else was said.

Grandma Goldberg made all the children's clothes and was known as the Queen because she dressed so well. Annette was always dressed 'to the nines' in the latest fashions by her mother's talented hands. Ironically, Annette struggled with anything to do with sewing, other than mending or a hem … and even that was not fun for her!

Annette grew up enjoying family and friends and she wanted to make something of herself, so, as a young adult, she decided to attend secretarial school at nights in Jersey City.

Divine intervention happened when Annette's best friend, Silvia, asked her to go on a double date. After asking for permission and getting all gussied up, she opened the door to her future, Larry Weintraub. He was handsome, with dark hair and complexion, and a bit shy. They felt an instant attraction.

Much to the chagrin of both families, they fell in love immediately. Grandpa Goldberg liked Larry, but Grandma Goldberg did not, saying, "Annette, you need someone happier and more creative." Her mother felt he was too serious and moody for her tender special flower.

Grandpa Weintraub was also against their relationship, but for different reasons. He needed Larry to help rebuild the watchmaking shop and to care for his mother and sisters. But, Larry and Annette's marriage was meant to be. With cautious approval, they were wed in 1942 after he earned his chemical engineering degree at Cooper Union.

When the draft caught up with him he chose to enlist in the Navy. For the next four years the couple moved wherever they were sent. Once WWII ended, Annette and Larry returned to New Jersey to consider their next move.

Larry was approached with a unique job offer. In theory, it sounded like a dream come true; the reality was that they had to move across the country to the recently opened secret city of Los Alamos, New Mexico. It was the opportunity of a lifetime for an entry level research job, but the personal price was high: leave behind all they knew—family, friends, culture, religious centers—and move to a secluded mesa top in the middle of nowhere, doing secret work for the U.S. government.

No one on either side of the family supported this move. Grandpa Weintraub told Larry, "If you go, you will be doing the work of the devil and I won't have any part of it. Follow God, Larry, or all is lost! I need help caring for your mother and sisters. Be a good son and respect your father. I demand it!"

Larry was tired of the meddling family and the congested living in the city. He accepted the profitable job offer. Annette didn't want to go, but she loved Larry and respected his decision.

Larry went alone to New Mexico to start the job and get their new life started, with Annette to follow. Shortly after his departure Annette found out she was pregnant. Youth gave her the strength to overcome the temporary separation, but the family continually tried to talk her out of going away. The stress was not good for the pregnancy, and she became anemic and weak. One night she stayed at work too long and was forced to take the bus home in the rain. She caught a chill, ended up in the hospital, and lost the baby.

Everyone blamed Larry. Annette suffered a deep depression, during which she decided to join her husband in New Mexico as soon as possible. Larry was also depressed over the loss of their first child and was elated to hear his beloved was coming soon. He needed his 'cheney' (Yiddish for beloved) close. Larry had secured a small government house and awaited her arrival.

Annette boarded the train alone and started one of the hardest journeys of her life. Tears filled her eyes when she watched her family and friends disappear in slow motion, as she left her past and rode toward the future. She settled into her seat on the train.

Four days later, the train stopped in the middle of nowhere. There was a small wooden shack with a sign that said "Lamy, New Mexico, population 10." A young army officer got on board and called out, "Mrs. Weintraub, Mrs. Weintraub." Annette froze.

This young man couldn't be looking for her, but she slowly raised her hand to get his attention. He walked up to her, "I am here on behalf of Larry Weintraub to pick up his wife, Annette, and am charged with taking her to Los Alamos, which is about 60 miles away."

Annette got off the train, feeling in shock at her surroundings. Dirt beneath her high heels made her unsteady as she took the officer's arm to be led away to the vehicle. *There is absolutely nothing here except dirt. Where are the stores, the train station, the theaters, and the people? This air is so dry,* she thought as she coughed. *Please wake me up from this awful nightmare.*

The officer didn't say much and left her to her own thoughts as they headed toward the mountains in the distance. As they got closer to the blue-green mountains they followed a steep, narrow road that appeared to be hanging on the edge of an endless winding cliff. Annette removed her gloves and clenched the door and seat as they swerved back and forth. *I am sure I'm going to die on this road before I make it to Larry.*

Finally, they reached the top of a flat-topped plateau (called a mesa, she learned) and stopped at a guard tower and gate with armed soldiers who checked her papers and let them proceed through. It was a mess—dirt roads, no sidewalks, little square houses tucked up against magnificent wilderness with mountains encircling them. *Please, please let me wake up,* she thought. They pulled up to a long, official-looking trailer.

"Cheney, Cheney!" There was her handsome Larry, smiling and waving at her. She was awake and knew at once that this was the beginning of her new life.

Larry was beaming with pride as they entered the nondescript government house that resembled a shoe box. "Cheney," he said affectionately, "this is our new home." And with that, she put her fancy dresses and shoes away at the back of the closet and never wore them again.

* * *

I knew my father had it tough, but didn't think he should treat me the same way. Couldn't he see the parallels with his own desire to escape his strict father's demands? I often wished I had grandparents to stick up for me. But I had only met one grandfather when I was seven years old, too little to remember much. The relatives I did meet from the east coast seemed so foreign and sophisticated compared to people I encountered in my small home town. On the few occasions when I visited they'd say things like, "Fix yourself up, you look so frumpy." I constantly fought my weight already, taking after my mother's body type. Their comments hurt and I didn't try to know them better.

As I reflected on my feelings about Dad, the argument receded and the beauty of Los Alamos calmed me. The fresh scent of juniper filled the mountain air as I looked for piñon nuts. They were my favorite, with their subtle sweet flavor that reminded me of the essence of the earth and native peoples. The nuts brought back fond memories. Every year our family would grab a sheet and wander on the mesas looking for big piñon trees. The sheet would be placed under the tree, and my father and brothers would shake the branches, releasing the nuts from their cone hideaways. On a good year, the nuts were big, juicy, and plentiful. Other years they were scarce, little, and dry. Every seven years, the trees would have a bountiful harvest and we would feast on them, putting them in candy, cookies, pancakes and whatever else we could dream up. Once we got the nuts home, we would slowly roast them in the oven, giving them a delectable toasty flavor. Dad always did fun things with us and wasn't afraid to explore. We had fun back then, I remembered somberly.

Watching two ravens circle in the currents of the canyon, I felt a twinge of guilt for being so rude to my parents. I loved my mother dearly, but ever since I became a teenager, I hated my father. He placed so many restrictions on me, rules that my brothers never had to follow. I had to be home earlier, had stricter rules on whom I hung out with, and wasn't allowed to date, none of which applied to my brothers. Dad criticized anything cute I wore and I was regularly grounded for any infractions of Weintraub law. Then, one by one, each brother left the house for college and I was left alone with my parents. Feeling watched, under their magnifying glass, arguments increased daily. Everyone was stressed.

I resented the fact I couldn't even go to the football games to play my trumpet in the school band on Friday nights since I had to attend services at the Jewish Center. Dad wanted us all to have the same Jewish upbringing as his, which was impossible in a remote town with few Jews. It was hard waking up Christmas morning, knowing all my friends were having a warm family holiday while my brothers and I delivered the morning paper in the snow to all the happy present-opening families. I didn't like having different holidays. When I had to miss school for Rosh Hashanah and fast for Yom Kippur, I always felt like an outsider. I was tired of feeling like an outcast and decided it was time to take charge of my destiny.

My eyes scanned the canyons and mountains I had roamed with my brothers as a kid. I'd always felt much more akin to the animals and Native people who'd lived here before the science labs came. The spirit of the land captured me and I was enchanted by the wilderness, which I knew like the back of my hand. My brothers and friends and I were always sledding in the canyons, sighting wolves and cougars that sauntered through town, washing the dog with tomato juice after a night's encounter with a skunk. I loved the butterscotch-vanilla scent of the towering ponderosa pines; witnessing the impenetrable depth of a new moon sky with bazillions of stars and constellations made me feel small as a speck of sand. As a young teenager, I felt the sciences dismembered all of that, and there was no way I was going to be a part of this crime.

Adventure and travel had always filled my heart. I loved the family camping vacations all over the United States when Dad would load us up and venture off for weeks at a time. Mom never was fond of roughing it, but she loved seeing the sights and laughing with the family. Dad would cook over a fire-pit and teach us about survival in the wilderness. I loved being by Dad's side, helping. He was so much fun then. What happened to us? I hit puberty and that's when everything went to hell. Dad stopped being so close and started criticizing everything I thought and did. He wouldn't let me do what the boys did and it pissed me off. I had to say what was on my mind; it only seemed fair.

I thought back to a day when I was thirteen. Feeling my independence, I'd had an epiphany. Lying on my back on this same canyon overlook, watching the ravens circle in the currents, I felt a deep spiritual presence within me. The looming thunderheads shone with the brilliant colors of the sunset as the full moon rose on the opposite horizon. Suddenly I knew what was in the bottom of my soul and knew my destiny. I had the soul of a gypsy and I was meant to travel, to be close to nature, and to follow my artistic talents. In a flash, it was so clear.

* * *

It was hard, very hard, when Annette and Larry, aged 21 and 22, arrived in Los Alamos in 1945. The town had just been opened to the public after being government run during the course of the atom bomb development. Larry had the perfect credentials for research at the labs and immediately hit it off with his co-workers. Annette knew no one and felt very isolated. She cried all the time when Larry was at work and only cheered up when he finally got home, happy just to have someone to talk to. She gradually met other wives, some content, most not. Everyone felt very secluded and cut off from society at large.

Over the years, Annette and the other wives became each other's substitute family, developing close-knit relationships stronger than most families. The town itself was basic and vastly in need of improvement. In the beginning, the roads were dirt, often turning into foot-deep mud after snowmelt and during the summer rainy season. Houses were basic boxes or trailers of shabby construction. Most shopping, post, and medical business had to be done in Santa Fe, requiring an hour's drive off 'the hill.'

Surrounded by the beauty of the Jemez Mountains, with their red rock mesas and canyons that took one's breath away, bears, wolves, cougars, skunks, hawks, ravens, and countless other critters were part of the everyday life of this little town. It was surrounded by ancient native ruins that provided the backdrop for many weekend outings.

The four seasons were magical, but winter was the most difficult. Two to three feet of snow would drop at the end of October and not disappear until May. Summers were ideal, with green grass, fruit trees, and lazy days ending with magnificent sunsets. Fall brought the colors of the changing aspens, framed with a turquoise sky, and the fresh scent of pine. Annette learned to love the beauty, but it took many, many years.

The labs became a mix of government and private employees who all required strict confidential security clearance to work there. Even plumbers and electricians were not immune. Potential applicants' families, friends, neighbors, employers, and teachers would receive official government visits and interviews regarding their relationships and knowledge of these potential employees. These were the Cold War years.

Once hired, the employee was bound under contract to secrecy and only allowed to talk to co-workers regarding their work. They couldn't even talk about this work to other workers in other groups; this was to ensure the secrecy of the research projects. Larry used to tell Annette that no one knew who to trust because informers and spies were everywhere. Each work group became family to one another, and few socialized outside of that circle, which made their bonds even stronger. Larry was under threat of losing his job if he shared information, even with Annette. It was frustrating for her, but she made the best of it. He was a dedicated husband and she was his world.

She began to accept and embrace this new life, wearing local traditional Native American jewelry and Mexican skirts with peasant blouses.

They lost their second baby. He was one month old when he died.

Annette was depressed at the second loss, but her new friends stayed close and helped. She decided to get a job as a secretary to help busy her mind. Her skills were excellent and she landed a job in the document division of the patent office, working for Ralph Smith at Los Alamos National Labs; later she was a secretary to Edward Teller and Freddy De Hoffman, both nuclear physicists who had worked on the Manhattan Project. Teller also worked on the hydrogen bomb. Annette was proud, enjoyed the hubbub of the work environment and being privy to the internal notations and communications of these very powerful scientists. She overcame her grief and excelled in her job.

Communication was irregular with the families back home, who missed Annette and Larry, but life went on. Larry would receive regular letters from his father denigrating him for his choice to work in the sciences and predicting he was going to hell if he didn't change his ways. It was no wonder Larry didn't want much to do with his family.

After Annette and Larry's loss of two babies, finally, a son was born—Rick. He was exactly what Larry needed. They were so proud and happy. A period of bliss followed for several years. Rick was the first generation New Mexican in the family. Larry missed his religious studies and congregation from out East and wanted his son raised Jewish. He had met other Jews through work, and they all decided to meet for Sabbath prayer and studies. It started with seven men, who then brought their wives and families together for holidays. Soon, an old building was bought and deemed the Jewish synagogue. After five years, they had a congregation of fifteen families. Each father would take charge for a month at a time and run services. There was no rabbi in Los Alamos, so they did what they could.

Larry was a complicated man. He had a deeply religious spirit and was somehow able to combine it with the 'devil' of science. Since Annette's Jewish upbringing was very liberal, his strict ways were hard to enforce. She did what she could to be a good Jewish wife, but frankly, she wasn't much for organized religion. So, she focused on Jewish cooking and excelled. Her matzo balls were to die for and won many synagogue recipe contests. Social life consisted of potluck dinners and bridge games with their circle of friends.

Annette's next pregnancy was difficult. She was in bed often and her friends helped care for Rick on the bad days. She had a dream one night that her mother was coming to visit, but couldn't find her way. The next day she lost this baby, a girl. She was devastated. She'd been waiting for a daughter, but it wasn't to be. This was her third lost child and it was taking a toll on her spirit. The little family made one trip back East, to visit their families.

Annette saw the greatest changes in herself. The family saw it too. They saw a mature woman full of confidence, a committed wife and loving mother, who didn't dress as fancy as before. She still liked to look nice, but her styles were more relaxed. She still had her ever-present radiant smile, outlined with the usual red lipstick, but she had given up high heels and hats. She had put on a little weight from the pregnancies, but had a voluptuous figure still. Her mother made all her favorite meals, and they ate out at all their favorite restaurants. Then they went to his family, which was not so much fun.

Grandpa Weintraub was smitten with Rick but still angry with Larry for his choice of profession and for abandoning the family. He displayed his bitterness to his son regularly, and Larry withdrew and became moody. As the visit wore on, all three became anxious to leave. Annette was surprised that she was excited to go home—maybe she *was* losing her city ways. She gave her parents and siblings hugs and watched the family, waving somberly until they were out of sight. The mood in the car was quiet until, finally, upon seeing the mountains, they knew they were truly home.

* * *

Annette and Larry knew they wanted another child and Rick needed a sibling. Their blessings were answered double-fold with twin boys, Howard and Doug. Larry helped when he was home, but Annette took the lion's share of caretaking. This was in the era when bottles and diapers were boiled and nothing was convenient. Non-stop mothering wore her out, but the family was happy and healthy. Once the twins started walking and talking, they took over. It seemed as though they were in cahoots with each other. They would escape Mom and take off in opposite directions out the front door, sneak into cupboards, and wind up in the hospital from eating something bad, beating each other up, or breaking bones. It was endless.

Yet, Annette still wanted a girl. It was likely she would have another boy but she knew a girl was possible since she had lost the one girl baby and so decided to try one more time.

Finally, her wishes were answered with me, Nancy. Mom would no longer be alone in this family of males.

When I was a baby, until I grew to be a young girl, Mom use to say, "My girl is so sweet and never does anything wrong. Those boys, though, especially the twins, are trouble makers and are going to turn my hair white."

I was cute and loved to entertain to receive smiles and candies. I loved making people laugh and being the center of action. In grade school, I participated in plays, sports, and Girl Scouts. Going against Mom and Dad only led to spankings and groundings, so I tried my best to obey.

Rick was ten years older than I, so he wasn't around as much when I was growing up, but the twins were five years older and responsible for babysitting regularly. Rick resented babysitting, and I would always rat on him, but the younger boys thought I was cute and mostly didn't mind. The twins were mischievous and constantly playing jokes on me, getting into things they shouldn't, and pushing their luck. At first I was just a tag-along, but in time I learned from them, and when my teens hit—watch out world! Maybe it was being the youngest of four, the only girl, or perhaps it was just my nature, but I was much more gregarious than my siblings. I acted much more like another little boy, but Mom would not give up trying to sway, or if need be, force me to see the beauty of the 'feminine' side of life. It never worked.

Mom saw the gypsy spirit in me early, but she tried to redirect me and ignore its presence. When I came in after that day on the mesa and told her of the epiphany that I was born to be a gypsy, Mom almost choked. Immediately, she told me that gypsies were nothing to aspire to, they were thieves, and she tried convincing me that wasn't my path. Mom had a premonition of trouble ahead.

East Coast to the Southwest – Mom's style really changed!

Dad and Mom and the twins

Rick, Doug, Howard, and me circa 1959

Chapter 3

Escape Plan

Melinda, they won't let me go. I'm pissed. Why can't I be from *your* family? I'd love having a couple of sisters and supportive parents," I complained, as she looked into her bowl of melting ice cream.

"Yeah, but your brothers are cooler than my sisters ... and cute! Maybe my parents can talk to yours since we've lived abroad before," Melinda responded. She shoveled another dripping spoonful of ice cream into her mouth.

Answering Melinda's spoonful with my own, I thought out loud. "They won't listen. They are so stubborn. At least Dad is, maybe Mom can talk him into it. But Mom hates Mexico—it's dirty, she keeps saying. We got in a terrible argument and Dad grounded me for life."

"I hate your Dad; he's so mean to you. He never lets you do anything other than study. Let me talk to Mommy and Daddy to see if they will talk to them," Melinda said, tasting my ice cream.

"We can try, but I'm not optimistic. Dad's pretty set against the whole plan. I have to figure out something else," I replied with conviction, swiping a taste from her bowl.

Melinda and I had been friends since we were five years old. We lived around the block from one another and were a constant presence in each other's households. Together we roamed the canyons, shared all secrets, went on family vacations together, and were inseparable. I loved visiting Melinda's home, where life was centered on Melinda and her two older sisters. Like most girls, they played dolls and dress-up. I learned about what girls do from these games but still always felt different.

Frank and Shirley Han were from Minnesota and the nicest people I knew. They were so different from my parents. There was much less fighting and conflict in their home. The Hans loved me and welcomed me like a daughter.

Sometimes Mom would complain, "Nancy, you are never home. You shouldn't be over there so much." But she also hoped I might become less of a tomboy if I spent more time around girls. After raising three sons, Mom was so excited to finally get a daughter with whom she could share feminine activities. She tried to entice me into shopping for pretty clothes, but I would say, "This dress is scratchy, that dress looks so dorky, the other dress is too girly…" Mom would reply, "I'm so frustrated that my only girl doesn't like pretty dresses and prefers her brother's hand-me-down jeans and sweatshirts." I would shrug my shoulders and give a half smile. What could I say, it was true.

Mom was also jealous of Shirley Han, who had girls galore to enjoy; she even wished she could go over there and join in the female goings-on. "It's not fair. My life has been so much harder with three boys. Isn't Nan obligated to provide me some type of womanly satisfaction through shopping and primping?" Mom mused. More conflict followed when I would respond, "I'm not going to become girly; I like being a tomboy and I'm proud of it."

I enjoyed playing at the Hans, but I, like my brothers, was more adventurous. They liked getting dirty, climbing cliffs, playing with bugs, getting mischievous. They didn't seem as flighty as girls. The boys weren't pressured to shop with Mom and were granted more freedoms. Girls seemed fragile to me and I wasn't like that; my brothers made me tough, which in due time became a blessing.

Melinda and I approached her parents about talking to my parents about Mexico; hesitantly, the Hans agreed to speak with them. "Nancy, it is not our way to meddle in another family's decision, but since we would be visiting when you are in San Miguel, perhaps that information would settle them about your going. I will talk to them," Frank diplomatically said.

"Thank you, thank you, thank you. I owe you, big time!" I chirped with glee.

As I had feared, the talk didn't help and caused my parents some resentment toward the Hans.

"Melinda, I'm going anyway, I'm nineteen and don't need permission. I will use my savings and wait tables until we leave. I won't tell them until a couple of days ahead so I won't have to hear their complaints so long," I proclaimed with confidence.

"Oh, I don't know Nancy, what if they send the police after you?" Melinda snapped, twisting her hair with worry.

"They can, but I'll be long gone in another country and they won't be able to touch me!" the rebel in me proclaimed. "They will see in time that I'm okay and they'll be happy I've become fluent in Spanish and will have some new art skills when I join the work force. Maybe I'll even return to the university afterward. I'll pretend I've given in, work on the sly, and then—blam, off I go!"

"My parents aren't going to like that, Nancy. Lies are not okay."

"I'll tell them my parents are considering it but haven't made a final decision. Once we get close, they will have to deal with it, you'll see," the rebel concluded.

"Okay," Melinda hesitantly agreed, looking uneasy. "Your father deserves it, but not your mom. She's a sweetie, and I feel bad for her."

I had to agree, and also had a bad feeling in my gut. I took after my Dad's headstrong nature and wanted to follow my own gypsy yearnings, so I proceeded with the plan anyway.

My parents were surprised when I gave in so suddenly, but happily accepted my declaration with relief. They were proud I was going to work and start becoming a responsible young adult. The Hans hoped for the Weintraubs' reconsideration and proceeded to get Melinda's travel plans arranged. I made all my own travel arrangements, applied to the Instituto, and worked like a dog to get the money I needed for the trip.

Finally, the day came for me to tell my parents. After helping with dinner and dishes and acting the good respectful daughter, I sweetly requested, "Mom and Dad, can we discuss something in the den?" Both parents looked at each other with foreboding, nodded, and followed me.

"I love you both dearly and truly want your blessings for what I'm about to say. I am leaving for Mexico with Melinda on Saturday. I have made all the arrangements and earned the money to do it. I am going with or without your approval and wanted to show you respect by telling you what I'm doing instead of leaving a letter on the bureau."

Both parents gasped. Dad turned beet red and Mom turned pale white. They both were silent, which threw me, as I was accustomed to fights and yelling. My dad looked at me with hatred and Mom hung her head. Silence continued. Rebelliously, I remained silent, my chin jutting forward in defiance.

Finally Dad took a deep breath and quietly said, "I see there is nothing we can do to stop you, but know this decision will forever change our relationship. There will be no more financial help, and I now consider you an adult with all the responsibilities and consequences of your actions. You have hurt your mother and me beyond reason, so don't expect our blessings for your impudent behavior." With that, he got up and walked out.

I later learned that he was preoccupied with how familiar this felt, how similar to his own departure from family so long ago. He told me, years later, "This must have been how my father felt when I made my choice to leave home."

Mom burst into tears. "Please darling, don't do this, PLEASE! What if something happens to you down there and you don't come home?"

"Oh, Mom, don't get so dramatic. I will be fine. I am just going to school, only in another location. I promise to call and write regularly. The Hans will be coming down and can report. I love you, Mom. I'm sorry it had to be this way, but I am a young lady now and you have to learn to let go."

That made Mom cry even harder as she remembered all she let go of in leaving her family on the east coast so long ago. I approached her, and we both cried and hugged as if we would never see each other again.

Mom confided later that she and Dad clung to each other in bed as they hadn't in a long time. Few words were spoken between them except when Dad looked deep into her eyes and said, "We've come a long ways, Cheney," and lovingly kissed her.

Chapter 4

We've All Been There

After my big announcement about Mexico, I went to bed, but was far too distraught for sleep, even though I'd got what I wanted. Thoughts circled endlessly in my head. *That was weird. Dad didn't even yell or protest when I told him I was going. I feel bad doing this to Mom, she is such a sweetie. Why couldn't they just be supportive like the Hans? Now I feel so guilty.*

After suffering from that cycle for more than two hours, I bundled up and went outside to watch the stars. Luckily it was a moonless night, so the universe was brilliant with stars. I counted ten falling stars, and each wish was the same—bring peace to our hearts. Peace was everywhere else but there. When I saw a skunk scurry across the street, I finally returned to my bed and a fitful sleep.

I was up before everyone and left a note to say I was going for a walk. When I returned, my dad had left for work and Mom was doing the dishes with a heavy heart.

"Hey, Mom."

"Hi darling." I always loved when Mom called me that.

I slowly approached Mom and put an arm around her. "You okay?"

"I'll survive. I guess."

"I'm sorry for not doing what you want me to."

"We've all been there, darling, just give us time."

I wondered what that meant. I didn't know at the time they'd also gone against their parents. My heart eased a millimeter, and I buried my head in Mom's embrace. "I'll make you both proud of me, just wait and see."

The next week was tense and uncomfortable at home. Dad barely said a word and Mom moped. My guilt kicked in and I occupied myself as best I could to prepare for the trip. I thought often about Mom's comment 'We've all been there', but it didn't seem the time to probe.

* * *

I told Melinda all of this.

"That is weird," she said, "but now you get to go! I can't believe it. I never thought it would work out."

"I told you I was going, didn't I?" My inner rebel answered a bit curtly.

"Jeez, don't take it out on me. I'm your ally!"

"Sorry, guess I'm just out of sorts. I should be excited to go, but now I just have a heavy heart," I replied with my head in my hands.

Melinda came over and gave me one of those hugs that make everything better ... for the moment. I cried heartily in my friend's embrace, thinking how I wished I had a sister. I was sure she would be much more understanding than my three brothers. Their responses when I called to tell them what had happened were, "You asked for it. Why do you always have to start problems?"

"Great support in this family," I thought resentfully. "I'm going to Mexico, and at least Melinda and her family think it's a good idea. I'll show them how enriching an experience living abroad is. Everyone in my family is so conventional. No one has a gypsy spirit like me."

Nights were the worst, with endless cycles of guilt, but I was stubborn and defiant and didn't budge on my decision. My gypsy soul, whom I'd discovered on the canyon overlook, took the lead.

Finally, departure day arrived. The plan was that the Hans would drive us to El Paso where we two nineteen-year-old girls would cross the border at Juarez, catch a taxi to the train station and get 'all aboard' for a two day trip to Mexico City. From there we would take a bus to San Miguel de Allende, secure an apartment, and start school. It sounded so straightforward to the two of us, brimming with excitement.

"Nan, again, I am not in favor of this. I just need to say that," Dad said, tensely. "You call us weekly on Sunday nights, and I also expect a letter as frequently." His angry eyes suddenly turned glassy and sad, and with a broken voice he ended with, "I love you."

I couldn't believe Dad said that to me. I hadn't heard it since I was nine when he wouldn't let me sit on his lap anymore, which broke my heart. Then he said, "I love you always honey, remember that," which helped the hurt. The memories made me burst out in tears and hug Dad as long as he would let me.

Mom watched us embrace, and her tears let loose. "Darling, we love you, be safe and call … I love you … come home soon if it doesn't work out." We hugged each other for a long time, crying.

"I'll call and write regularly. I love you guys … don't worry, I'll be fine." I choked out the farewells between tears as the Hans's car pulled away. I turned to watch them get smaller and smaller in front of their home. They had their arms around each other and Mom's head was buried in Dad's shoulder. I fought back tears for a long time and everyone in the car remained silent. It was hard not to wonder whether this was the right move. I was hurting Mom and Dad as I never had before. I felt like such a bad daughter.

I compared myself to Melinda, who was doing the same thing and didn't have to bear any guilt at all. It wasn't fair, and that's when I started looking ahead to the adventure. Five hours of desert driving helped me process all that had just occurred. As I dozed into sleep, I pondered Mom's words once again. 'We've all been there, darling', and I wondered.

Chapter 5

Crossing Over

I woke up to see the Organ Mountains, and my spirit felt lighter after my deep slumber in the moving car. "Hello, sleeping beauty, ready for some food?" Shirley gently questioned. All the Hans were looking at me.

"Sure," I simply replied. I was feeling awkward and disoriented from sleep and the emotional hangover of leaving. "Where are we?"

Frank looked in the rearview mirror at me. "Outside of Las Cruces, and it's about thirty more miles to El Paso where we will spend the night. If you are hungry now we can stop or wait until we get to the hotel, Peanut." Mr. Han had always referred to me as Peanut since I was smaller than his daughters and was one of the 'peanut gallery.' I loved the endearment, coming from a father figure and so different from the critical tone of my own father.

"I can wait, so whatever you all want to do is fine," I replied, trying to not be a burden. The Hans were all much more relaxed and happy than when we'd departed, and it infected my mood. *This is really happening, wow!* I thought as my gypsy took the stage.

"Let's find some green chile enchiladas with an egg in El Paso," Frank offered. It was tradition on special occasions to take Melinda and me thirty miles from Los Alamos to Española to the Rio Grande Café for this dish. Sometimes they would take the old '57 Ford pickup and we rode in the back. Going home, we would cuddle under a sleeping bag and count falling stars. The most we ever counted in one trip was twenty. Now, everyone agreed to the suggestion and we eagerly forged ahead to El Paso.

* * *

My thoughts took over again. *This family is so different from mine. Like the time Melinda and I took the Ford booney riding among the mesas and piñon trees and we broke the axel. Mr. Han initially was cross but then laughed; my Dad would have killed us.* I was thankful for their presence in my life; they showed me what peaceful love was, and it nurtured my gypsy spirit.

I'd always had a fondness for the arts and speaking Spanish, so when a high school friend told me that her family had just returned from the art and Spanish institute in San Miguel de Allende, Mexico, I knew I had a destiny to fulfill there.

In the '60s and '70s, my parents would take the family to Juarez, Mexico, as an adventure, to shop and eat. It was tourist friendly and safe in those times. I was fascinated with the differences of cultures and my heart felt attuned to the people. My free spirit later wanted to return.

Melinda wanted to help fulfill this Mexican destiny, but she would miss her new love. "Come on Melinda, he'll be here when we get back, just think of the fun we'll have." I had just broken up with my first boyfriend and was looking forward to exploring something new in my life. Melinda finally got on board with the idea, even though she knew French and would have preferred a trip to France. But, Mexico was closer and cheaper, so the plan had been hatched.

* * *

We successfully arrived in El Paso, found enchiladas, and then settled into bed at the hotel. Before sleep, Shirley bent over to kiss my forehead goodnight and quietly said, "Don't you worry, Nancy, your parents love you and will see everything will be okay." I needed that and slept soundly until morning.

Excitement filled Melinda and me as we hoisted our backpacks and said goodbye to the Hans. We looked at one another, hugged, then trudged over the bridge to Juarez, nervous but happy.

All our paperwork was in order and the crossing was uneventful but still overwhelming. As we crossed the river, a sour smell invaded our nostrils, a scent which I would call 'the smell of Mexico' by the end of the trip. Cars, people, sounds, dogs, and colorful art blended together into an energy that danced around us. People were everywhere, and everyone turned to watch these two young *hueras* (light skinned girls) with big packs on their backs and eyes like saucers.

"What is everyone looking at, Nancy?"

"Us, the *gringas*! Get used to it, girl—it's only just begun," I answered. One of the first things I realized, once we crossed the border was how all the men noticed Melinda. She had long honey-blond hair to her waist and fair Scandinavian skin. No one seemed to even see me, as I blended in with my dark hair and complexion. It made me jealous, because Melinda always was the one the boys went after. I felt it was time for things to change.

"What if we can't find a taxi? What if no one understands us? What if we get lost?" Melinda rambled.

"Don't worry, I know Spanish and everything is fine," I confidently replied. Leading an adventure was my forte, and it felt good to comfort Melinda after all her family had done for me. I had been taking Spanish since seventh grade and had gotten comfortable with my classroom studies. It was very different in practice though, and after much repeating and hand signals, we found a taxi to take us to the train station.

I went out of my way to speak Spanish to handsome young men, but it always backfired because they wanted to be introduced to Melinda. Resentment built slowly in me and would show its ugly head more and more frequently as our adventures progressed. Melinda was scared of the men and wasn't interested one iota because she already missed Brian, her new love. I was the free spirit in search of amorous adventures.

The taxi, after seeming to drive through every alleyway in Juarez, took us to the station and we boarded the train to Mexico City. We felt an equal mix of excitement and fright. Men of all ages and types watched the two *gringas* with interest, hoping to share our seat. At first it was fun and flattering, but then became bothersome.

Once in the train car, we decided to settle in by a young couple from Germany—just for foreigner's comradery—and prepared for the long two-day journey. The couple offered us a beer and the fun began. Once the beer was opened, others from the train drifted to the growing circle to join in.

"*Señorita, toma conmigo, tengo una botella de tequila solemente para ti,*" invited a drunk old Mexican man, infatuated with me (of course the old men always liked me). He convinced us to take shots from his newly opened tequila bottle. From that point on, the remainder of the first day's travel was a blur but lots of fun. As I got looser, so did my ability to speak

Spanish. I was speaking Spanish with anyone who would join and felt on top of the world. I was the center of the party, just as I craved to be.

Melinda, on the other hand, became quiet and withdrawn.

"What's up *chica*? Why so quiet?" I smiled and handed her a beer.

"Thanks, but I'm good. I just can't understand half of what's being said and I'm tired. Go have fun, I'll just doze."

"C'mon, Melinda, the fun has just begun!"

"Really, I'm fine. Go."

I looked at her, shrugged, and returned to the party thinking, "Hm, something is up."

Finally, I had enough and returned to Melinda's side. We slept soundly through the night, even though the snoring was widespread, and elsewhere the party continued. Once sunrise awoke us, we dug in our food bag for granola bars and oranges, offering some to the hungover German couple. The train had traveled deep into the desert of Mexico, and only occasionally was there any sign of life—animal or vegetable. Everyone was quietly dozing, reading, or looking out the windows for most of the day. A familiar partier would pass with a smile and nod but continue on their mission or rambling without stopping to visit. The old man with the tequila was lost in a heap of blankets for the remainder of the journey.

When there was a passenger stop, vendors would line the train windows outside, selling all types of unknown foods and curios. We bought sodas and *tortas* from them and were astounded how poor and dirty everyone looked. We passed homes in the middle of nowhere that consisted of a hillside with pots and pans tacked into the dirt embankments. That was it. That was their home. How could they possibly survive with so little? What did they eat, what happened in storms, or births of babies, or making love? Dumbfounded by what we saw, we were speechless.

Melinda had already written her first letters home, one to her parents and one to Brian. I wasn't ready yet; I had a week before mine was due.

The night was quiet, and early the next morning we arrived in the biggest, dirtiest, most polluted city we had ever seen, Mexico City. For miles and miles coming into the metropolis we saw a mishmash of pallet homes, dirty babies, begging mothers, crowds of people, and traffic. Then the train station appeared and we left our passing friends and stepped out into the quagmire.

"Yuk, this is depressing. We've got to get out of here as quickly as possible," I said with Melinda's quick agreement. We were disgusted and scared, so upon disembarking we got directions and were able to walk to the bus station. Of course people stared, but it wasn't as bad as we'd imagined, as it seemed everyone was preoccupied with their own dilemmas. Unfortunately, the last bus had already left, so we had to find a hotel and stay the night. After a few inquiries, a woman led us to a hotel close by, and we gave her a dollar, which lit her smile from ear to ear.

"Can you believe how just a dollar means the world to her?" Melinda noted. We would come to learn that even a peso was a big deal to most. Once we dropped our packs and settled into the room, we agreed to go exploring and find some dinner.

We felt so light, not having to lug our backpacks, and found walking was helpful after the cramped days in the train. The city was a total contrast, with fancy new architecture located right next to hovels and destitute society. Beggars walked next to men in fine suits, and filthy children played in the filthy water alongside curbs outside expensive restaurants. No one seemed to notice the contrast. Or if they did, they were used to it and seemingly indifferent.

With an exhale I urgently said, "I've got to find a park or somewhere with flowers and trees. These streets are grossing me out."

"Me too—ask someone," was Melinda's immediate response.

"*Las Avenidas de Las Americas es muy cerca y muy bonita, amigas, sigueme y voy a mostraré.*" The handsome young student led us to the main boulevard in the city and pointed us in the direction where beautiful parks and museums were located. I smiled and felt the rush of speaking in Spanish to this handsome man, actually understanding him, plus he seemed to look at me more than Melinda. That was a refreshing change.

Just as we were beginning to doubt his directions, a magnificent statue appeared in the middle of the street and a vast park behind it.

"Yeah! This looks like a find," exclaimed Melinda, and we forged ahead with enthusiasm. At the entrance, we found all sorts of food vendors, but one caught our attention. He had huge orange fruits on a stick, cut with the flesh peeling off like a magnificent flower.

"*Que es esto, señor?*" I asked, wanting to know what it was. It was a mango the size of a softball with lime and chili sprinkled on it and was the first of many to come. A mess to eat, but ambrosia. Next, we had *paletas*, homemade popsicles, I had coconut or *coco* and Melinda had pineapple or *piña*. We walked through the beautiful park with fountains, statues, and flowers, both sampling new foods and people watching, just what we needed.

Art museums were everywhere and I was in heaven, being in close proximity to such beautiful expressions of art. I saw the huge murals of Diego Rivera, a famous Mexican revolutionary artist. I always had a passionate soul connection to the arts in all forms. Art spoke to my spirit and ran in my veins.

Once the sun began to get lower, we hiked back to our hotel room, tummies full, worn out, and happy. We slept like *bambinos* and woke up early the next morning to catch the bus. It was crowded, but we were able to sit next to one another, beside a mother traveling with her three children. The kids were so well behaved and obeyed every nod and wink from their mother.

"You would never see this happen at home. The kids are so belligerent and out of control, I wonder how she does it," Melinda observed.

"She probably beats them when no one is watching," I halfway joked.

It was wonderful leaving Mexico City to head toward our destination, and we finally relaxed. Something ignited within me—a joy, energy, a power—my gypsy spirit. I thought about my family but my intense guilt was starting to ease, and happy feelings about my decision increased. Melinda was also happier and not so down about leaving her boyfriend and beloved parents. The adventure was a reality now, with a long road ahead to explore.

With every conversation in Spanish, my confidence grew and my self-esteem soared, savoring the attentions of these handsome dark Mexican men. My dark features and appearance, along with speaking Spanish, allowed me to feel as if I were a part of the culture, more than Melinda, who definitely looked and acted like a foreigner. Even though the men seemed more attracted to her, I was the one they talked to.

The bus trip was uneventful and each stop looked like the previous one. Everyone was dirt poor, selling something, with flocks of children in tow. Each pueblo (town) had a Zócalo (plaza) in its center where people congregated. Girls and boys flirted under the watchful eyes of adults, while vendors sold jicama with lime and chili. Dogs lay in the middle of streets and would lift a lazy eye when a vehicle slowly avoided them. Each town seemed to have its specialty commerce item to supply to other pueblos. No one was in a hurry.

The landscape started changing to hills with increasing scrub bushes, trees, and the appearance of rambling rivers alongside the highway. The bus rose out of the plains toward our destination, and we watched eagerly with each passing town and commented quietly between ourselves.

At last San Miguel de Allende came into view.

"Oh my God, it's beautiful!" we both exclaimed at the same time.

The town was tucked into the side of hills covered with trees and bushes, but not so dense that the dry and rocky earth was obscured. The roads of the town were narrow and cobblestone, lined by rock buildings with arches, big wooden doorways, vines, big green leafy trees and flowers. The center of town had the traditional Zócalo bordered by one of the oldest churches in the area, which overlooked the scene with its tall white steeple. Cobblestone streets exited the Zócalo on every side, and some went up the hillside while others went down. In the distance, homes lined the slopes, and we wondered what amazing views they must have.

"Can you believe it, Melinda? This is more beautiful than I could imagine. The architecture, the streets, the greenery … I will make beautiful art here." I felt blessed.

"This is magical, Nancy. I can't believe this is where we are going to live."

The station appeared and the bus let off its passengers. We hoisted the heavy packs on our backs, wondering how we were going to find an apartment.

"Maybe we should find Instituto Allende and see if they have a bulletin board for apartments," suggested Melinda.

"Great idea!" I looked for someone to ask directions. Turning, I bumped right into a middle aged Mexican man dressed completely in black. He supported his bulky one-legged body with a rickety cane. He had a patch over one eye, a black Zorro-type hat and looked like a bandito in an old western movie. I jumped back and tried to not show my fear.

"*Señoritas*, you need home?" he asked in pigeon English. "I have, come follow me, *por favor*."

We were caught totally by surprise, thinking this was an evil man up to no good.

"*No gracias, señor. Adios.*" We turned to leave quickly.

"*Señoritas*, really, I'm okay. I find all the *gringos* apartments. Ask him." He pointed to an equally suspicious character, half the size of him, sporting a big sombrero who nodded his head in agreement. "I know a beautiful home up the hill, cheap, follow me."

He turned and started hobbling off, waving for us to follow, "Come, come, I am okay, I have a cheap home for you up the hill, I know many gringos here, they will tell you El Negro is a good man." Half-pint followed him, also waving and encouraging us to follow.

"What do you think, Melinda? This is too coincidental—he just happens to know of an apartment when that's exactly what we need."

"He scares me; I think we should do what we said and find the Instituto."

"Yeah, I agree," I said, and we turned to go.

"*Señoritas*, really, ask anyone about El Negro. I am known here, you are safe with me. What could I do to you?" he pleaded from across the yard looking down at his one leg and pointing at his patched eye.

We looked at each other, shrugged and agreed there was not much he could do to us, so we finally agreed to follow him and his friend. El Negro talked the whole time about San Miguel and all the gringos he knew as we slowly climbed the steepest cobblestone street up the hill.

"Behind all these walls are beautiful homes and courtyards," El Negro said, referring to the seemingly endless stone walls and doors that lined the street. "Gardens with flowers, fountains, *aye*, such beauty, you will see."

The streets were very narrow with uneven cobblestones. Women were out, sweeping sidewalks; children in school uniforms passed, gossiping to one another, and at the corner a man walked his huge pig leashed like a dog, while others herded their chickens. Melinda and I were speechless and just looked at each other with open mouths.

We continued climbing this steep street with El Negro continually repeating, "Just a little bit more." It was slow going and everyone was huffing and puffing.

We were just about to jump ship when we finally reached the top of the street where the town clock was loudly donging away in front of us, forcing us both to cover our ears.

El Negro had a crooked smile on his face as he watched us two *gringas*. "You'll learn to love that. Come, come, it's the second door down this street." We continued to hesitantly follow him. When we got to the door, he told us to wait outside while he entered. He was gone for a long time and we almost left when the big wooden door opened and a middle aged woman with her hair in a tight bun, apron on, and broom in hand invited us in. She didn't speak English, so I did all the talking and translating back to Melinda.

"She's the maid of the household, and they have the upper floor of one side of their house for rent. It's only two hundred a month! Let's at least look at it, don't you think?'"

We looked over her shoulder and saw El Negro comfortably sipping coffee and eating a sweet at a table behind her. He smiled and waved. The house was enormous with a courtyard, exactly like he had told us. The indoor hallway was lined on either side with birds in cages as far as the eye could see. The maid took us up the stairs and opened the door to the apartment. It was huge. There were two bedrooms, two baths, kitchen, living area, and another complete room that could be whatever you wanted it to be. The best part was that it had a big picture window overlooking the quaint town below. The maid led us up one more flight to the top of the building where clothes were hanging on lines and flowers and plants were growing abundantly.

"She says we can use the roof too. She does a lot of chores up here and for a small fee would do our laundry. Also, for a fee, she will cook for us. Can you believe this? Are we in a dream?"

From the roof, the view was incredible. Not only could we see everything going on in the town below, but the hills beyond rose splendidly in the distance. It would be easy to hike to them when an escape or nature time was needed.

"There are some rules to follow. No boy visitors. No music or noise after nine p.m. Rent is due on the first. No going into other parts of the house where the family lives. I think we should take it don't you?"

"Yes, let's sign the rental agreement."

The three of us went to the kitchen where El Negro sat. There, we signed an agreement, got keys, and paid partial rent. I gave El Negro ten dollars and we retired to our apartment to unpack our meager belongings from our backpacks.

"Can you believe how that happened? No one will believe us when we tell them. This was meant to be," exclaimed my blossoming gypsy.

We both agreed to go explore and find a phone to call home. I was actually looking forward to talking to my parents and letting them know everything was fine.

The hike down the street was far easier than the hike up. There was only one place on that side of town with a phone for foreigners. It resembled a big closet with a counter and phone on the wall and was open only a few hours whenever the owners felt like it and when they had an international line open. Well, neither was happening, so we went in search of food and a margarita.

After a few inquiries we found the Americanos hangout, El Paragua. All sorts of interesting people were in there and most seemed as if they had been there awhile. Melinda and I were sharing some nachos and margaritas, when a very lovely woman with long blond hair, dressed in a tunic and pants, approached us.

"Up for some company?"

Happy for the opportunity to meet a local American, we quickly rearranged ourselves to include her at the table.

"My name is Maggie and I go to the Instituto."

Introductions were made and a friendship began. Maggie was from Maine and had been there for six months. She told us in three months she had plans to travel south. Would we like to join her? She said she was traveling alone and we looked like good travel buddies.

"Too soon for us, Maggie, but I'll keep it in mind," I was intrigued. I hadn't even thought of traveling elsewhere, but it sounded inviting.

Maggie shared another margarita and introduced us to some other Instituto students. Melinda and I quickly accepted her offer to take us to the school the following day to sign up for classes. Maggie's interests were clay and weaving, and she raved about the Institute. She had become very fluent in Spanish, and had also started taking classes at Bellas Artes, another art school. This one was attended by local Mexicans and *gringos* who had been there for a while. "Classes are better over there, more indigenous and less bourgeois. Americans can be so self-righteous sometimes, you know?" We both nodded even though we didn't know.

I thought to myself, *Sounds as if I would like Bellas Artes; I'll check into it later.*

Melinda and Maggie hit it off, maybe something to do with both being light skinned, blond and of Scandinavian descent. I wanted Melinda to feel more comfortable so I was happy they'd met. We made a meeting place at a *panadería* (bakery) for breakfast the next day. We walked arm in arm, slowly weaving back up the hill to our new apartment, arriving just before nine. The key turned loudly, opening the wooden door and squeaking loudly to announce our arrival. Giggling with embarrassment, we snuck upstairs, fell into our beds and slept soundly.

I was dreaming about being attacked by birds when the pre-dawn light woke me, only to realize every bird in every cage was tweeting their little lungs out. The noise was deafening. I went to the courtyard window and saw at least seventy cages of colorful little birds joyfully singing and flitting about. Never before had I seen anything like it; I felt hypnotized. Melinda stumbled out a little later, confused and irritated.

"What the hell is this? I can't handle this first thing in the morning.

How long has this been going on? When are they going to stop?"

"Calm down, they are just little birdies singing about the beauty of another day. I think they are cute. Don't you ever want to sing your little tweety song?" I nudged.

"Not this early in the morning; I don't like it," a crabby Melinda answered. I ignored her and tried to cheer her up as we sat down in front of the window overlooking the city. Once we watched the sun rise over the town, Melinda was back to her cheerful self and we got ready to meet Maggie.

Town was bustling with kids walking to school, vendors selling breakfasts, and livestock traversing the streets. "We are going to lose weight on this hill, Melinda! Up and down, up and down, up and down."

Maggie was sitting at the Zócalo outside the *panadería*. "You have to get here early to get the best goods; they sell out fast." The aroma was like the hug of a lover, irresistible. We picked out a bag of goodies and a cup of *café con leche*, which was mostly milk with a little strong coffee in it. This new tradition would become a daily ritual and add many pounds to our waists, even though we walked up and down the hills. We three joined others with the same tradition and sat on benches in the Zócalo eating, drinking, socializing, and waking up.

The Instituto was a fifteen minute walk from the Zócalo. A big arched entryway opened into a courtyard filled with flowers, plants, birds, and milling students.

Melinda and I felt as if we had entered a dream; everything was like a beautiful fairy tale. Most everyone wore colorful, indigenous clothing with big straw hats, scarves, and embroidered bags of one type or another. People were friendly, happy, and the smiles on their faces seemed permanent. Works of art were displayed everywhere, and most carried their current projects in hand. With every new sight, the gypsy in me gained confidence.

I signed up for jewelry making, weaving, batik, and Spanish, while Melinda did pottery, weaving and sketching. The grounds were charming and designed to inspire. Classrooms represented the art being taught, with weaving looms, clay wheels and tables, dye baths and wash basins, and welding torches for jewelry. We were wide-eyed and smiling throughout the tour and looked forward to returning the next day to start our classes.

We stopped to see if the phones were available before returning to the apartment and were in luck.

"MOM, DAD! It's me. I'm great and it is incredible here!" I proceeded to tell them about our trip, of course leaving out any worrisome details. Mom was so relieved to hear from us and Dad mostly listened. We made it brief and I promised to write.

After the call, I heard something different in their voices but couldn't quite put a finger on it. Maybe it was because they had gone to San Diego. Maybe they were glad I was gone and they didn't have to deal with me anymore. Maybe they were enjoying having an empty nest. Something in that gave me relief, but also a sense of being alone. "I hope I haven't burned my bridges of love," I thought with a twinge of melancholy. Suddenly, a wave of regret washed over me, and the great distance between us made me feel vulnerable. What if something did happen? I tucked those thoughts away and focused on my new life.

We wearily trudged up the hill toward home. "Say, why don't we buy some Kahlua and milk? We can sit on the roof and watch the sunset!" Melinda suggested, and a nightly tradition commenced. Hazy clouds made an unbelievable sunset over the perfect scene below, and the two of us toasted one another and our adventures ahead.

Chapter 6

Inspired

I watched as Señor Bandera, the instructor, took the batik and removed wax from the cloth with an old iron and newspaper. The gunky layers of wax melted away, slowly but surely. We had just spent the last week preparing the cloth, creating a design, dying it multiple times and applying a layer of wax after each dye bath. The class exclaimed as the image appeared. Five different dye baths blended at the broken edges of wax where the fabric was exposed and stayed pure where the wax sealed the dye in. Before each dye bath, the students crushed the waxed fabric to create crackles. These would spread over the entire design and could be seen once the wax was ironed off.

"Fabulous, absolutely fabulous," I said in awe. Something about doing this batik art touched my core. The process was totally messy and difficult, but captivating. My first piece was exceptional. I had found a Mayan pattern of an Indian smoking a pipe and started with white fabric then set wax on part of the design. Next, I did two versions of blue dye with wax between each bath and ended with two versions of purple. The crackles and color were perfect; everyone wanted my work and asked if I would sell it. My gypsy spirit soared with pride.

I was on fire as I showed my artwork to friends at El Paragua over a margarita. "You have to think backward to get your colors because you have to apply it light to dark. Then applying the wax—have you ever tried drawing with hot wax? It's very hard to control. The dye baths are also difficult. To create the color you want, along with how it combines with the previous ones, is quite messy. I love the layering. As each color is applied with the dye bath, the design becomes this accumulation of wax applications and it somewhat obscures the design, so you have to intuit where you put it. Then, after you are done, you have this piece of fabric covered with gluey gloppy wax that has totally hidden the design and you get to crumple, beat, and crunch it mercilessly. And, once you iron off the wax, a masterpiece waits, seemingly created by itself without any help from the artist."

Everyone loved my work and agreed it could be sold. I enjoyed being the center of attention, especially as it was related to my art. This was a subject that excited my mind along with my heart. The batik class kindled something magical within me. The smell of the hot wax, the long outdoor tables used to rinse the fabrics between dye baths, the clothesline where everyone's creations hung waiting for the next process, the instructor who was knowledgeable and encouraging, the vats of colorful dye waiting to cling to the threads of fabric ... it went on and on. I was in love with batik.

I felt as if I were drinking from the fountain of life as I immersed myself in the arts. Something in me finally received the nourishment it needed, and I blossomed. Everyone noticed. "Nancy, you look radiant today, do you have a new lover?" "Nancy, are you on drugs, you seem high!" "Nancy, you are glowing, do you have a fever?"

I just smiled as my heart expanded in joy.

"I've finally found my passion. I've tried doing and being what everyone else wants me to be and it's kept me numb. I am an artist. I'm finding fulfillment in creating and witnessing beauty. Other artists recognize this in me and understand its importance. Conventional studies aren't me, they just fool me into thinking I should be something I am not," I thought out loud as I sat on the rooftop one evening at sunset with Melinda.

"That's true, but how will you make a living? It's almost impossible to find a job as an artist."

"See, you are stuck there too. Vision and belief, you have to have vision and belief. Make it happen and don't accept any other option. Keep your eye on the prize. Just do it. Create your own reality. Be true to your heart," I retorted as I sipped my Kalua and milk.

"Sounds good in theory, much harder in practice," she responded with a sip.

"I will not let anything squash what has been ignited in my soul. Art is my destiny."

"Okie Dokie Smokie, whatever you say," Melinda skeptically replied, and we both looked off to the sunset and were quiet.

The two of us had been spending too much time together, so it was a blessing we had different classes and were developing different friendships. Melinda hung out mostly with Maggie when she wasn't staying home to read or write letters to Brian and her parents. She was terribly homesick all the time and fought bouts of depression. I didn't feel that way in the least and continually tried to inspire Melinda to shake it off and smell the roses, which seemed to make her resentful and more depressed. Even when we were out having fun, Melinda seemed aloof and had a fake smile on her face.

After trying everything I could think of, I gave up, followed my own advice, and left Melinda home to read. I started spending more time at the Instituto working after class on my projects.

At first, weaving class was exciting. The big looms clunked and banged along in class and created a percussion concert when everyone was working. Shifting the pedals to change the row and throwing the shuttle of yarn through took practice to not get caught in the strings of the waft and I wasn't very good at that. We had to learn how to string the looms, which was very tedious and I didn't like that part of it either. Creating the designs required keeping count and not missing a stroke, also not my forte. I did like the many different yarns and colors though, so that kept my interest.

Melinda, on the other hand, loved weaving. It was predictable; she liked the detail and control, and had a knack for it. Maggie helped her thread the loom and included her in other projects she was doing. Weaving became Melinda's focus and a way to have a life apart from me.

One day the class did a field trip to the local yarn factory where the spinning and dying was done. As we walked into a big metal barn, hundreds of skeins of yarn, of all colors and types, hung from the ceiling. It was beautiful to see the yarn's subtle variations in all colors of the rainbow, and more. We walked amongst them, touching and learning about the different types. Then we got to choose the yarns we wanted to use for the class project, a blanket. The other room was filled with spinning wheels, where a troop of women sat quietly working to the hum of the wheels. It was all very captivating.

I chose maroon, peach and purple. Melinda chose variations of browns. That, in itself, spoke volumes. There was an unspoken blanket weaving competition going on. I created a fairly challenging pattern, while Melinda's was simple. My wool was soft to the touch. Melinda's was bumpy and rough. Both were beautiful works of art at the end, but we each felt our own was better.

What was going on? Why were we competing? We had never done that before. One night the answer came out in a fight.

"I feel so left out all the time. You speak Spanish and know what's going on, and I always have to ask or I feel like a dork in the corner. You are so happy, and I miss Brian and my parents. Art turns you on, and I don't care about it. Everyone likes you; you are funny, interesting, pretty ... I hate myself." Tears poured out of Melinda.

"What do you mean? All the guys want to know you and they think you are a goddess, while I interpret their love for you. You have a boyfriend and wonderful parents. You have their support for who you are. You are so nice, and I'm the trouble maker!"

After getting it all out on the table, we both were quiet for a while.

I broke the silence and embraced Melinda. "Guess we needed that, huh? I'm sorry; I love you and don't want anything or anyone to get in the way of our friendship. We've known each other too long to allow that." We had a good cry and decided to go out to eat.

Over a margarita, I ate tortilla soup and Melinda had chicken. We laughed, shared stories, got tipsy and walked arm in arm back up the hill, one more time. All was back in order, at least between the two of us.

The next day, I woke up groggy and heavy, chalking it up to the margaritas. In Spanish class, suddenly I started getting chills, feeling dizzy, and left to throw up in the bathroom. It took everything I was made of to make it through the morning's class. Exhausted, freezing, and nauseated, I dragged myself back up the hill and collapsed in bed, only getting up to evacuate from one end of my body or the other. This scenario went on for a week and a half. The tortilla soup had left me with salmonella poisoning.

A local doctor gave Melinda some pills to stem the raging tide, but said I would just have to ride it out. After three weeks, I finally started to perk up. Weakness ruled, and I was pale and gaunt. It took another two weeks to get back to my old self. My appetite and stomach never seemed to be the same again. Everything was inspected, re-inspected, washed, re-washed. Absolutely no risks were taken, and rarely did I eat out. Food wasn't as much fun; I left the experimenting up to Melinda who seemed to have an iron gut.

"Whew, that was like dying and coming back to life," I told my friends at El Paragua upon finally returning to my routines. "Just let me do art—that's all I care about." And that is precisely what I did.

Works of batik sprung from me like water from a faucet. Mexican and Mayan patterns became my vocabulary and color was the conversation. I couldn't get enough of it and with each piece, my body and spirit got stronger and my confidence soared. I felt possessed and couldn't figure out why, but I followed the desire of my inner gypsy. My friends and classmates watched and wondered what was driving this art mania. The results were so magnificent, no one got in my way.

I lost interest in the school social scene and became more drawn to the locals, with whom I could speak Spanish and be part of a culture that felt and lived the arts. The Americans seemed to be trying to impress each other with their coolness, but it felt so shallow to me.

"Why don't you hang out with us at El Paragua anymore?" Melinda asked defensively.

"I don't know, I just want to explore something else. Don't worry, I'll be fine," I responded. I didn't want to tell her that I thought it was elite to only hang out with the Americans, who acted as if they were better than, or scared of, the people whose country they'd decided to live in.

I began hanging out in the Zócalo or at parks where the locals were and was thrilled to converse in this language that opened up a passionate and free new me. Somehow, it was easier to express my heart and desires in Spanish. It felt more flowing, expressive, and colorful than linear choppy English. It was as if Spanish was an art that had the textures, creativity, and beauty that complimented my batik, and now I had two new treasures that opened up my gypsy self. The Mexicans recognized my passion and were drawn to my energy and saw me as one of them. I found many new friends with whom I preferred to spend my time.

"I don't like these new friends of yours—be careful. We don't know who they are. You know they just want money or for you to marry them and take them home to start their new lives in the land of milk and honey," Melinda angrily said to me when I came home one afternoon in the company of three young Mexican men.

"You know nothing about them. We talk about art, religion, family, government, and whatever else. We feel like *compadres* and just want to learn from each other. You are jealous."

"I am not at all. They scare me and I'm afraid they are going to hurt you. Then what … oh, Mr. and Mrs. Weintraub, your daughter is missing, but other than that everything is hunky dory. Care about someone else other than yourself for a change. You always have to push it beyond reason, Nancy. You think you know everything. I agree with your parents, you *are* a pain in the ass." She turned and walked out.

I was caught off guard. Melinda had very rarely spoken to me like that before and it made me think. *She's missing Brian and her parents. She's not into this culture; it's just not her. Art isn't her thing and she doesn't like seeing me so happy from all that is making her depressed. What can I do to help? Maybe it will help when her parents visit next week. Maybe some trips together to some other towns. She does like to travel. Maybe I should spend more time with Melinda; she probably feels I've abandoned her.*

"Melinda, how about just the two of us go to Querétaro this weekend and check out the opal capital of the world?" I asked, entering her room.

Looking up with red swollen eyes, Melinda smiled and embraced me as she approached. "That sounds fun, I'd love to. I've missed you, Nancy. It seems like you don't even like me anymore and have forgotten I'm even here."

"I'm sorry. I have been very selfish and careless with our friendship. Let's do some traveling together. Maybe we can talk to Maggie and get some ideas about good places to go in southern Mexico and maybe even Guatemala!"

"What about your parents? They would never agree to that."

"Maybe if I tell them we are going with a group of students. Your parents will see how good we are down here, and their report to my parents will help."

So, the friendship once again survived the throes of growing up, and a new energy infused the two of us. I continued to nurture my Mexican friendships but made sure I found time for Melinda. The blanket weaving war became the mutual appreciation society and we spent time banging on the looms together, seeing beauty in our different styles.

The Hans arrived for a week-long visit during the reconciliation of our relationship. They stayed in the apartment and were delighted at what they found. The school, friends, art, location, and even the morning tweeting of birds made them proud of what we two girls had created.

"I had no doubt about what you two could do when left to your own choices. You have shown maturity and responsibility. Your parents would be proud too, if they could witness this themselves. You have both grown, it's obvious," Shirley proudly stated.

"I am amazed, I knew you two could do it, but this is even better than I could have ever imagined. You go, girls!" Frank high-fived us, and

Melinda beamed with pride.

I couldn't believe the kudos I was receiving from the Hans. The validation for all our efforts made my confidence surge. "My parents will never get the chance to see the real me because they are too busy wanting me to be someone else," I reflected with a flash of anger. "I know what I'm doing and know what's right for me—travel."

The visit was a whirlwind of activity and calmed Melinda tremendously. The Hans loved everything about our lives and treated us to a few nights in a hotel. Discussion about further travels was supported by the Hans because they felt that type of education was elemental to character development. They agreed to talk to my parents, to encourage their support for the travel idea.

Giving me a big bear hug, Frank said, "Don't worry. After seeing the pictures of your lives down here, they will see how much you've grown and the good decisions you've made. Give them time. They are Old World people and have a hard time accepting the new ways."

"Girls I am so proud of you. Stay away from lukewarm food, it breeds salmonella." I nodded enthusiastically in agreement. "And honey bun, cheer up, you'll be home soon in the arms of Brian. Life goes on, and don't let any guy take you away from living your life. Love you tons," Shirley declared as she wiped a tear from Melinda's eyes.

"It was a great visit and nice to be around people who know us so well after being around strangers for so long, don't you think, Melinda?" I said. I linked arms with her as we watched them drive away. She couldn't respond past the tears.

She is such an emotional girl, I thought. *My tears usually come from anger and frustration as opposed to love. I am missing the folks, though; I would love for them to come visit just to see for themselves. I miss hearing Mom call me darling.*

My Batiks

Eagle Sight

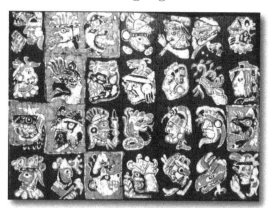

Mayan Men

Chapter 7

A Fling

"Darling, I've gotten a job!" Mom spoke excitedly during our weekly call. After only a month of looking, she'd landed a medical transcriptionist job at the hospital. Since she knew shorthand, they scooped her up and trained her for the position. Mom was elated and I could tell she was feeling some relief from the depression.

Mom had more news. "You know your father has been so frustrated at work—well, he's found a new position at J Division. It involves more travel, and he's invited me to go along with him to Chicago!"

I congratulated them both, glad to hear their lives were moving in positive directions.

"Nan, there's one more thing. Your father and I have decided that you can take some time to travel. The Hans gave us such a favorable review of what you two girls have done, we think it's okay."

Ecstatic to have their approval for the first time since I'd left, I had tears in my eyes when she hung up the phone. With a much lighter heart, I headed toward the Zócalo to meet up with Melinda for a festive evening out.

Most residents of San Miguel de Allende met Sunday nights at the Zócalo. Girls dressed up, of course modestly, coming from very traditional homes, and got an opportunity to walk in promenade fashion at the plaza. Girls circled one way, and boys went the opposite direction. If a certain connection was made, they could visit within view of their chaperones. It was the best time of the week for the locals, and the energy was lively and joyful. Parents and chaperones visited one another and got an opportunity to catch up with the latest gossip. Vendors sold every type of food and aromas filled the air. The church was lit up, watching over the scene like the father of the family.

Musical groups roamed the Zócalo playing for tips, a beer, or just for fun. Mariachi bands dressed in beautiful bolero jackets, studded pants, and wide sombreros blared their trumpets and strummed bass guitars, led by a forceful lead singer. Eight or more men would play to the crowds, evoking their sentiments to cheer and toss coins in their guitar cases.

Ranchero bands, usually a trio, were lower key. They dressed in blue jeans, cowboy shirts, and cowboy hats and only played guitars, with a singer melodically singing ballads. They would play more intimately to smaller parties away from the crowds.

On occasion throughout the evening, the Mariachis would approach the Rancheros and compete for a location. The Mariachi always won with their grandeur and sheer loudness. We laughed as we watched one huge group of horns blow away a humble trio.

"Poor guys, they have no hope with those pompous Mariachis." I watched as the trio left the corner to their victors. Out of the corner of my eye, I noticed a very cute Mexican boy and his two friends looking at us. "Melinda, don't look now, but we are getting the eye from some cuties over there."

Melinda was conflicted. She was flattered and a little tempted, but loyal. Wherever we went, the Mexican men always came on strong and wanted us to marry and take them home to the States. She didn't like that at all. They were fascinated with her blond hair and wanted to touch it, which frightened her.

Every once in awhile a very nice and proper man would approach us and sincerely just want to talk and be friends, but that was the exception. I seemed to meet more of this type, probably since I could speak Spanish. "It seems like we both want what the other has, you want the guys to be more attracted, and I want them to be friends," Melinda murmured as she saw the trio walking toward us.

"*Hola Señoritas, quieren compania?*" one of the cuties asked as he had his eye on me.

I was feeling social and was very attracted to him. "*Si, pero mi amiga no hablas Español, puede hablar Ingles?*" After finding out they could speak broken English, we found a bench to sit on and visit over a *paleta*. Melinda was relaxed and enjoyed herself for the first time. They were students and with a bit of English, she found common ground with them.

The first young man, Jesus, hit it off immediately with me. "Jesus is a common name here?" I couldn't believe his name was Jesus, although pronounced hey-sus. *Ironic. Here I am a Jew and I'm interested in a guy named Jesus, Mom and Dad would NOT approve.* Guilty thoughts nudged me. *But he's so cute and nice.*

The boys walked us up the hill to our apartment and said goodbye. "Melinda, you did great tonight. You actually practiced your Spanish and it sounded good. The guys were nice and not too forward, don't you think?"

"Yeah, I did do well tonight. I was relaxed and it helped they knew some English too. That was fun, I think that is the first time I let my guard down and it felt good!" Melinda was bright and smiling.

"Maybe we are finally getting to know the culture better, and we're not on pins and needles, wondering what's going on all the time." We embraced and hit the sack.

After school the next day, I found Jesus waiting at the apartment door. I was pleasantly surprised and agreed to go for a walk with him. This became a regular routine and I found myself falling for the guy. Melinda was comfortable with him and the three of us would do things together, which helped me feel that I wasn't abandoning my friend.

After a month, Jesus wanted to take me to see his uncle's apartment on the hill. It was one of those beautiful homes on the hillside overlooking San Miguel de Allende that I had always wanted to see, so I agreed. Well, as it turned out, his uncle was out of town and Jesus just happened to have the key. Once inside the beautiful home, he made the moves on me and got me to the bed before I even knew what was happening.

My first love had been in high school. Once we went to college I lost my virginity to him. Of course Mom and Dad knew nothing of this. We hadn't used protection so I knew we were playing a game of Russian roulette. I didn't like having sex and felt overcome with guilt. That led to our breakup and I hadn't been with another.

When the decision was made to go to Mexico, I'd decided to get birth control, just because you never know. So, I went to the family clinic and got an IUD. After it was inserted, I had never felt such pain before in this part of my body and wondered if this was a good decision, but wasn't about to have it removed, knowing that would be equally painful. The doctor told me it would take a while, but eventually my body would adapt, and it finally did.

So, here I was with Jesus, a guy I really liked and was attracted to, but didn't want to go this far this fast. "Not yet Jesus, not yet." I pushed him away, but he kept grabbing and saying he loved me. Finally, I gave in. We had fast, guilt-filled sex and quickly left the apartment.

We continued to see each other, but Jesus became more and more demanding to have sex. Against my better judgement I started sneaking him into our apartment, but it just felt worse and worse.

"Why can't I say no? I like him, just not having sex; I'm not ready for this. But on the other hand, it's nice to be held. Why can't we just lie together without the sex?"

Melinda listened to me over coffee. "I don't have an answer for you, Nancy, but follow your conscience because that's what you have to live with. I have had sex with Brian, but we love each other and it's not the basis of our relationship. I think Jesus likes you, but likes sex more."

"I think you are right, Melinda. It's time to end this; it's not what I want." I got up and went to find Jesus. He was not happy and called regularly for a while, but then finally got the message and left me alone. Unfortunately, I was also left alone with a vaginal infection.

I waited outside the doctor's office, worried about the pain and itching I felt. The doctor finally saw me, asked about the symptoms and gave me a bottle of pills. Never once did he take my vital signs or give an examination, but simply presented the diagnosis and sent me out the door. After a week, the infection appeared to go away, along with my desire to ever be intimate again.

Once again, my life became art, art, and more art—and travel.

Chapter 8

Puerta Vallarta

D o you want to go with my sister, Diane, and me to Puerto Vallarta for the weekend?" Jenny was a friend from my jewelry class. "It won't cost much and we can share expenses."

Melinda and I looked at each other and agreed without debate. They were friends; Jenny's sister had traveled regularly and we had heard about Puerto Vallarta from many. The weather would only get hotter as we approached spring so this was a good time to go.

We met Friday noon at the bus and met Diane, who was attending the other art school, Bellas Artes. Diane was five years older than Jenny and exuded confidence. I was very impressed to learn she had been a card dealer in Las Vegas for the last five years and knew her way around.

The bus ride was spent getting to know each other, snacking, and figuring out a plan for once we arrived.

"I've stayed at a youth hostel named Jorge's before. It's cheap, clean, safe, and many foreigners stay there. Once we get there we'll ask around because I don't remember exactly where it was,"

Melinda, Jenny, and I nodded in agreement to Diane's proposal.

It was easy to find once we arrived and was a well-known hangout. The hostel had a courtyard surrounded by bougainvillea, tropical plants, palm trees, and chirpy birds. Rooms were basic but comfortable and we quickly got settled and set off to find some food.

"You want to try some peyote? My friend hooked me up before I left." Diane was holding a piña colada in her hand as we all munched on nachos. "I've got enough for everyone; I'm going to do it on the beach tomorrow."

"I've never done it before, what is it like?" I asked.

"Well, it tastes nasty and makes you sick at first, but once that's over, oh my God, it is amazing. It's nothing like pot or acid. It's spiritual. The Native people use it for religious purposes. There is no hallucinating; it's as if you have a direct connection to the higher powers of yourself and the universe. I totally love it."

Melinda and I had smoked pot, but tried nothing else other than liquor. We were both interested to experiment, especially since it wasn't a chemical drug, but natural. Somehow, that seemed more acceptable and less scary. My gypsy liked the idea of a spiritual adventure and was seeking something deeper. The next morning we would take it and go to the beach for the remainder of the day.

That evening we sat around a fire pit with other travelers and listened to stories until late in the night. Everyone was already feeling high just from our happy excursion. Finally, we all went to bed in anxious anticipation of the next day's adventure.

"Argh, this is horrible!" Melinda gagged as she took her first bite of the peyote button.

"I've never seen buttons this big; it's at least 3 inches across and so juicy. The ones I've seen my friends do in New Mexico are drier and less than an inch in diameter," I said. "Ready or not, here I go … yechhhhh!" My face twisted as I took the first bite.

It took about thirty minutes to gag the peyote down. It truly was the worst thing I had ever eaten. Then Jenny and I lost our cookies, but Melinda and Diane didn't. I was disappointed, thinking I wasn't going to feel anything since I threw it up, but soon I felt the high coming on.

The four of us left the hostel with only our swimsuits, towels and bottles of water. Grins were nonstop on our faces as we headed to the beach before the high really set in.

Diane knew the best resorts in Puerta Vallarta and led our foursome to a luxurious pool and bar area. The bar was surrounded on one side by the pool and the other by the deck. Guests could swim up to the bar and drink while sitting in the pool. Piña Coladas were served in hollowed out pineapples with flower garnishes popping out the top. Other drinks were served from coconuts, pitchers, and grand size glasses all decked out with bouquets of flowers. Quite impressive. Beautiful tropical plants, flowers, and birds helped create a jungle atmosphere for the guests. The beach was close, and bathroom facilities or refreshments were readily available. It was definitely a slice of paradise, and very expensive. Diane and Jenny headed to the bar at the pool and Melinda and I headed to the beach.

The peyote was coming on strong, so we decided to lie on the beach to watch the waves. The area was a beautiful tropical utopia; on peyote, everything took on spectacular dimensions. We watched the detailed patterns and colors of the ocean mixing and merging to the symphony of crashing and surging waves. Palm trees, flowers, and birds completed the composition. It was magnificently awesome. We were as speechless and stoned as we could be. We were sure people knew we were high but we didn't care in the least.

After an hour, Melinda and I decided to walk down the short beach. It turned into a journey of noticing every shell, palm tree, grain of sand, cloud, sound, and how it all fit into the cosmos. We talked about the origins of man, nature, and enlightenment. We felt the native spirits within, and I was the closet to the feelings I had that day on the mesa in New Mexico when my gypsy spirit and purpose were revealed. This was awesome.

After our timeless walk and spiritual enlightenment, we decided to find Diane and Jenny and use the facilities. I didn't want to go far from the beach as I didn't find peace in the resort scene. The two still sat at the pool bar and were in the company of two men who were tall, skinny, and not very good looking. They both wore blue jeans, cowboy shirts and cowboy hats.

"Hi y'all. I'm Mike and this is Dave." The thick Texas drawl was like a twang of a guitar.

After introductions, Diane explained that Mike won a week-long trip to Puerta Vallarta from work. They had unlimited use of the bar, room service, and whatever else the resort had to offer. The men were alone and invited us to party with them to take full advantage of their windfall.

"So, order a drink, food, whatever you want, girls. Live it up!" Diane was far into party mode, super high from the peyote and some cocktails. "Let's go up to their room and order room service, whatever we want; we'll never get a chance like this again."

Everyone wanted to go but me. I wasn't hungry, only thirsty for water. I really just wanted to be close to the ocean and nature, nothing else. For the remainder of the day, that's where I stayed. The others came to check on me, but mostly they partied at the resort.

It's so ironic, here I am at this world renowned resort with the opportunity to have anything I desire for free, and all I want is water and being on this beach. I watched the glorious scene in front of me. "This is absolutely perfect."

My experience was profoundly spiritual. The oneness with nature filled my soul with a peace I had never experienced before. I pulled out my small sketchbook and oil pastels and got lost in the textures and colors of the ocean.

As the sun was setting, I was beginning to get cold and come down from the day-long high. The others were feeling the same way; they came to gather me up, and our foursome linked arms to float back to the hostel. "What an incredible day, I feel like I got to live paradise inside and out today. Thanks, Diane." I sat in front of the fire pit and glowed in the flames with the others. Everyone else was also appreciative, but more for the partying they'd had with the Texans and opportunity to enjoy the windfall of their free resort trip.

The peyote sparked feelings deep within me. I felt as if I had communed with my ancestors and received insights of life and knowledge. Intense, but no words seemed appropriate to describe or share, so I kept it to myself. *Definitely a 'trip' to remember. Peyote is a religious experience and I look forward to my next one.*

We had to catch the bus early the next morning, so we gathered our bags and hit the road. I closed my eyes on the bus and slept until we arrived back in San Miguel de Allende.

Chapter 9

A Shift

The trips, both to Puerta Vallarta and the peyote, changed me. I felt restless and wanted to see more places. Speaking Spanish was becoming second nature, which increased my confidence to communicate and lead some travel adventures.

Melinda was antsy to head home to New Mexico. She missed Brian terribly and wanted to be home before school started in the fall at the university. I had friends of all nationalities trying to convince me to stay and pursue more education in San Miguel, but I was unsure what I wanted. Home was calling me to return to my university education, but the gypsy was tempted to stay.

"Melinda, I think it's time we plan our travel. Classes are almost over and it's time to sign up for more or head home. Once the trip is over, you can go home and I'll decide what I'm going to do."

Melinda agreed immediately, and seemed relieved to know home was in her near future. "I've really enjoyed this, Nancy, I'm just so homesick. So, let's talk to Maggie and forge our travel plan."

It didn't take long to choose the route; this had been the basis of many conversations since we arrived. We would travel by bus wherever we went and stay in youth hostels. Our friends gave us lists of places to stay and things to see, so after an evening the itinerary was set.

First we would go to the east side of Mexico to the ruins at Palenque. From there we would head up to the Yucatán to see more ruins and the beautiful clear waters of the Caribbean at Isla Mujeres. A bus would take us to Guatemala's ruins at Tikal and would be followed by the one and only flight, to Guatemala City. We would then get on the bus again to Antigua and Lake Atitlán to see the weavings for which the area is known. Then we would head north and cross back into Mexico by San Cristóbal de Las Casas. Oaxaca and Barra de Navidad would be the last stops before heading home to San Miguel. Melinda would then prepare for her departure to the States. I was trying to convince Melinda to visit Taxco, the pueblo of red roofs and silver, but wasn't having any luck.

"I'm already taking more time to do this trip than I want, so don't push your luck." Melinda was getting crabby as we hunched over the map.

Great start. She is going to be impatient the whole time, I thought.

We made arrangements to move out of the apartment upon departure. If I decided to stay, I would move in with Jenny. We spoke with our parents, informed them of the plan and got itineraries to them.

"But Nan, you don't list any hotels or names of places you'll be staying," Mom complained.

"We don't know them, but everyone who has been there has said there are youth hostels everywhere and lots of foreign travelers to direct us. I'll call at every stop, I promise."

"This isn't what you told us, Nan. You said you'd be traveling with a group of students." Dad sounded angry.

"Well, the timing isn't right for most of them, but we will be meeting some here and there. Like when we go to Palenque, Maggie is going to be there. Then in Antigua, Jenny will meet us. I have a few other friends who are still working out their plans, but promise to intersect with us as we go. I'll call regularly so you'll know where we are." I felt like I was back-paddling on an upward stream.

"I think you should just come home now. Enough is enough, and you have been getting your way all along. It's time for you to take your responsibilities in hand and get back to civilization and your studies." Dad was furious now.

"Dad, I may not even come home. There is a chance I will stay down here and go to school longer." I dropped the bomb.

Everything went from bad to worse, leaving everyone crying or shouting. The next day a calmer me called back to try and smooth over the prior conversation, but I was still met with a prickly father and weepy mother.

"Guys, I'm going to do this and the more you say no, the more my decision to stay will be firm. So, please, just accept this." I had made up my mind; I had to follow my gypsy heart.

Left with no choice in the matter, Dad hung up and Mom pleaded for me to be safe and call regularly.

"Darling, I love you. When you get home I want us to spend time together. I need you," Mom sobbed.

"That sounds good, Mom. I miss you too. Don't worry, everything will be fine and we'll pick up right where we left off. I need to do this. My gypsy is in control and my destiny will be revealed through this trip, I feel it." I hung up, feeling anxious but strong.

Chapter 10

Backpacking Vagabonds

I was wearing a bright homemade batik shirt and pants with a scarf around my head and a large yellow backpack, while Melinda wore a long skirt with boots and a big red backpack as we boarded the bus. We had moved out of the apartment and said goodbye to the friends as we headed south. First stop, Palenque.

The scenery became more dense and full of jungle as we headed south past Mexico City. Wherever we went, the native people stared at the two of us as if we were from another planet. Always friendlier once I spoke Spanish, people would gladly visit or invite us for a meal.

Other foreign travelers were easy to find along the journey and were great story tellers of fact and fiction. Sometimes we would share a bus ride, but usually we kept each other company at the youth hostels over a meal or around a night-time gathering by a fire. The rooms were all very cheap and ran a steep three American dollars a night, which included breakfast. Rooms were clean and everyone had sleeping bags. We met people who had been traveling all over the world for five years and were still going.

I was in my element. The stories, cultures, personalities, and wisdom of this environment inspired my very soul. The different customs and lives opened new doors of opportunity for all the many ways life could be. The places everyone had been, I wanted to witness myself. The University of New Mexico was feeling like a box.

Bus travel was long, crowded, and unpredictable. Some towns didn't get bus service daily, so we had to stay a night or two until it arrived.

Other buses broke down, and passengers would wait on the side of the road until another one rescued them. It wreaked havoc with our timetable and infuriated Melinda, who was wishing she was already home. I didn't mind, it gave me time to see different places and speak Spanish with the locals.

The Palenque ruins were deep in the jungle. It was very hot and humid and we spent more time drinking watermelon juice than climbing the ruins. Many foreigners came to this destination and I felt proud to be one of them. Even though the ruins were incredible and exotic, the heat forced us inside most of the time, so we decided to cut it short and head for the Yucatan.

The water was as clear as tap water as we looked down from the ferry taking us to Isla Mujeres. The inviting turquoise water and a breeze kept the heat manageable. Once we disembarked, a flock of kids descended to help us find a hotel. Another youth hostel was located near the beach, and the two of us settled in for four days of rest, swimming, shopping, and rejecting Mexican men. Melinda and I would hike miles down the beach for our solitude, but always, the men would follow.

I was always planning the exit strategy from the oncoming men and Melinda was quick to follow. In each place, Melinda's impatience to keep moving got us back on the bus. Each day brought a new adventure.

Belize had been recommended as the place to cross into Guatemala. Again, a crowded bus ride. In Belize City we uneasily watched military tanks patrolling the streets, as British Colonial rule was coming to an end and local government was taking over. The country contained a curious combination of cultures. Everyone spoke English with a British accent, including the large black population who had been brought over during times of slavery. We found English products in the stores and stocked up on drugstore items.

The next day we took a bus through dense jungle to the Guatemala border, an area heavily patrolled by military tanks. No one seemed to mind except us; we were freaked out by their presence and happy to be walking away from the border to enter Guatemala and prepare for a long ride to Guatemala's ruins at Tikal.

That was definitely the longest, bumpiest, curviest, most crowded bus ride yet. People had their birds, chickens, reptiles, and whatever livestock they could manage on the bus. For most of the twenty-four hour ride, we had to stand and were almost hallucinating from exhaustion.

At one mountainous stop, the driver unloaded luggage and packages.

A big drum was being removed from the bus when it got out of hand and fell. The lid burst off, sending an explosion of chocolate syrup into the crowd before it lay on its side with a river of chocolate streaming into the village. Children were screaming and laughing in the mess, looking like chocolate covered peanuts by the time the bus finally pulled out. I had a great time with my sketchbook on this scene.

The Tikal ruins sat in the midst of the deepest jungle we had ever seen. Monkeys and toucans screamed in the trees. Locals told us there were many ruins in the area that hadn't been excavated because the jungle vegetation grew so fast and it was too hard to keep trimming it back. The Tikal ruins required people to cut back growth daily, just to keep them exposed. Climbing on the ruins and learning about the Mayans was captivating.

"I feel like I'm on another planet, everything is so strange." Looking up at a toucan in a tree, I noticed Melinda's mood. "So, Mel, you okay?"

"I want to go home *now*, Nancy, I don't want to do this anymore. It's interesting and fun, but I'm tired and want to go home."

"But we're only halfway through the trip."

"Maybe I should catch the next bus to a city and fly home."

"What! That's crazy. Listen, you are tired. Let's rest and you'll feel better in the morning."

"I don't think so. I'm done."

A sinking feeling filled me; I knew she was serious. The next morning it was decided we would shorten our visits, get to Oaxaca, and Melinda would fly back to San Miguel alone and prepare to head home. I would travel on my own for a while after Melinda left. Not the plan I wanted, but a compromise I could live with.

Guatemala City was huge and dirty; the hostel was several city bus rides from the airport, and the people were much less friendly than at our previous stops. We were approached to buy drugs, which frightened both of us. We got out as early as possible the next day.

Next stop was Antigua, a quaint town tucked between small mountains. An art school there attracted foreigners and gave it a 'hip' ambiance. I immediately loved what I saw and felt comfortable with the people, both native and foreign. Melinda also felt comfortable in this small town atmosphere and seemed to relax in comparison to the other destinations. After checking in at the local youth hostel, we proceeded to explore.

"*Hola chicas*, where are you from?" The broken English came from a handsome young man dressed in jeans and a denim coat. He was very dark and appeared to have Indian heritage.

I felt immediately drawn to him, as if I already knew him. *"Somos Americanos, pero estabamos estudiando en San Miguel de Allende. Habla Ingles?"*

"Oh, art students from San Miguel. My name is César," he quickly replied.

Introductions were made and César informed us he was a native of Antigua and offered to give us a tour, which was most appreciated. We felt comfortable with him and didn't feel the pressure men usually gave us. He worked at the art school and had many friends from all over the world. During the tour, César and I hit it off and talked nonstop. After a shared meal, Melinda excused herself and returned to the hostel.

César and I talked until early in the morning. An undeniable attraction between the two of us led me to invite him to spend the night in my very small bed. I didn't know what it was about him, but I felt as if it was love at first sight. Our souls connected and we felt the same on many of the subjects we shared. We didn't have sex, just held each other. *Who is this guy and what is it about him that draws me so strongly to him?* I thought as I nodded off.

The next day César offered to accompany us to Lago Atitlán to visit the many villages around the lake where back strap weavings were done. Each village had its own weaving pattern and we wanted to get a sample of each type. We were happy to have his company, especially me.

César knew the area well and after a two hour bus ride, we found a hotel for the night. The next day we would hike around the five mile lake and stop at each of the seven villages to look at weavings. A good meal was shared and we went to bed.

Again we shared a night of holding one another without sex. I really appreciated he wasn't pushy to have sex and was happy to just cuddle. I felt I loved him already. It was very exciting, but also very scary, because we would be parting ways and I wasn't looking forward to experiencing lost love. César's feelings were the same. He continually referred to how comfortable he was with me and how he felt as if he had known me all his life. It was strangely wonderful.

The next day was filled with hiking and viewing weavings. César knew people around the lake and was able to bring us right to the homes where weavings were available to view and buy. Each village's patterns were incredibly intricate and colorful. Women, along with children as young as five years old, were doing the back strap weaving. The strings of the weavings were secured to trees and pulled tight and attached around the backs of the weavers, thus back strap weaving.

"*Puedo tomar su fotografía?*" I asked a young girl tied to a tree with her weaving as I pointed at my camera. Very shy, the girl nodded with her hand open to receive some money. "They know even a photo is worth money!" I happily dropped a few coins in her hand, took the picture and bought one of her weavings. By the end of the visit, the girl gave me an adoring hug and wanted to leave with us.

"*Lo siento, niña, pero debe quedar con su mama!*" César broke the news that she couldn't go and placed a kiss on her forehead as they turned to go. My heart ached watching how sweet César was with the child, "He'll be a good father to someone someday. If only it were with me." My heart was already starting to moan over the end of the love affair.

A pile of beautiful weavings were strewn out over our entire room and we examined and appreciated our bounty. We had to be very careful how much we purchased on this trip because it had to be carried in our backpacks, which were already stuffed. Luckily, we could wear some of the woven shirts and skirts, which we had already put on.

"Beautiful women, you are both beautiful women. I am the envy of my friends!" César flattered us.

"Ah, and you are the handsome man escorting the beautiful women; my friends would also be envious," I lovingly replied.

"Mushy, mushy, mushy. I need my handsome man by my side soon or I will die of sadness. I'll see you two in the morning. Thanks, César, for taking us around today. You are a good man. Nancy has good taste." Smiling, Melinda turned away from us with a tear in her eye.

Another ideal night was spent together, both cherishing this new friendship and not talking about the future days ahead.

César took us to the Mercado the next morning for breakfast. We had the traditional drink of rice and milk served steaming hot in a big glass. It came in vanilla or chocolate and satisfied our hunger completely.

This market was so different from most we had been to in Mexico. In Mexico, they were noisy and vendors came at you greedily. But here in Guatemala, it was so quiet. Vendors smiled and nodded without saying a word or chasing us for a sale. César said the Guatemaltecos were known as *los tranquilos*, the tranquil ones. That expressed it exactly for me; I had felt that energy since we crossed into Guatemala.

I savored the time with César the next day and was happy when he told me he would take the bus partway to the border with us. I could have those precious hours with him before our departure.

The bus was crowded but quiet. César and I sat close, holding hands and smiling soulfully at one another. We promised to write and hoped one day to see each other again. Once he stepped off the bus, I quietly cried. Locals on the bus watched and saw the lovers' separation and were particularly friendly to me for the remainder of the ride. I couldn't believe I felt so strongly toward him. *Doubtful, but maybe, just maybe, I will see him again.* My hope lessened the pain in my heart and soul. Now I understood what Melinda had been enduring. I turned to her and gave her a big hug as we quietly watched the landscape pass.

The border crossing between Guatemala and Mexico was nothing more than a shack in the middle of remote mountains. A few travelers got off and were whisked away by their greeting parties, leaving us two *Americanas* alone at the border shack. The bus turned around and headed back from where it had just come, as the border was the destination point. Two big, unkempt, non-smiling guards told us to enter the shack to process our paperwork, both of them eyeballing two traveling girls.

"*Por qué estan viajas solas?*" A greasy, arrogant guard was suspicious of two females traveling by themselves.

"We are headed home after traveling. We are students from San Miguel de Allende and now are heading to the United States." I responded in Spanish with confidence and a smile.

He turned to his coworker and they spoke between themselves. We expected a quick stamp on our passports and then to find our way to the bus station about five miles away.

The guards approached, both looking us up and down, especially Melinda with her long blond hair.

"*Venga conmigo!*" The first guard approached Melinda, took her arm and led her away to a room and closed the door. The other guard led me to another room.

"Where are you taking us, why are you separating us?" I got nervous as I saw Melinda taken away. I was wishing César was still with us.

"*Necesito sus papeles.*" I handed him my papers as he asked.

This is weird and scary, maybe I'm over reacting, but this does not seem safe. They are officials, so they can't get away with much, or can they? Thoughts went around and around in my head but I tried to remain calm.

Meanwhile, the guard totally disassembled my backpack, supposedly looking for drugs.

"Where is my friend?" Over an hour had passed and I was getting frantic and worried something was happening to Melinda. The guard wouldn't say much and would go in and out of the room. If only César was here he could make it right. Another frantic hour passed and I yelled to the guard, demanding to see my friend.

Suddenly, as if nothing had happened out of the ordinary, the guard came in, handed me the stamped passport, and led me and my backpack to where Melinda was standing, looking pale and frightened. He released the two of us to cross the border.

"Are you okay, did they hurt you?" I was panicked as I hurled questions at Melinda.

"I'm fine. He didn't do anything but watch me and tear apart my backpack. I thought he was going to do something, but finally, he just told me to go. That was awful, let's get out of here before they change their minds."

"What did they want with us? I thought we were surely going to be raped. It's as if they were just playing mind games with us. Let's book." Melinda and I took off down the road, not caring where it took us, just as long as it was far from the two creeps. We went over and over our experience, trying to make some sense of it and didn't unlock arms for the entire five-mile walk to the bus stop. We waited another three hours for the bus but didn't mind; at least we were away from the guards.

For the first time since I left home I realized how at risk we were in another country. So far, most experiences had been within our control, but the border crossing proved how helpless the two of us potentially could be. Rules and laws were only theory here and totally at the authority of whatever power-hungry officials deemed they could get away with, which was a lot. My naiveté was exposed.

I realized I missed the comfort and security of the United States. Maybe the University of New Mexico in the fall wasn't such a bad idea after all. Dazed and confused, we fell into the deep sleep of exhaustion.

The next stop was San Cristóbal de Las Casas, a beautiful little pueblo where every mode of transportation was crowded to the max. People and packages rode on the top of the bus! People held on to anything that moved, including burros, cows, and horses. This was the town norm, and everyone was doing their morning routine. Conversations around us were in many different Indian dialects. The terrain was mountainous jungle, humid but not too hot. We found the local hostel, settled in, and went to the mercado for food. Beautiful fruits, vegetables, and flowers lined streets that resembled Shangri-La. A big, domed white church was at the center of the Zócalo, and lines of colorfully painted buildings were where people gathered to talk and trade goods.

The men dressed in wonderful light white muslin tunics and pants with colorful ribbons sewed on the sides and front. Their hats were flat sombreros with the same colorful ribbons dangling around the circumference of the hat hanging around their heads. This was their everyday wear but it looked as if they were dressed for a very special occasion. Again, I missed César.

The day passed quickly and the next day we left for Oaxaca to get Melinda on a flight home. We were thoughtful and quiet, knowing this was the end of the road for our travel abroad together. I was nervous to travel alone after the border incident, but I had met many single female travelers on the road and knew I would be okay if I was alert and stayed in public areas.

"Well, this will be our last stop together so let's do something special, Melinda."

"Like what? It's all been so special."

"Let's buy a surprise for each other to represent this trip together."

"That's a good idea. We'll go to the Mercado once we get settled. We won't have much time because my flight leaves early in the morning. I'm so excited to get home. I'm sorry if I've been such a drag, wanting to go home, but I can't help it."

"I know, Melinda. You have real love in your life. Great parents, a boyfriend … lots to look forward to. And you know what? I have great parents too. They are just old fashioned, but they love me and have done a lot for me. I'll find my love one day; I just have more living to do first." We agreed that I would call often while on my own.

Oaxaca was a bustling city, but manageable. We found a hotel room over the Mercado and sat for hours watching all the action below from our window. The moment was filled with sentiments of departure and we felt private and not inclined to get out in the crowd. Finally, we wanted to go find our special gifts for one another so we entered the moving mass below.

After combing the Mercado, we both found our gifts and decided to present them over a margarita and dinner, the last dinner.

"Oh my goodness, Melinda, this is beautiful and far too expensive." I examined the opal and silver pendant in the shape of a flying bird. The opal was a large specimen and carried the iridescent blues and greens I loved. Not only was it my birthstone but my favorite colors.

"The bird is you, Nancy. You want to soar and have your wings wide open to catch currents of opportunity." Melinda smiled to see me captivated by her gift. "Wear it and always know I am with you in spirit, you know, birds of a feather flock together!"

"Thank you so much, Melinda. I love this and will always treasure it as I do our friendship. Now, open mine."

Melinda opened a small ring box that contained two gems, one garnet and the other amber. The ring was two separate silver puzzle rings that when fit perfectly together, became one. "This is you and me, Melinda, I am the garnet and you are the amber. We are interwoven and ultimately are separate beauties, but live together as a whole and complement each other."

"It's perfect, Nancy. It is us, isn't it? Forever sisters!" We lifted our margaritas and toasted our friendship.

Neither of us was in the mood to do anything other than stay quiet and together, so we returned to the hotel, arms linked, and prepared for an early morning departure.

I watched as Melinda boarded the plane, waving goodbye the entire time. It was a very difficult parting and we both had red eyes and heavy hearts.

"Well, it's just me now." I felt vulnerability mixed with excitement. I went back to the hotel and, for the remainder of the day, sat window watching the Mercado drama below. I ran out only to make a phone call home to reassure the parents. Predictably, both Mom and Dad were worried and tried to talk me into cutting my plans short when I told them I would be traveling for another month yet.

I agreed to call again the next night, then curled up with a Mexico map to plot my next chapter. I wanted to see the ocean again and had heard about Puerto Escondido. It would be a difficult bus ride, which I definitely was getting tired of, so I decided to splurge and take a short flight there and then return to bus travel. From there, I would travel up the coast toward Acapulco, stopping wherever I wanted, then turn inland toward Mexico City, stopping at Taxco first. After that, I'd see how much money I had left and either locate a few more places to stop or head back to San Miguel de Allende to pack up and head home. Content with my plan, I fell into a fitful sleep.

I hadn't felt like a lone traveler until I departed from the plane and looked for a place to stay. Melinda had always been by my side, and even though we got stared at wherever we went, I felt safety in her company.

Now, people looked at me over and over, looking, I assumed, to see who I was with, because no woman of right mind would be traveling by herself. I stroked my bird pendant and it brought peace.

"It is dangerous to travel alone, let me help you find a safe place to stay, a safe place to eat, a safe place to be …" Everyone told me the same thing and I responded that I was fine. The suspicious looking men were told my husband was in the store and I was waiting for him.

Near Puerto Escondido was a small village called Barra de Navidad. According to Jenny, there was a beautiful beach there where foreign travelers hung out and one could hang a hammock between palm trees instead of staying in a hotel. That sounded great to me, so I asked around about getting there. Barra de Navidad was very small, with only a few buildings making up the town. The beach where all the gringos stayed was a short walk from the bus drop so I hoisted my yellow backpack and followed the trail pointed out by a Mexican of few words.

Sure enough, the beach was heavily occupied by palm trees and one area had hammocks hanging between them. Where were all the travelers? No one was around except a young Mexican boy. Chapo introduced himself in Spanish and showed me where I could hang my hammock, then showed me to the trail through the palm tree forest. I felt funny leaving my stuff hanging in the hammock as I walked away, but Chapo convinced me it was okay and he would look after it. After I gave him some pesos, he left me as the trail entered an absolutely stunning beach. It was endless and clean with pounding surf. In the distance I saw a small party of travelers swimming, surfing, and sun bathing. I wanted some time to myself, so I chose to walk the opposite direction for a while before approaching any of the beach group.

No one in the world knows where I am. I walked, pondering my situation. It felt great to have time to myself without worrying about anyone or anything. *I can't believe how I've learned and changed from my time abroad. I'm inspired to share my art and maybe even teach batik. My Spanish is fluent enough that I even dream in Spanish. I will combine this all somehow in my future, I'm ready to soar.*

My experience had released joy in my gypsy soul and now was time to follow its wishes. I enjoyed traveling by myself and doing what I wanted, when I wanted, and how I wanted. I realized it had exhausted and drained me to be the constant translator, and I'd felt responsible for Melinda's unhappiness. The liberation from that burden was immense. Very simply, I loved *my* life.

The only troublesome feeling was the continual heartache from missing César, but it was just not meant to be. Lost in thought, I had wandered far from the group and decided I better turn around. After spending a few hours on my own I was ready to meet the travelers and maybe share a meal with them. The group was six men and three women from Germany, Australia, Switzerland, and Canada. We all shared a meal and stories by a fire under the stars. Everyone fell within the same age range and shared the wanderlust I felt. I noted to myself that now I had stories to share around the fire and was no longer an amateur traveler. Some had more travel experience and others had less, which made me feel proud of myself.

Sleeping in a hammock swinging between two palm trees under the stars with waves pounding off the shore fulfilled a fantasy and etched a memory deep in my heart and soul. Nice people, basic food, good stories, and simplicity. I loved it and felt my real spirit spring forth. I really liked this person I was becoming. My self-esteem had always been riddled with guilt, comparisons, or denial; now it was a blossoming flower—beautiful, full of color and confidence. *Mom and Dad will be proud to see how I've grown.* I wished on a falling star and fell into a peaceful sleep swaying gently in the hammock.

The next two days repeated the first. I took time to sketch, journal, and walk, exploring and nurturing this new sense of self. A quick phone call to the folks was made nightly to put everyone at ease.

The couple from Australia was leaving on a bus the next morning and I decided to head north with them to my next adventure. Barra de Navidad had been significant to me, as I felt a very imperceptible shift deep within, which brought me closer to my power. The time alone in nature allowed me to catch up and assimilate my experiences of the past nine months. I felt stronger, more confident, and sure of myself. I was ready to go home, go to school, and make something of myself.

The bus ride to Acapulco went through thick jungle, and not much could be seen other than trees. I used this time to draw in my sketchbook and write in my journal. People on the bus became subjects for the drawings and posed happily. If they really wanted the sketch, I gave it to them, but I wanted to keep most for future reference. Acapulco was huge and I didn't look forward to spending even one night there, but the Australians offered to have me to join them at their hotel. It was a little more expensive, but I thought it was worth it to not be lost in such a big city alone. The couple was kind enough to treat me to a meal as they saw

I was counting pennies. We found a beautiful place overlooking the city and watched the sunset and city lights before retiring to the hotel.

I hadn't had such a comfortable room since the Hans took Melinda and me to a hotel in San Miguel de Allende. It was more expensive, but I was starting to feel ready to head back home and would save money by not stopping in so many places. Barra de Navidad changed me. I'd found what I had been looking for—myself. Now I could start the next chapter of life at home.

"Mom, I'm coming home sooner than planned. I have one more stop in Taxco, and then I'll go to San Miguel, pack my stuff, and catch a bus to the border. Do you think someone can pick me up in El Paso, or should I take a bus from there?" I was getting excited to see Mom.

"Oh darling, that is the best news I've had since you left. We'll come to El Paso and pick you up, just let us know when you get closer to knowing the exact time. Work has been very busy and I could use a break, especially to see my baby!" Apparently, Dad was nodding in agreement. "How are you?"

"Great, Mom, I have so much to tell you. My gypsy has wings now and I'm ready to fly home!"

I could imagine my father's wince and the conversation between them afterward. Mom would want more time with me; he would want me to follow some version of his idea of 'being on track' and both would be happy to see the youngest of their kids all grown up.

After I hung up, I took an extra-long hot shower and watched a movie on TV; what decadence after sparse living for so long. *Well, I know I can live like a vagabond if I need to and be quite happy. In fact, I prefer it; it keeps me humble and not relying on material things for my happiness. But, it is nice to have this once in a while.* I snuggled into the soft cozy bed and fell asleep before the movie ended.

The Australians shared a taxi with me and dropped me off at the bus station on their way to the airport. Addresses and hugs were exchanged and we traded wishes for safety, health, and future visits. I was on my way to Taxco!

* * *

Infused with new excitement, purpose, and quenched worry, I wanted to make the most of the time before I got home. Focused on being present every moment of the day nurtured my new confidence and joy. Speaking only Spanish gave direct access to my gypsy self and expressed my thoughts perfectly. People were surprised to hear a *gringa* speak their language so well and asked regularly if I was Mexicana.

Taxco was known for its silver and its red roofs. The pueblo was a beautiful sight, as the bus came around the winding bend up the mountain. Tucked up against hillsides, every building was white with red clay tile roofs, and bougainvillea of every color framed most homes.

The next day I explored the town. Every shop, vendor, and corner was selling silver jewelry in every shape, size, and form. I treated myself to a bracelet, bought a pin for Mom and a necklace for Mrs. Han. After shopping, I found a small park with a fountain and lush flowers and trees.

I took out my sketch pad. Across the fountain from me, two middle-aged gentlemen were in a lively conversation using their hands and arms. By their appearance and animated gesture, I wondered if they were Italian. Could I capture them on paper? The men were intrigued as they noticed me continually looking up at them and then down to my paper. After thirty minutes of steady sketching, I stood up to stretch. "Time for some food." I gathered my bag and took the path toward town, passing near the gentlemen.

"Hello young lady." The man had an accent and sparkling eyes. "What have you been drawing?"

I had to admit I'd been sketching them. They introduced themselves as Frank and Giuseppe and confirmed they were Italian. They were on their way to Acapulco on business, stopping in Taxco mainly to buy silver gifts for their wives. I was relieved when they mentioned wives. They admired my drawing, and we had an afternoon of delightful conversation. When they invited me to have dinner with them, I happily accepted. It was like visiting with a couple of older uncles. Over coffee and dessert, Frank informed me he had a gift for me. Intriguing ...

"Nancy, my family is from a long line of gypsies in Italy. We have always been in the arts trade and well, fortune telling." Frank looked directly at me with conviction. "I don't do it often, but occasionally someone touches me, and the calling is there. You are someone I would like to give this gift to, I would like to read your palms and tell your fortune. What do you think?"

"Wow! I've never met a real gypsy, but I've always felt I had that spirit." I told them about my experience on the mesa as a teenager and how it had driven me since.

"I felt that in you, my dear. You do have a gypsy spirit; we can always recognize one another." Giuseppe nodded in agreement as Frank spoke. "Giuseppe and I have known each other's families for generations and have been part of the same historical gypsy lineage. So, what do you say?"

"I would be honored." I was humbled and my instinct beamed with excitement.

Frank reached for my hands and we three drew close as he examined every aspect, front and back. For five minutes he didn't say a word, just worked his eyebrows up and down.

"Well, Nancy, you have very unique lines." He told me I would have two very significant relationships in my life. My life would be full of heart and art. I was strong willed and would travel many places. Three children would be in my life. "But, this line worries me," he said as he traced the line by my thumb "This is your life line. It is strong, but there is a significant break in it. The lines barely parallel each other where they break, see it here?"

I looked at my hand and saw how the life line totally separated, then continued a half inch up. The lines did not connect, but overlapped in a faint parallel. "What does that show?"

"Well, there is going to be something very significant and dangerous that happens to you, potentially life threatening. It will be in the near future. Beware, be careful. It does seem you will survive, but it will be close and I don't feel a hundred percent that all will be okay. Please child, be careful, these lines are unusual and I have never seen anything like this before, and I've done many." Frank looked at me with care and concern, as did Giuseppe.

I didn't know what to say or think. He seemed serious. Did I really believe in this stuff? Were these guys playing with me? I couldn't take it too seriously, but didn't want to offend them either. "I'll be careful, don't worry. I'll be fine."

They walked me to my hotel and we took turns to embrace one another.

"Thank you for the good company. Here, take the sketch." I reached for my sketchbook.

"No, no, you keep it to remember us and to remember what I told you." Frank lightly kissed me on the cheek, took Giuseppe's arm and led him away.

Frank's words came back to me. Two significant relationships in my life ... unconsciously, I noted his warning of danger but really didn't want to give it too much acknowledgement. Once in my room, I became melancholy as I realized my trip was coming to an end.

The next morning I boarded the bus which would travel straight through to San Miguel de Allende. After packing up, I would take one more bus ride to Juarez, cross the border, and meet Mom and Dad. Part of me was excited and the other was sad it was ending.

This had been the best time of my life and I didn't know when I would be able to travel again for a long while. It would be okay though; now it was time to get on with school. Maybe I would meet my first significant relationship this summer; it would help me get over César.

My journal was becoming a book. I wrote furiously in it for the first part of the bus ride. Sometimes I would add a sketch or doodle to the words or tape a postcard or photo on its pages. "When I get home, I will collage the cover and enter it into the first edition of *Travels with Nancy*." This journal and my sketchbook were the most valuable possessions I owned. It was proof of my coming of age and of using my gypsy wings for the first time in my life. These conversations, feelings, stories, and art ideas would become a map for my future as I referred back to them for inspiration or notions for action. It would also help me feel César was near.

The long ride made me very grateful to see the church steeple of San Miguel de Allende appear in the distance. Descending off the bus and putting my foot on the ground washed me with a sense of relief to be somewhere familiar. The plan was to stay at Jenny's before leaving for the U.S. I hadn't realized my internal radar had been beeping to keep me safe in all the unfamiliar territory I had been in. It turned off the moment I touched ground in San Miguel de Allende, my home away from home.

Jenny wasn't home, but her new roommate was there to let me in. After introductions, I put my pack down and decided I'd better go make some phone calls. Mom was ecstatic to hear I was back to San Miguel. "I'll phone you in a few days with exact dates and times Mom, but I need a few days to get myself together here first." I felt so much older than when I left home as the rebel.

Jenny couldn't get over how good I looked. "You look older and more beautiful. Did you fall in love?"

"Funny you should say that." Jenny and I spent hours catching up over the travel stories. It was a good time and with each day, I was more prepared to head home and start my new life, not as a rebel.

After a week, everything was in order for my departure from

San Miguel and journey to the border. The next day I would board a Chihuahuenese Bus (Mexican version of a Greyhound Bus) and in two days' time would arrive in Juarez. I would taxi to the border and meet my parents on the other side, where we would stay the night in El Paso before driving home the next day to Los Alamos. This was such a straightforward simple itinerary, I was almost disappointed after all the complicated travel plans I had just completed.

A piece of cake, I thought as I put my journal and sketchbook, along with a book and snacks, into my small bag to carry on the bus. My big yellow backpack was stuffed to the seams with all I'd accumulated since I left on this journey. Batiks, weavings, Mexican shirts and skirts, jewelry, and everything else I owned were fit into the well-worn backpack that would be below in the luggage compartment.

I told Jenny, "I will be glad to not lug this heavy backpack anymore. I am really tired of that aspect of travel and will do it differently next time, something with wheels! And it definitely will not be yellow; it will be blue or green."

Chapter 11

Homeward Bound

May 12, 1977

J enny and Maggie walked with me to the bus station and we hugged.
"Keep up with that beautiful batik, and don't crush too many hearts!" Jenny had a tear in her eye.

"Say hi to Melinda for us; we'll miss you, and if we ever pass through your town, we'll go for a margarita. Be good. Be safe!" Maggie waved enthusiastically.

"Write! I hope our paths cross again! Do art!" I yelled out the window by my seat.

The bus left a cloud of diesel to choke the crowd. I watched my two friends turn up the familiar street heading to the Instituto and wondered if I had made the right decision. *Those two have been here for years and seem very happy. I could do the same. But for some reason, I'm pulled to go home. Got to listen to my heart. Bye, César, wherever you are!* I settled into my seat and watched pensively as San Miguel de Allende disappeared. Once I couldn't see it any more, I turned forward to watch the landscape until I dozed off.

Awakened by my growling stomach, I rummaged through my bag for some food. After eating an orange and a sandwich, I took notice of the other passengers on the bus. People got on at every stop, and now the bus had about twenty people, but most were sitting up front by the driver. I always preferred sitting closer to the back, with more privacy.

"All these Mexican bus drivers have religious saints watching them on the dashboard, framed by rows of colorful dingle-bobs, how tacky, and what's with that?" I mused. "And they all drive like bats out of hell, even though they don't get to their destinations any faster."

A few seats behind me, on the other side of the aisle, two cute Mexican boys were watching me. At first, I ignored them, but after a few hours decided to start a conversation. They were on their way to Chihuahua to visit their brothers and possibly work in the family business, making boots. Both were very sweet and funny, so I enjoyed passing the time by telling stories with them. The boys moved directly across the aisle from me and left empty seats between us which I was happy about. I wanted some time to myself to let this new chapter unfold.

The bus would arrive in Juarez midday tomorrow, Sunday. Luckily, the bus was a luxury style, the best one I had been on since arriving in Mexico, probably because it went to the United States border. The average count was thirty passengers, so the bus was never completely full. These things mattered to me, as I knew the more passengers, the more stinky the bathrooms would be by the end of the ride.

The sketchbook and journal occupied me, as did lively conversation with the two cute Mexican boys. I missed César. He was so different from these two boys. He had an artist's soul and was more mature. I sighed and decided to look through my sketchbook at my drawings from Antigua. A sketch of César looked back at me. It wasn't exact, but did capture his resemblance and mood. "At least I have this." Somber thoughts filled me. Not wanting to get depressed, I closed the sketchbook and watched the next small town appear on the horizon.

A *torta* was handed to me through the bus window by a vendor before the bus started rolling again. It was midafternoon now and we had been on the road six hours. That was the problem with buses; they stopped at every single town, doubling the length of the trip. I had learned patience throughout my travels, but for some reason, wasn't as patient this time. A light rain started falling as we passed through the middle of nowhere.

Excitement flowed through me, as I knew I would see Mom and Dad … tomorrow. *Wow, it's been over ten months since I've seen them! I wonder if I'll look different to them. I think I put on weight eating all those pastries and fried food. I know Mom will be happy to see me and forgive me. I wonder when I'll see Rick, Howard and Doug. Howard moved to California for a job, so maybe I can go visit him before school starts.* My thoughts went round and round in wonder.

The two Mexican cuties asked me to share some of their pastries and the three of us returned to storytelling and making each other laugh.

Suddenly both boys' eyes grew huge, as they stared and pointed out the window behind me.

I turned to look as we entered a curve. The movement of the bus was different, as if it were floating. Suddenly, the landscape was above and the sky was below; time stood still. The bus flew off the highway down an embankment. I instinctively tucked.

My life flashed before me and somehow I understood. Everything changed and I wouldn't be seeing Mom, Dad, my brothers …

Blackness, loud crunching, windows breaking, grinding metal, more loud crunching, silence.

* * *

I felt myself rolling to my back then slowly, sound entered my ears. The noise of whirring tires came first. Groans, screams and crying filled the air. My eyes opened to the blue sky above. What happened? Increased groaning, screaming, crying. An uncanny peace filled me.

I tried to turn my head, but my body refused to move. Terror replaced the peace. Sounds and smells invaded my paralyzed world. The smell of dirt mixed with smoke and diesel filled my nostrils. Methodically, I attempted to move different parts of my body, but only my eyes could move. I heard blood-curdling cries and my eyes focused on the bus, which was lying on its roof fifty yards away. The tires whirred without contact to the pavement. The driver screamed as people tried to pull him out; he was pinned under the bus. As I watched, his form became limp. It became obvious he'd died when everyone backed off and left him there.

Bodies were strewn everywhere; groans, cries and whimpers continued to fill the air. *Why can't I move anything?* I desperately fought the fatigue that washed over me. I couldn't. I closed my eyes. Time stopped. Next time I opened them, which seemed an eternity, nothing had changed. I tried to talk; nothing came out. A few people walked around the bodies, dazed and confused. Again, exhaustion consumed me and I closed my eyes.

"*Señorita! Señorita!*" The two Mexican boys were talking to me, so I opened my eyes and smiled innocently. "What happened?" I mumbled. The boys said the bus wrecked and they were waiting for help. They would look for my backpack and put it by me. "Journal, sketchbook, please," I managed to whisper. That was all I really cared about. They told me to lie still and they would return. *No problem, especially since I can't seem to move,* I thought helplessly before dozing off again. An awkward detachment permeated me. I felt millions of miles away.

"*Señorita! Señorita!*" Again the two boys tried to rouse me. "*Aquí está su backpack, no podemos encontrar sus otras cosas pero vamos a continuar a buscarlos.*" They looked at me so seriously, and I just wanted to assure them all was well. I was happy they found my backpack, but was frantic for them to locate my journal and sketchbook.

"So tired, so, so, tired." I kept falling in and out of consciousness. Endless desert surrounded us and no one was coming to help. *Where are they? Why is it taking so long? Why can't I move?* The thoughts cycled over and over; nothing happened for an eternity as I drifted in and out.

The boys returned after a long time (I later learned it was about forty-five minutes). Since no help had come, travelers were stopping to put accident victims in their vehicles and take them to the nearest town, Fresnillo. An old couple offered to take me, so a group surrounded me for the transfer. By now I was barely conscious but understood what was going to happen before I went unconscious again.

Pain engulfed every square inch of my existence, and torrential screams exploded out of me as I was picked up and carried to the car. Never in my life had I felt such agony. The torment was relentless as the group pushed, pulled, and jostled me. The last thing I remembered was finally being laid in the back seat of a beat up sedan with an old man and woman looking at me with tenderness and worry from the front seat. Unconsciousness was my welcomed friend.

The next time my eyes opened, I was in a stark grey hospital room shared with many others in beds lined up in rows. Moans, cries, and a sickening stench filled my senses.

"Agua." I quietly croaked. *Please, someone bring me water I'm soooo thirsty,* I thought over and over, but no one helped. Whenever I awoke, I saw no one other than those moaning from their beds. My throat was parched. Finally, a nurse found me with my eyes open and excitedly brought a doctor over.

"*Como esta, como se siente?*" The doctor asked, but I only could nod with my eyes and say *agua.* They continued to question me but I just fell back into unconsciousness.

I had no idea how much time passed, but it was dark outside and I still didn't have water. I was increasingly distressed that everyone refused to give me even one drop of water. "*Por favor, sólo una gota.*" I just wanted a drop.

My eyes opened to a circle of young girls looking at me. They were nurses in training, helping the critical patients. The students asked if they could do anything for me.

"*Agua.*" But no one would help. One student saw my misery and ultimately got the okay to occasionally give me, literally, *a* drop of water. She explained to me they didn't know what my injuries were and it could be fatal to let me drink water. At least someone explained it to me. *Injuries, what injuries?* Maybe a broken shoulder because there was extreme pain there.

No one spoke English in this hospital, and they didn't know what to do with this American in their midst. It was a small, stark government clinic with few supplies and abilities. The last thing they wanted was to have an American die here; it presented great complications. I spoke in Spanish whenever I did speak, but that wasn't very much. I would nod, smile and mutter answers while conscious, but that never lasted long. On one occasion when I was conscious they managed to get my name. The only phone number I could remember was my brother's, and I happily gave it to them, and then went unconscious again.

Pain exploded, shattering the tranquility of the darkness, as I felt hands moving me from the bed. "Nooooooo!!!!!!!" My scream filled the room.

"We have to get x-rays and don't have the machine here in the clinic, so we will transport you to the Red Cross where there is one," One of the trainee nurses explained in Spanish to me. I cared about nothing but the excruciating pain.

Comfortably unconscious, I was transported to the Red Cross. I remembered waking in a vehicle momentarily, then welcomed the darkness once again.

"NNNNNNNNOOOOOOOOOO!!!!!!!!!" Again hands were moving me.

"You must get up on the table so we can get x-rays, you can do it…." the voice in Spanish said.

"I can't, *no puedo*……ahhhhhhhhhhh" I wanted them to leave me alone, but they wouldn't. They assisted me onto the table as I fought with unconsciousness and agony. That was the last thing I remembered.

"Nurse, give her another shot of pain killer," someone ordered in Spanish.

"*Pobrecita, tanto mucho dolor.*" A sweet voice was accompanied by a stroking hand on my forehead, an attempt to ease the pain.

My awareness consisted of the sounds around me, the antiseptic smell of a hospital, thirst, pain—constant and extreme—then darkness.

The room was bright as I heard voices and opened my eyes. I was back in the grey room at the clinic where a woman with a blood-soaked bandage around her head was being led out of the room. As she left, two nurses were saying to each other how it was lucky the woman was able to go home, although she probably wouldn't survive. There were few people in the room with me now.

"*Agua.*" My garbled request was returned with one drop of water.

"She's awake, doctor." I heard a comment in Spanish.

A group of people surrounded the bed and looked at me very sadly.

"*No se preocupa, estoy bien.*" I didn't want them to be worried; I was fine.

"*Muy seriousa, chica.*" The doctor looked at me solemnly, as though I was going to die.

"*Estoy bien, no se preocupa.*" I whispered. What was everyone so worried about? I smiled and closed my eyes, thinking about how bad my shoulder felt.

Waking Up

Chapter 12

Dad To the Rescue

Hello, is this Rick Weintraub?" A man's voice was on the line. "Yes, may I help you?" Rick thought it was someone selling something and almost hung up.

"Rick, my name is Mr. Smythe and I am a missionary in Fresnillo, Mexico. On Sunday, I was notified by the San Jose Clinic that an American had been in a serious bus wreck between here and Zacatecas, and we think it might be your sister. What is her name?"

"Uh, you're kidding, oh my God, uh, her name is Weintraub, Nancy Weintraub. Pat, come here, Nancy's been in a bus wreck in Mexico!" Rick reeled from the news and alerted his wife to pick up the other line.

"Yes, that's her. Luckily, she speaks Spanish and was able to give us your number. The problem is no one in the hospital speaks English so I am acting as translator and advocate to get your sister home. She is in critical condition, but they can't do anything for two reasons. The clinic doesn't have capabilities for surgery, and it's against the law to do anything without consent from U.S. officials and the family."

"Oh my God, what's wrong with her?" Rick was pale.

"Well, that's part of the problem. They are not sure. They know she has internal injuries, but don't have the means to know without doing surgery. The Red Cross took an x-ray and saw there was massive internal bleeding. Time is of the essence to get care for her. Can someone come down here to get her?"

"Yes, give me contact information and where she is." Rick saw Pat writing down all the numbers as he was already figuring out the next step. "Thank you for helping Mr. Smythe, we'll be in touch in a few hours."

"Great, meanwhile I'll go to the clinic to find out the latest, I'll be by the phone in two hours." Mr. Smythe was already gathering his bag to head out.

"Jeez, Pat, this is Tuesday and the accident happened Sunday! I can't believe this; what a nightmare. I'd better call Mom and Dad."

He explained about the call from Mexico; the phone was silent on the other end. "That's all I know, Dad. What do you want me to do? Pat found out Fresnillo is a tiny town north of San Miguel de Allende about three hundred miles."

"Oh my God, that's all you know? I have to tell your Mom. Give me a minute. I'm in shock." Dad hung his head.

"What's wrong, Larry?" Mom saw his reaction. "What happened? Tell me! It's Nan, isn't it, Lar talk to me."

"Son, I'll call you back, but please start looking for flights to Fresnillo. I'll call you back."

"Cheney, calm down. Listen. Nancy has been in an accident." Dad knew Mom was going to fall to pieces and he would have to be strong for her and everyone, so he put his frenzied emotions aside as he told her. She did fall to pieces, but Dad was already in planning mode.

He would have to get to Albuquerque first to take any kind of flight out, so he headed to the bedroom to pack a bag. Mom was crying and wild with distress. "Please dear, I know how hard this is, but we've got to pull ourselves together. Time is of the essence."

She responded and helped, even though she was crying the whole time. "Pack a bag, Cheney. Come to Albuquerque with me and you can stay at Rick and Pat's until we know our next step."

Dad phoned his boss, Mr. Hew, and told him of the emergency. "Larry, whatever I can do to help, just let me know. If you can bring her here to Los Alamos, I can help with whatever security clearances you may need."

That may come in handy, Dad thought. "Rick, what have you found out?" Dad asked when he called back.

"Well, Dad, it's not good because the town is in the middle of nowhere. First you will have to fly to Guanajuato, take a short flight to Zacatecas, and then bus it from there." Rick delivered the bad news.

"Nothing is quicker? How long would that take? We're coming

down. Keep looking—see you soon." Dad didn't like what he heard. At that speed it could be Thursday before he could even arrive at the clinic.

"Sir, I'm sorry, there is no other way to get there unless you have a private airplane and diplomatic connections," the airline operator stated. "Book the flight for 9 p.m. departure tonight for one adult, you say? Okay, that's flight 234 to Guanajuato arriving tomorrow, Wed. May15th, 1977 at 10 a.m."

Rick and Pat decided to book what they could and get Dad on the way. He called Mr. Smythe to tell him the arrangements up to this point.

"I can drive to Guanajuato and pick him up; that would be the fastest way. Plane service to Zacatecas is slim and it's about a five hour drive compared to twelve hours by bus. They stop everywhere." His offer was accepted.

There was no change in my status, I still bordered on critical to fatal.

* * *

Dad and Mom arrived around four in the afternoon at Rick and Pat's Albuquerque house and got caught up with the plan. Mom had become despondent and cried continually.

"Son, please stay by your mom. I'm worried about her. Have you contacted your brothers?" Rick nodded. "What about the flight to Guanajuato, has that been booked?"

"Yes, Dad." Rick and Dad went to the den, while Pat made a cup of tea for Mom and tried to give her comfort. "Damn Mexico, I knew something was going to happen. She shouldn't have gone. It's my fault for letting her ... my baby, my baby ..." Mom cried hysterically.

"Mom, calm down. We don't even know anything yet, calm down." Pat attempted to console her, but it was useless. This was just how it was going to be, so she decided to help with the plans and let Mom have some quiet.

Travel arrangements were complete, at least getting there. Getting me home would be tricky, crossing international borders and taking me to Los Alamos without security clearances. Luckily, Dad had a passport.

Rick took charge. "Just get there, Dad. We can help arrange everything after we know what's needed. We'll call the Los Alamos Medical Center and Bernalillo Hospital to see what we need to do to prepare for her arrival."

"I prefer Los Alamos, Rick. This is going to be a long haul and it would be better if Mom and I can be home, plus the care is far superior there and we know everyone, especially with your Mom working at the hospital."

Rick had had many conflicts with his father, but a newfound respect emerged as he watched the clear-headed and forward thinking of his dad under such duress. The phone rang.

Rick answered and handed it to his father. "Mr. Weintraub, your daughter's internal bleeding is steady, and the doctor does not feel very favorable about her survival. I need you to know that, so you have no illusions as to the reality of the situation. She may not make it until you arrive, so be prepared." Mr. Smythe did not mince words.

"I understand. Thank you for helping us, and I'll see you tomorrow at the Guanajuato airport. My son says you'll have a sign with my name on it?" Dad spoke quietly; he didn't want to upset Mom further. He hung up the phone, telling Rick and Pat what Mr. Smythe said. Everyone was quiet and somber.

Pat put together sandwiches but everyone only nibbled. Both Howard and Doug called for an update and were told to be prepared to fly home at any moment. Mom clung to Dad as he went to the door. "I'll call regularly, dearest. I love you. Keep the faith and all will be well. Take care." Dad planted a firm and lingering kiss on his wife as he left the house. Rick took his dad to the airport, hugged him for the first time since he was a boy, and they both shed a tear as he turned to get on the plane.

Chapter 13

In Limbo

I opened my eyes. "*Agua.*" The pain geared up again so I asked for pain medication, "*Medicina de dolor, por favor.*"

My world revolved around pain, pain meds, drops of water, and assistance from the sweet nurses. I tried to talk with them when conscious, but just couldn't stay awake or summon the energy to speak. *I wish they wouldn't be so worried. I am fine, but they won't believe me.* Thoughts came and went. *My shoulder hurts terribly … maybe it's broken.* I fell asleep again.

"Dad is coming tomorrow?" I managed to respond to the nice missionary who visited and helped to communicate with my family. I smiled and closed my eyes. The pain meds dulled my mind more than the pain itself, but that was better than nothing. Time held no meaning; only the present moment registered in my mind.

The airline staff knew about Mr. Weintraub's emergency and was very keen and responsive to his requests. The lights were turned off for the long night ahead. Thoughts circled round and round in his mind. He struggled with his anger for allowing me to talk him into going to Mexico in the first place. Then his eyes filled with tears at the thought of losing me and he tried to prepare as Mr. Smythe had advised. No plans or details could be made, so Dad just had to sit with it. He recited his Hebrew prayers to calm himself and provide focus. Thanking the airline staff as he disembarked, Dad was exhausted from a fitful night without sleep.

The airport in Guanajuato was chaotic. "Who would have ever thought I would be here," Dad thought with melancholy.

Immediately he saw a gentleman with his name on a sign and approached him.

"Mr. Smythe?"

"Yes, pleased to meet you Mr. Weintraub. Please call me Jeff. I'm so sorry to meet you under these circumstances."

"Yes, and call me Larry. I only have a carry-on, so no need to go to the baggage terminal."

"Great, that will save time. Your daughter is still in the same condition, which is better than what it could be. My car is not far. It will take us about five hours to get to Fresnillo."

"Show me the way."

The two men hit it off immediately. Even though Dad was Jewish, he always respected anyone dedicated to the spiritual life. After being filled in on all details about Nancy, the conversation turned to their personal lives; family, religion, military, children, wives. Dad watched the countryside of Mexico pass as Jeff gave him a crash course on his life and experiences in Mexico. Jeff invited Dad to stay with him in his small home, an offer which was gratefully accepted.

The highway passed through endless desert. They came around a curve midway between Zacatecas and Fresnillo. "This is where the accident happened." Jeff pointed at the bus still lying on its back off the embankment with various trash and parts strewn across the dirt. "We learned Nancy was riding on the left side of the bus, and when it rolled down the hill, the window broke and she flew out. It is very lucky she wasn't crushed by the bus, because many were."

"How many were on the bus?" Dad felt sick to his stomach to imagine his little baby lying in the middle of this place, hurt.

"There were about thirty people. About ten died, ten were critical, and ten walked away. Those on the left side of the bus got it worst. I spoke with two young Mexican boys sitting on the right side who survived. They told me they tumbled inside the bus and the seats cushioned their impact. The boys had been sitting by your daughter and helped her after the wreck. They were able to get her pack and put it by her. It easily could have been stolen."

"Why did the bus go off the road?"

"Well, the bus drivers here in Mexico all drive too fast. It had been raining, and as the driver entered the curve, he didn't slow down, so the bus hydroplaned off the road. It could have been totally avoided, but these drivers often figure since they have a picture of their saints on the dashboards, they are protected. This is not an unusual occurrence; it happens all the time. Many Mexicans die every year in bus wrecks. What was unusual about this one was that an American was on the bus."

"Why doesn't somebody do something about it?" Dad was angry to hear it had been avoidable.

"No good answer for you, Larry. Mexico is untamed and does what it wants, how it wants, when it wants. There are few controls or regulations enforced. The accident happened far away from anywhere with ambulances, so drivers passing through picked up the hurt and brought them to Fresnillo, the closest town. Big cities are equipped, but no one else has resources. Mexicans are accustomed to this lifestyle and don't have the same expectations we do. Their world is ordered very differently. For example, the other critical patients brought to the clinic died for lack of means to pay for their care. Those with concussions or broken bones were sent home to the families to care for them the best they could. Some made it, many have not. Life is much harder here. Nancy is lucky to have you, because she would die here if she had to stay."

Tears welled up in Dad's eyes. It was too much to see the scene of the accident and to hear the background of the event. He broke down and sobbed. Jeff reached over and put his hand on Dad's shoulder and they remained quiet through the empty desert.

"We are almost there, Larry."

He nodded and watched with intent as they entered the poor desolate town. They pulled up to a block building off a side street with a faded sign saying San Jose Clinic. After parking, Jeff led Dad inside. It was stark, with cement grey bare walls and meager simple tables and chairs. It smelled of antiseptic mixed with sickness. Everyone knew who he was, they nodded and smiled with compassion. Dr. Gonzales walked up to greet them, reached out to shake Dad's hand and then a quick embrace. Dad was already surprised at the warmth of the people.

Jeff interpreted the doctor's words. With every moment, the reality of this situation sunk in deeper for Dad. No one spoke English, for starters; he was going to be totally reliant on Jeff. He wasn't used to that; he was always able to take care of himself.

"The doctor says your daughter is in a very precarious state. He knows there is internal bleeding, but not much more than that without further tests, which they can't do here. He has stitched up two areas on her head where there were gashes, but the skull is intact. She has extensive scrapes and cuts. They had to cut her clothing off when she came in and Nancy keeps asking for her shirt, but it was torn beyond repair. We need to get her home as quickly as possible. After you see her, we will work out a plan for departure. The doctor says to prepare to see her. She can't speak much or stay awake long, so a short visit is best."

His baby laid so still with her eyes closed. He had to watch for her chest going up and down to make sure she was breathing. Nancy looked different but he couldn't put his finger on what it was, maybe she had put on some weight. One of the nurses assisted them on the visit and approached the bedside.

"*Nancy, su papa esta aqui! Despiertase.*" Shaking my arm lightly, the nurse tried to rouse me.

My eyes flickered several times and my mouth was moving, as if I wanted to say something. "*Agua.*"

The nurse put the allotted drop of water in my mouth. "Ummm." I swallowed with difficulty, and then opened my eyes slowly. I looked at the nurse and smiled.

"*Nancy, su papa.*" The nurse brought Dad to my view.

"Hi Cheney." Dad choked out the words softly.

It took a moment for me to focus and understand who was standing in front of me. "Dad? *Como esta?*" I spoke as if he were the patient.

"I'm fine honey. I'm here to bring you home."

"*Bueno, como esta Mom?*"

"Mom misses you, and she is ... fine. I love you." Dad was holding back tears.

"*Te amo Dad, necesito dormir.*" I closed my eyes with a smile.

"What did she say, Jeff?" Dad was surprised to hear the Spanish response.

"She said, 'I love you, Dad, I need to sleep.' She only speaks in Spanish." Jeff watched Dad absorb the scene and backed off to allow him some private time with me.

"Give me just a moment, and then we can make our plan." Dad picked up my hand and stroked it. He closed his eyes and said a few prayers in Yiddish while tears streamed down his face. The staff watched from a distance, some also with tears in their eyes; they had become very fond of me.

Dad pulled himself together, gave me a kiss on the forehead, and turned to Jeff and the doctor.

"Dr. Gonzales invited us to his home for lunch. We can start figuring out what is next." Jeff took his arm and led him out.

Dad was quiet as the three walked a few blocks to the doctor's house. It was modest but nicer than most of the surrounding ones. As they entered, the aromas made Dad's stomach growl; he realized he hadn't eaten since he left home. The doctor's wife gave him a heartfelt hug as she led him to the table for soup, tortillas, beans, rice, and steak fajitas.

"Why is Nancy so bloated, Doctor?" Dad took a sip of soup.

"He says it's internal bleeding. If you were to see her abdomen, she almost appears pregnant."

"Oh my God, how am I going to get her home?" Dad saw the formidable task ahead and was feeling overwhelmed.

"The doctor has some connections in Mexico City for an air ambulance and the name of someone for you to talk to. They also have a doctor who can travel with you, but the only problem is that he doesn't have papers to cross the border. He suggests you get to the border and deal with it once you get there. There is no time to take the usual lines of authority, and he will help however necessary."

"Can the plane fly all the way to Los Alamos, New Mexico?" Dad was listening carefully as he took a bite of the fajita. The food was helping him feel better.

"It can, but we will need air clearances. Nancy needs to have a doctor travel with her the whole way. She is too fragile and it is entirely possible for her to … well, um … die in flight."

Dad was quiet. After a wonderful meal and cup of coffee, he was ready to go to Jeff's home to make phone calls. "*Gracias, Señora Gonzales, Doctor*," Dad embraced both and turned to follow Jeff.

The remainder of the afternoon was spent on the phone, having frustrating conversations with officials who didn't seem to have any answers about anything. The air ambulance could arrive Friday morning, but they didn't have any medical personnel who could go with them. If Dad could get air clearance, they would go all the way to Los Alamos.

Dad called his boss to work on the air clearance for landing in Los Alamos. Jeff called Immigration to find out about getting a doctor, who didn't have papers, to travel with them. Dad would ask Rick to contact the Los Alamos Medical Center to notify and prepare for their arrival. If all went well, they could have Nancy to the hospital by late Friday night, the Sabbath.

"Sweetheart, how are you?" Dad knew the family was anxious to hear from him.

"Larry, I've been crazy worrying about you. How is Nan, what's going on? I love you," Mom rattled on.

"Nan says hi and she loves you," He wasn't about to tell her the sordid details. "She is still fragile, but we are working to get her home by Friday night."

"Friday night? This is only Wednesday. Can't it happen faster?" Her frantic tone filled his ears. His exhaustion, worry, and fear couldn't handle this right now so after a few more 'It will be okays,' he asked to speak to Rick.

"Hi son, is your mother holding up?"

"Not really, Dad. She's been really crazy and I don't know how to calm her down."

"Well, I need you to contact the Los Alamos Medical Center and let them know we are shooting for a Friday night arrival. Maybe you can start with Mom's boss, Dr. Linneber, and ask her if she can help in any way since she will be the acting cardiologist. Maybe she also has some ideas for Mom, like a sedative or something to calm her down. Rick, Nancy is really bad and it will be a miracle if we can get her home alive. Just need you to know this."

Rick held in his reaction as he turned away from Mom. "Okay, Dad, will do." Inside, he was panicking. "Anything else?"

"Have you contacted your brothers?"

"Yes, Howard has a flight booked for Saturday and Doug will be here on Friday."

"Good. We are going to need all the help we can get. Put in some prayers for your sister, Rick. I'll call you tomorrow morning for an update."

Rick had never heard this tone in his father, and it filled him with dread.

Dad and Jeff had made all the progress they could for the time being; they decided to stop by the clinic once more and then return to Jeff's home for a light bite and bed.

"Dad, *Crei estaba un sueno, pero estas aqui!*"

"She said she thought it was a dream, but you are here." Jeff's interpreting was a godsend.

"How are you, Cheney?" Dad stroked my cheek.

"*Estoy muy bien, y tu? Tengo dolor en mi hombro.*"

"She said, very well, and you? My shoulder hurts." Jeff smiled.

"Anxious to take you home to see Mom."

I smiled and closed my eyes.

"They just gave her the pain meds so she'll be out now for a while. We might as well go home."

Dad wanted to sit by my bedside for a while, so he told Jeff to go ahead; he knew where the house was and would join him there later. He welcomed some time to walk and clear his head.

There was only one other patient in the room with me now. There had been eight and Dad wondered how many of them survived. As he stared at his baby, he reminisced about bringing me home from the hospital nineteen years ago and how happy Mom had been.

Nan was so different from the boys, he thought. She liked sports more than they did and he had always called her 'his jock.' The good times flooded his memory and outweighed the troublesome times, which were many. None of it mattered though; what mattered was how precious she was and hopefully how his prayers got answered. "Nan please make it, baby. We need you, be tough ... Mom needs you."

He let go of my hand and lightly kissed me goodnight. "I love you, Keppe." He hadn't used the Yiddish endearment since I was young and it warmed his heart.

The clinic staff kindly bade him goodnight as he mustered a smile for them. The town was unexpectedly active. Dad thought once it got dark, everyone would be inside, as in Los Alamos, but people, including children, were milling about talking and taking care of their business. Here, they followed the traditional siesta schedule from two to five in the afternoon, when families were home eating and relaxing. Businesses would close during that time and reopen from five to nine. Everyone he passed smiled and said *hola*. He felt they knew who he was and what he was going through from their acknowledgements of him.

Later, Jeff told him everybody knows everything about each other in this town, and since the accident greatly affected Fresnillo they did know about Nancy and who he was.

Dad slowly wandered, breathing in the cool desert air. He was tired, so very tired, but the fresh air cleared his mind and he had a second wind by the time he arrived at Jeff's home. A plate of fruit and pastries were on the table and they sat down to a light snack.

"Why has God done this, Jeff? What have I done to deserve this? I'm a good hardworking man and have tried to be a good father. Where have I gone wrong?" Dad had his head resting in his hands after they retired to the living room.

"Larry, I don't have the answers you are looking for, but I do know God has a plan and we just have to have faith in that."

They shared their beliefs about God, hoping to find some solace and answers. "Jeff, thank you so much for your hospitality and support. Our spiritual discussion has been like healing salve on an open wound."

"Anytime, friend. Now, why don't we have a beer on the porch? Maybe that will help you sleep."

The beer went down easily and made Dad drowsy. He slept deeply.

I was fretful that night, waking continually in pain and raging thirst. "*Mas agua por favor, tengo sed.*" I moaned loudly and wasn't as lucid as I had been. The nurse was worried and called the doctor at home; he promptly came in.

After a quick exam he saw my blood pressure had gone down and the internal bleeding made my abdomen more swollen and hard. He knew there wasn't much he could do for me, so he increased the pain killer to make me more comfortable. It helped calm me for the remainder of the night.

The next morning, the doctor made a few more calls to expedite the air ambulance and locate someone to travel with them. Finally, his contact in León found a resident available for travel, but he, too, lacked papers to cross the border. The doctor made arrangements for the resident to come to Fresnillo in the afternoon to review the case and prepare for the trip. The plane would arrive at six a.m. the next day.

Dad came in early to see his Nan and heard about the difficult night. I didn't wake at all while he was there and he noted my bigger belly. He hid how frantic he felt inside and focused on travel arrangements.

"Dad, I need the name and number of the doctor there. The hospital is preparing for Nancy's arrival, and they need to speak with the doctor." Rick had a pile of notes in front of him.

"He only speaks Spanish, though. I'll get Jeff to translate. Have them call this afternoon at two p.m."

"Great. It looks like they have a good team in Los Alamos. All three doctors worked in MASH units in the military and are well prepared for saving lives."

"Rick, we are going to need that. I just hope we can get her there in time; she's taken a turn for the worse. How's Mom holding up?"

"Well, Dr. Linneber prescribed a sedative and Pat has gone to get it. Mom is a mess; she's in bed at the moment. Hopefully, some rest will help. Doug will arrive here tomorrow morning and then we will all drive up to Los Alamos to meet you when you get there."

"My boss is working on air clearance for the ambulance and we may have trouble at the border. The doctor coming with us doesn't have papers. What else could go wrong, Rick? I feel as though for every step forward I take ten backwards."

"I know, Dad, I know. If it helps anything, you are not alone, Dad. There are a lot of people helping us."

"You're right, Rick. You wouldn't believe how nice people are here; I don't know where we'd be without all their efforts and heart. I love you, son."

"I love you too, Dad." Rick wasn't used to this side of Dad, he had always been so strict and serious.

"Well, I'll call later after Mom wakes up and give you the final plan before we take off tomorrow. Wish me luck."

"Good luck, Dad. Give Nancy a kiss from all of us." Rick hung up and hung his head.

* * *

It had been good to speak with Rick; it gave Dad some peace and strength.

"Dad? *Donde esta Dad?*" I woke with a jolt. The nurse ran over, happy to hear my voice.

"*Su papa esta aqui, espero un momento … Doctor, ella esta despierta.*" After comforting me, the nurse ran for the doctor to let him know I was awake, and then went for Mr. Weintraub.

"*Hola Nancy, como se sientes esta manana?*" The doctor wanted to hear the quality of my speech.

"*Quiero ver mi papa.*" My voice was low but clear. I wanted to see my father.

"Cheney, I'm here," Dad took my hand and looked closely into my eyes.

"Dad? Is that you?"

Everyone gasped; this was the first English I had spoken since my arrival.

"Yes baby. I'm here to take you home."

"Good. *Estoy lista. Cuando?*" I was ready and wanted to know when.

"Tomorrow, baby. Stay strong. I love you."

"I'm fine, Dad, *no se preocupa.*" I tried to comfort him before I closed my eyes and dozed off.

"That is the most she's said at one time for a while. Maybe she's gathering some energy since you are here. Also, somehow you are stimulating her to speak English." Jeff was hopeful as he addressed Dad.

"Perhaps, perhaps." Dad looked at me as I closed my eyes and wished he could have spoken longer with me. He was right there with me, but was missing me terribly.

"The doctor said it's not unusual for her to talk more as she gets worse. It's like getting better before it gets worse, so we need to prepare for a downturn."

"That is exactly what I didn't want to hear." Dad had never felt so helpless.

Jeff took Dad to a nearby café for breakfast and tried to cheer him up. There were people at every table eating and chatting. Occasionally, one would come over to greet Jeff and Dad and give them their blessings. It was the medicine Dad needed to not feel so alone with this burden.

"Jeff, can I take you home with me? You would be a wonderful addition to our family!" Dad spoke with heart.

"Thanks, Larry, I'll think about it." Jeff winked.

"I better call my boss to find out about the security clearances." Dad paid the bill and the two walked out, feeling a little livelier.

"Mr. Hew, any luck with the clearances?" Dad finally got him on the third try.

"Larry, no one will give me any direct answers, but I'm confident by the time you arrive, all will be in order."

"So you are saying to leave without knowledge of the clearances and just wait until we get to the border?" Dad did not like the sound of that at all.

"Yes, that is what I'm saying."

"Mr. Hew, with all due respect, my daughter is hanging on by a thread and may die coming home. If I have to wait for any delays and stupid politics, that may be the time needed to save her life. We are talking about my daughter's life, sir. Can't you please pull some strings?" His voice was emotional and stressed.

"Larry, I understand, really I do. It's all out of my hands. I will make a few more calls to inform them of the extreme emergency, but I'm afraid the wheels of progress are slow. You need to plan to leave anyway in the morning with or without knowledge of the clearances. Get your daughter home. I am ninety-nine percent sure they will be ready by the time you reach the border. I'm on your side, Larry. Take care of yourself, and everyone sends their prayers to you."

"Yes sir. Thank you." Dad felt as if he had the air kicked out of him. He slumped over the table with his head on his arms. Yiddish prayers filled his thoughts and soothed his heart. Jeff walked in and came over, put his arm around Dad and recited a prayer out loud. Dad wept, it was all too much.

It helped to get the tears out. Soon, Dad was ready to hit it again on behalf of his little baby.

"Dr. Gonzales called and said the resident has arrived and wants us to have a meeting." Jeff looked directly at Dad's eyes.

"Okay, it will be time for the conference call from the Los Alamos doctors too, so it's good the resident will be there. Listen Jeff, thanks, thanks a million. Somehow I will repay you for your kindness."

"Larry, just knowing you is payment enough. Now let's go see your little 'sheenie'."

"That's Cheney, c-h-e-n-e-y. Cheney. Now I've taught the Catholic boy a bit of Yiddish!" Dad grinned and turned to the door, following Jeff.

* * *

"Larry, the nurse said Nancy keeps waking up and asking for you. At least she's remembering your presence." Jeff had spoken to the staff.

Dad walked up to me and touched my cheek.

"Dad, Dad is that you? I want to go home" I startled him with my English and immediate response.

"Hi, baby, I'm here. We are going home soon. How are you?"

"I hurt, Dad; please get water, I'm so thirsty. They won't give me water." I was agitated.

"Calm down, baby, I'll get you water and something for the pain." Before he finished his remark, I closed my eyes but a frown remained.

Once he got the nurse to help, he joined Jeff and Dr. Gonzales. A young man stood up as he entered the room and walked over with his hand extended.

"*Hola Señor Weintraub, me llamo Ricardo Anaya y me voy contigo en el avion.*" He was the resident joining them for travel.

The four men sat around a table and discussed my condition and the plan for departure.

"I'm afraid my boss can't promise anything related to the air clearances, but he has advised us to go anyway. Hopefully, by the time we get to the border, the orders will be there. There's nothing else he can do." Jeff translated what Dad told them, and both doctors' eyebrows went up on hearing the news. The two spoke between themselves for a little while then shrugged their shoulders as if saying, what else can we do? The phone rang and Doctor Gonzales answered.

"It's the medical team at Los Alamos." Jeff took the phone to translate. The conversation was a three-way effort. Jeff translated the questions and answers of the three Los Alamos doctors, the two Mexican doctors, and Dad's concerns. Everyone sighed as the phone call ended with a sense of accomplishment.

"I need some fresh air, but I want to visit Nancy first." Dad was bleary eyed.

"The doctors have invited us out for dinner and a beer, would you like to do that?" Jeff questioned.

"Sure. After I visit Nancy, I need to call home then I can meet for dinner."

* * *

"Sweetie, I'm here." Dad spoke softly in my ear but I didn't respond. Finally, after a few tries, I fluttered my eyes.

"*Agua.*" My dry voice squeaked. Dad gave me the drop of water. "Ummm." I swallowed.

"*No siento bien. Quiero regresar a mi hogar.*" I reverted back to Spanish and quickly closed my eyes.

Dad worried. After trying to stir me again, he gave up and spent time reciting his Yiddish prayers. Feeling calmed, he nodded to the staff as he walked out. "I need a miracle, God, maybe even two. My baby ..." Dad choked up as he walked to Jeff's house.

Since Dad was a marathon runner, he focused on his breathing and envisioned himself running in the beautiful mountains surrounding Los Alamos, pretending to be in his daily routine. "I will go running with my little jock when I get her home and back to normal." Somehow the hope helped him gather will. As he approached Jeff's humble abode he prepared for the next difficulty, speaking to Mom.

* * *

"Rick, we had our conversation with the Los Alamos doctors and they are as ready as possible. I'm going to take off without clearances tomorrow morning at six. You call the hospital once you arrive in Los Alamos; they will know where we are and when we'll arrive. So, prayers are the only thing left for us to do. How's Mom?" Dad's voice was exhausted but determined.

"Sounds good, Dad. Mom is up and quiet, so I guess that's the sedative helping. She wants to talk to you. Here she is ..." Rick handed over the phone.

"Hi Cheney, how is the love of my life?" Dad tried his best to stay upbeat and positive.

"I miss you, Lar. When are you coming in? How is Nan?" Mom's voice was slow and subdued.

"I miss you, too. We arrive tomorrow sometime later in the day. Nan is still critical, but everything will be okay. Everyone is so nice and helpful here, so I just have to get her home. We have our plan all figured out, so now we just do it."

"Lar, is my baby going to make it?" Mom started to cry.

"Yes honey, no fears, our girl is coming home. Everything is going to work out perfectly. You stay calm and take care of yourself; we don't need you getting sick too, okay?"

"Okay, Lar. I'll do my best. Please get home safely. I love you." Mom regained her composure.

"See you tomorrow—that sounds good doesn't it? I love you." Dad blew a kiss over the phone and hung up.

"Hey, Larry, did you talk to your family?" Jeff walked in briskly.

"Yes, all is as well as could be hoped. Annette is on sedatives and that seems to be helping. Well, is it dinner time? I'm ready to get some food. I can't think about anything else but six a.m. tomorrow. I hope all goes well ..." He was trying to be upbeat, but his worry showed through. "I want to see Nancy after dinner, too."

"Larry, everything is going to work out. I feel it." Jeff was also trying to mimic the positive attitude and hide his unease.

Jeff and Dad met Dr. Gonzales and Dr. Anaya at a small café that was as austere and as simple as the rest of the town. Dinner was subdued as they enjoyed the delicious enchiladas and a *cerveza*. Everyone was anticipating the next day, so they parted early to prepare final details.

"Jeff, I'm going to see Nancy. I'll see you back at the house shortly." Dad shook his hand and headed for the clinic with the doctors.

As they entered the clinic, a nurse drew Dr. Gonzales aside and talked to him, looking anxiously toward me. I hadn't woken up since midday and it was apparent I was getting worse.

Dr. Gonzales stood by the side of the bed, doing the few checks he could. He restrained a nervous shaking of his head. Dad watched and knew I was declining. He sat next to me after the doctor left and recited his prayers. I very still and bigger in the abdomen.

"Nan, just one more day to hold on for help. Please baby, hang in there, we need you to hang on."

My eyelids fluttered as if I heard but couldn't respond. Dad knew it was out of his hands. He kissed my forehead, said a prayer, and walked back to Jeff's house to prepare for the early morning departure.

Chapter 14

Into the Wild Blue Yonder

It was early morning and pitch black when they heard the sound of a small plane approaching the small primitive runway. The nurse ran to notify the staff; it was time to move me. Both doctors were huddled in a last minute conference, and Jeff stood shoulder to shoulder with Dad.

"Jeff, you are a godsend and definitely in the right line of work. You've bolstered my spirit on many occasions, and I would be worse for wear without your help. I'll call when we arrive and stay in contact with you. I have made a friend for life, and if you ever find yourself in the state of New Mexico, let me pay back some of the hospitality you have given me." Dad felt a bond with this man who'd been a stranger only two days ago.

"I hope our paths cross again. You are a fine man, Larry. Stay strong in spirit and heart. God will take care of the rest." Jeff turned toward Dad and the two embraced.

The clinic ambulance roared in at the same time the plane touched down. The pilot crawled out of the small four-seater and walked over to the doctors. Papers traded hands and conversation went non-stop as Jeff and Dad approached.

He introduced himself as Jose Castillo, in heavily accented English, much to Dad's relief. "My boss tells me by the time we get to the border the paperwork should be in order for the plane, as well as Dr. Anaya's papers."

"I hope so … well, let's go." It was obvious Jose worked under emergency conditions, which gave Dad confidence. "Dr. Gonzales, Dr.

Anaya and I will get onboard to accept the patient. You two, (pointing to Jeff and Dad) help the hospital staff carry her on the stretcher to lift her in."

After I was secured, Jose reported to Dad, "She hasn't woken up in nineteen hours and her blood pressure is down. The internal bleeding continues to swell her abdomen. We need to get going."

Dad waved at Jeff and the clinic staff, and then turned his attention to getting buckled in next to his girl. The plane was just big enough to carry the four of us. Take-off was loud and a bit wobbly, but once the plane gained altitude it became smoother and a little less noisy.

I didn't open my eyes. Even with pain medicine, I still was agitated from the clamor and jostling. Dad kept an eagle eye on me, as did Dr. Anaya. Conversation was sparse. Every dip and bump from the plane elicited a groan from me.

"Mr. Weintraub, we'll be at the border in thirty minutes. The tower is telling me I don't have clearance. They want me to land to speak with the officials." Jose wasn't fazed.

"I expected that. Can you explain our emergency? Tell them my boss has authorized our papers through someone at the border and will contact them as soon as we land."

"Will do." Jose shot off a ramble in Spanish and replied to Dad, "They aren't buying it and think we are doing something illegal. Don't worry; once we land we'll get it straight."

Jose was so calm and confident; Dad wasn't worried other than the moans coming from me and the increasing size of my abdomen.

The landing was rough and actually woke me for a split second. "*Donde estamos?*"

"*A la frontera.*" Dr. Anaya responded to the surprise awakening.

I sort of smiled and closed my eyes.

The officials escorted Dad and Dr. Anaya to a building, entrusting Jose to keep an eye on me. The airport interpreter conveyed the story to the Mexican officers, who at first were suspicious until they saw there truly was a dying girl on the plane. After an hour, the phone calls and papers necessary to get clearance were obtained, and the plane took off again.

"We lost an hour," Dad lamented.

"Don't worry sir, I'll make it up in air time." Again, Jose's confidence bolstered Dad. Meanwhile, Dr. Anaya got more and more concerned as my blood pressure dipped and the bloating increased.

"Dr. Anaya says we don't have much time. She's in rapid decline." Jose's nervousness showed through for the first time. "Sir, we have another problem, the weather up north shows a thunderstorm right where we are going. I may not be able to fly north of Albuquerque."

"What else, dear God, what else?" Dad knew he had to remain calm, but he felt like collapsing. "Well, what do you recommend?"

"I'll radio Albuquerque and ask if they think I can make it to Los Alamos, hold on …" Jose radioed and the storm was confirmed. It was a bad thunderstorm dropping in from the north, right where they were heading. Traffic control told him it would be risky, but with the emergency at hand, to proceed and they would radio if he needed to change course.

Dad saw the Sandia Mountains bordering Albuquerque in the distance, then he saw the storm. Black thunderheads with lightning loomed over the entire northern horizon. "Looks bad, Jose."

"Yes it does, Mr. Weintraub. Let me radio the tower." They told him hopefully he could outrun the storm and to go for it. He was directed to land in Santa Fe if he was having trouble.

Even before they passed Albuquerque the currents and turbulence increased, bumping the little plane relentlessly. Everyone held their breath. To make matters worse, lightning cracked right outside the windows. I whimpered from all the noise and movement. Once or twice my eyes suddenly opened wide and looked out the window at the dark clouds, pummeling rain and blinding lightning.

"What's happening!!!" I cried.

"It's okay, Nan, we're almost home." Dad had to yell to be heard. He took my hand, which seemed to calm me; I quieted down and closed my eyes again.

"Sir, I have to land in Santa Fe. The storm is too bad. I'm sorry!" Jose yelled out over the thunder.

"Whatever you think, Jose!" he yelled back. Dr. Anaya was checking my vitals with concern.

The little plane felt as if it was going to crash, the way it bumped and lurched in all directions. Dad and Dr. Anaya let out occasional gasps. Jose was focused. I moaned and breathed unevenly.

The airport tower radioed emergency instructions to Jose. Each minute felt like an eternity. The storm was not easing up; if anything it was getting worse. The plane continued in this manner for over twenty minutes, when Jose got permission to land and was guided in by the tower. It was impossible to see out the windows from the rain thrashing against them. Dad held me as we descended in the chaos, saying Yiddish prayers in my ear.

Finally, the plane landed with a few bounces at the Santa Fe airport. Everyone except Jose was in a state of shock, and it took a few minutes of deep breathing to relax and realize we were safe.

"Everyone okay?" Jose turned around as he turned off the engine.

"Thanks to your amazing flying skills—thank you, thank you, thank you. Whew, that was terrifying." Dad was shaken.

"*Estoy bien, pero Nancy esta peor, nececitamos moverla ahorita!*" Dr. Anaya warned I was worse and needed to be moved immediately.

Dad contemplated taking me to a Santa Fe hospital, but Los Alamos had better doctors and facilities. "The only hope is an ambulance at this point. I'll run in with Larry to make arrangements. Dr. Anaya will stay here with Nancy." Jose got up, opened the door, let the stairs down, and ran through the rain to the small airport building with Dad.

"What! Santa Fe Ambulances won't leave their district? What the hell! My daughter is dying. Make one exception PLEASE!" Dad couldn't believe what they were telling him, but they wouldn't budge. Finally, a woman approached to say Los Alamos was sending an ambulance and would be there in forty-five minutes. "Then it will be another forty-five minutes getting her back up there, this is CRAZY!" Dad walked away before he hit someone. He had never been so frustrated in his entire life. Jose came up to him to calm him down.

"Mr. Weintraub, hang in there. We've gotten this far and you're almost home. We are going to unload Nancy and keep her in the airport lobby where it is quieter and warmer. You stay by her side, which is mostly what she needs." Jose knew just how to calm Dad. "Once you leave on the ambulance, I will stay the night here and take Dr. Anaya back in the morning, if the weather permits."

"Thank you, Jose. You are another guardian angel in this saga. Stay in your profession—you are good at it. I want to thank Dr. Anaya too." Dad turned to see a group of men wheeling me in on a gurney with Dr. Anaya by my side. The trio stood around the gurney waiting for the ambulance to arrive amidst the torrential rain still descending outside. I continued to moan and then suddenly opened my eyes.

"Dad?"

"I'm here, Nan."

"*Donde estamos?*"

"We are in Santa Fe, Cheney."

I smiled and closed my eyes. Everyone was happy I was still responding. A distant siren grew closer and finally arrived at the doorway.

"Well, I guess this is it. Again, thank you two, I will keep you in my prayers. Get home to your loved ones safely. I owe so much to your kindness." Dad hugged both men as they wished him good luck.

The EMTs loaded me in the ambulance, with Dad by my side, and took off in the downpour to Los Alamos. Luckily the rain didn't delay them further and we climbed the mesa to Los Alamos forty-five minutes later. Dad was so happy to see his hometown, he felt like kissing the ground, even if it was muddy! The ambulance drew up to the emergency room and quickly unloaded the gurney with me on it. Somehow I knew I was home and opened my eyes as they wheeled me in the building. There was Mom, Rick, Pat, and Doug all smiling down at me as I passed them.

"Hi everyone, I'm home!" I said happily. Dad was shocked that I responded so clearly after all I had been through and how bad my condition was. He thought to himself, Nancy had perfect timing to do that in front of Mom.

The gurney was brought immediately into surgery. The last thing I saw were very bright lights, then two men putting a mask over my face and telling me to count backwards from a hundred. All went dark for a very long time.

PART 2

Chapter 15

Reality Altered

Dr. Eilert walked into the waiting room after I was taken into the surgical suite. "It's going to be awhile, Mr. and Mrs. Weintraub. She has extensive internal bleeding, so we are going to open her up but won't know what we are up against until we are in there. She is *very* critical, so I recommend you go home and we will keep you posted." His vague and curt response left the family in despair, but they thanked him and walked out, feeling as if they were in a dream.

"Lar, she sounds bad ..." Mom was trying to hold it together, but she fell apart and started sobbing. The family huddled around her, fighting back their tears.

"Let's go home." Dad, exhausted and anxious, just wanted to be in his own house after his traumatic venture. Once they were home, Dad started telling the tale of his trip while Pat and Doug put together sandwiches. The story was unbelievable and everyone hung onto his words.

The phone rang after two hours. "Mr. Weintraub, this is Dr. Eilert's nurse, to give you an update. Your daughter is in very serious condition and the doctor says her injuries are worse than they thought. She is hanging on, but may not make it through the surgery. Your daughter has a punctured lung, split liver, and ruptured gall bladder—all of which have been bleeding internally. They are placing tubes to drain the blood in the body cavity and one for the collapsed lung. Once that is done, the doctors will go from there. I will call you again as soon as the doctors know what they are up against. I am sorry for the bad news."

"Thank you, please call soon." It was worse than he'd thought and he didn't want to tell everyone, but they needed to know the truth, just in case …

After hearing what the nurse had said, Mom burst into hysteria. "I have to go to the hospital, my baby needs me." She headed to the door.

Dad took her in his arms, "You have to stay here, darling. They are in surgery and we can't do anything right now. Calm down, there is nothing we can do but stay strong right now." She fought to pull away, but he wouldn't let her and finally she collapsed, crying on his shoulder. Everyone was in shock and didn't have much to say after the report. Dad was tired and convinced Mom to rest with him on the couch for a while. Everyone followed suit as they waited for the next call. It came two hours later.

"Mr. Weintraub, the doctors are still in surgery, but I wanted to check in with you. We still have a long road ahead. They finally removed enough blood to take care of the injuries. They are working to repair the liver which split almost entirely across. It is going to be awhile before we can accurately assess your daughter's condition. Presently, she is totally on life support. There has been extensive blood loss and we are going to need blood donated. Please come in to have your blood types tested. She is AB positive. If you know anyone with that type, please have them come in, we need as much as possible. That's it for now and we need to see your family now for the blood." The nurse was in a hurry and hung up.

Everyone got into the car. As they came out of the house, their neighbors of twenty years, the Days, asked how things were going. After a brief synopsis, Dad asked their blood types. Luckily, Mr. Day was AB positive, so he hopped in the car with the Weintraubs.

It turned out only Dad was AB positive, so he and Mr. Day were able to give a pint each, but much more was needed. Rick, Doug, and Pat went to work, calling everyone they knew through the synagogue, schools, and neighbors to find more matches.

I had been in surgery six hours now, and the family decided to remain in the waiting room, hoping it would be completed soon. Occasionally, someone would come out and update. The liver had been repaired and now the gall bladder and lung were being worked on, but I was still failing.

A few more blood donors had been identified and were coming. The rabbi from the synagogue came in to stay with the family, which Dad really needed.

Finally, after eight hours of surgery, Dr. Eilert and Dr. Neuman entered the waiting room and introduced themselves to the family. Everyone encircled them to hear the news.

"Your daughter made it through the surgeries, which is exceptional. When she first came in, we estimated she had two hours left to live, so this is very significant. Nancy has youth on her side, which helps. There is extensive damage to the liver. It is the most vulnerable organ and we will be watching closely; she has turned yellow from all the bilirubin in her system. The gall bladder had ruptured and has been removed, so it is no longer bleeding into the body cavity. We have a tube in her lung to see if we can get the collapsed lung back. By no means are we out of the woods, but her blood pressure has gone up and seems to be holding steady, even though it is still very low. That will take some time. It is a waiting game at this point and I can't make any promises, other than she made it through the surgeries. She still has a long way to go and could decline again at any time. You can see her in recovery, but be prepared for many tubes, bandages, and blood." Doctor Eilert and Doctor Neuman looked exhausted and quickly left the stunned family.

Mom cried and the family hugged before going in to recovery to see me. They were only allowed to go in two at a time, so Mom and Dad went first.

I looked like a science project with fourteen tubes coming out of my body. My skin was as yellow as dark urine and I had a respirator down my throat. Blood-soaked bandages and needles were everywhere; it was too much for Mom. She broke down sobbing and couldn't get control of herself. Nurses came around to take her out and try to calm her. Dad was stunned and had no words. Rick and Pat went next, and Doug went in alone. The doctors would meet with the family in the morning to give a complete report and consultation.

No one spoke in the car. They were told there was nothing for them to do but go home. Once home, Dad and Mom went to bed and everyone else sat listlessly, with occasional conversation.

Doug would drive to Albuquerque in the morning to pick up his twin, Howard, who was coming in from Livermore, California, where he had just landed a good job with the scientific research laboratories related to the Los Alamos labs. They hadn't seen each other in over six months, and Doug was looking forward to seeing him and having his best friend and twin brother near to help cope with this family trauma.

Dad tried to fall asleep, but he was wired and tired at the same time. Mom had a sedative and was resting, so he snuck out of bed and went to the kitchen. Rick and Doug were in the den watching the tube.

"Hey, Dad, couldn't sleep?" Doug's eyes were full of concern.

"Yeah, too worried. Anyone want a beer?" This was very unusual for Dad to ask. The boys agreed to join him. Dad needed to talk.

"Let's turn off the TV and sit on the porch," Rick suggested. Everyone grabbed a chair as it was tradition to sit out and watch stars in the deep midnight sky. The beers were quickly downed and Doug went in to get another round. This was extremely rare, but so was the situation. After the second beer, Dad finally relaxed.

"Do you boys believe in God?" Rick and Doug exchanged startled looks. Both stammered, but before they could answer, Dad continued. "I do … did … I don't know. I can't figure out why it would happen to this family. I have tried to live my life by loving God with dignity and respect, working hard, loving my family, and I have never intentionally tried to hurt anyone. I just want to understand why this would happen to such an innocent child. I know she has been going through the terrible teens, but this is an awful rough punishment. I feel angry at God for letting this happen." Dad started tearing up.

Doug was most like Dad and understood him better than anyone in the family, even Mom. He came over and gathered his dad in his arms and just held him and let him get the tears out. Rick came over and held his hand.

"Dad, I don't have an answer, but all I know is that you have us here to lean on. I love you Dad." Doug also teared up.

Rick, being the oldest, felt as if he had to hold it together for everyone. "Dad, we will get through this together. Nancy will make it. I feel it. You are exhausted; maybe with these beers, you can rest. Tomorrow will be another trying day, so please take care." Dad nodded and let Doug lead him back in the house to his bedroom.

"Goodnight son, I love you." Dad said it so easily, which also was unusual.

"I love you too, Dad. I'll see you in the morning. If you can't sleep, come get me and I'll hang out with you." Doug was in new territory with Dad, but felt the emotions were needed to help them process this nightmare.

Both Rick and Doug sat out a little longer under the stars, reviewing the amazing interaction with their dad. Neither had ever seen this side of him. It was unnerving and scary. Dad had always held it together and never ever questioned God. He had always been like a rock when it came to attending services, holidays, saying prayers, and enforcing attendance at the synagogue throughout their lives, even with resistance from all the children.

For our father to question God was like an earthquake, shaking the very foundation we'd learned to organize our lives by, even if we weren't devout within ourselves.

Morning came quickly, but Dad was up. "After a bite, I'm going to the hospital and I'll call after I get an update. Everyone else can come as they want. I'll see if they have gotten the blood they need; if not I'll call and you guys can get on the horn to find more. Mom is still waking up and please be sure she is put together before you bring her to the hospital, if you know what I mean." Everyone nodded.

"I'll swing by the hospital on my way to Albuquerque to pick up Howard. He comes in at noon, so I'll be back here by three at the latest. We'll go right to the hospital." Doug hugged Dad.

Mom was coming out of a deep sleep. She liked feeling ... nothing, but soon the nightmare of the situation descended on her like a tornado. Immediately upon remembering me, tears fell onto her pillow. She wanted it to be a dream, but it wasn't and she was going to have to get up and see her baby with tubes, bags of blood, catheters, needles sutured into her beautiful skin, and ... hopefully ... alive. "Oh God, why has this happened? Please let her live, please let her live. I need my baby, she is my joy and reason for living, don't take her from us. What have we done to deserve this? Oh God......" Mom lay in bed trying to find the energy to get up.

Rick knocked on the door. "Mom, are you up?"

"Yes, darling, come in."

"How are you this morning?" He could see she had been crying. She shrugged as a tear rolled down her cheek. "I just wanted to check on you. Dad left for the hospital and said he'd call us with an update. Doug just left for Albuquerque to pick up Howard. I was going to the store and wondered if you needed anything. Pat is here with coffee and breakfast when you're ready."

"Okay. I can't think of anything I want. I'll shower and get dressed. Rick, how are we going to make it through this? I may go crazy…"

"Mom, we are in this together. You lean on us to be strong for you. It's okay if you fall apart; this is your child and no one is judging you to behave in any certain way. It's going to be hard no matter what anyone says, so we just have to do what we can."

"God has forsaken us, Rick…."

"Mom, I don't know anything except we have each other. Please let that be your guiding light."

"Thanks, honey, I needed that. Well, let me get up. One step at a time." Rick came over and hugged her. Mom was strengthened by his action because he never liked showing his feelings. They smiled at one another and faced the day.

* * *

Dad always liked to walk to work and the hospital was on the same route. It was five miles, along streets lined with beautiful pine woods surrounded by mountains. The fresh air cleared his mind and energized his spirit. He arrived at the hospital at seven-thirty, before the morning traffic started.

Approaching the ICU, he heard the beeping and pumping of machines. The head nurse told him I was still unconscious and they were waiting for signs of improvement. The doctors were doing their rounds and would be in shortly.

Dad stood by his girl, watching the respirator breathe for me. He watched the blood drip into me from the IV tubes. He looked for any eye movement under my eyelids. He stroked my arm where there were no needles or tubes. "Cheney, I'm here. You be strong. We love you." He could have sworn he saw a slight eye movement.

"Mr. Weintraub?"

Dad turned to see the internist. "Hi, Dr. Lindberg."

"I am so sorry for your daughter. We will get her through this."

"Thanks, we are all going to get her through this."

"I just met with Dr. Eilert and Dr. Neuman about Nancy's case. We have some concerns about some potential complications. I'll be helping to diagnose and treat your daughter."

"What kind of complications?" Dad didn't like his tone, it sounded too serious.

"Oh, good, here are the doctors to explain." Dr. Lindberg turned to the doctors entering the room.

"Good morning, Mr. Weintraub. Give me a moment to look at Nancy and then we can go to the conference room to discuss the case." Dr. Eilert and Dr. Neuman did a quick check of me, talked to the charge nurse and accompanied Dad and Dr. Lindberg to a conference room.

"Well, Mr. Weintraub, your daughter is still very critical. We are waiting for some responses from her, but that is going to take a while. There are a few things going on you need to know. Other than the liver, gall bladder, and lung damage, your daughter is fighting a massive infection of her uterus. She has PID, Pelvic Inflammatory Disease, which occurs over a period of time when an infection is not treated."

"How did she get that?" Dad queried.

"She had an intrauterine device, an IUD, that we removed during surgery. The type she had was a Lippes Loop, which has a string that hangs down through the cervix. It is very common for impurities to basically crawl up the string and enter the uterus and cause infection. Do you know how long she's had it in? The extent of the infection tells us it's been there for a long time."

Dad was incensed to hear his daughter had an IUD; I had no right to be involved in that type of activity at this point in my life. I wasn't even married. "Doctor, I had no idea she had one," he admitted, embarrassed.

"Okay. We are treating the infection, but it is going to take a while since it is so pervasive. There is another complication. Nancy has salmonella poisoning and it's gone into her blood system, which is very dangerous. We have asked Dr. Lindberg to help us treat this, as it seems to be a strain she picked up in Mexico, and we haven't seen anything like this here."

Dad put his head in his hands. "My God, it just keeps getting worse ..."

Dr. Lindberg put his hand on Dad's shoulder. "Mr. Weintraub, I'm sure I can get this under control. I started my research last night and am preparing to call professionals in the field. What we think happened is Nancy picked up salmonella from something she ate. That alone will make her very sick, but usually, once the body gets immunity to the strain, it goes to the gall bladder and creates an enclosed environment where it goes dormant. It can remain there for the remainder of one's life and not affect the person any more. That is, unless the gall bladder is disturbed, which, in Nancy's case, ruptured, spilling the tainted blood directly into the body cavity and blood stream. Now, it is very dangerous. We will need to give her transfusions of clean blood and try, basically, to wash out the salmonella in conjunction with drug therapy. The problem is, we don't know what drug to use on this strain. We may have to try several until we find the one that works." Dr. Lindberg was straightforward without being as curt as Dr. Eilert.

Dad felt comfortable with him. "I don't know what to say. You are the doctors, and I trust your judgment. Please, just keep me informed. Nancy did get very sick about five months ago when she was in school. That must have been when she got the salmonella because I remember her saying she got sick after eating out with Melinda." Dad needed something to give him hope, "What are the chances of Nancy waking up today?"

"We can't tell, but I'm not going to mislead you, Mr. Weintraub. Your daughter is very fragile. It's a waiting game to see if the surgeries were enough to carry her through. You must realize, she still may not make it." Dr. Eilert didn't want to say it, but he had to tell the truth.

Dad nodded solemnly and fought back a tear. "So, we can wait here and be near her?"

"Of course. We will keep you posted. It may be difficult to wait around but feel free to come and go as you want. If the nurses need to do a procedure, they will ask you to leave temporarily. We ask that you and your family be quiet. Any other questions?" Dr. Eilert and Dr. Neuman got up to continue their rounds after Dad shook his head.

"Mr. Weintraub, would you like to join me in the cafeteria for a cup of coffee?" Dr. Lindberg asked.

"That would be very nice. I could use some company." The two men walked to the hospital cafeteria and Dad told him about his emergency trip to Mexico. Dr. Lindberg was very interested in the saga and the two felt a camaraderie.

As Dr. Lindberg got up to leave, Dad heard his name called.

"Mr. Weintraub!" It was Melinda and her parents. They all embraced and sat down to get the news on me. Dad filled them in on my status and then a quick rendition of the trip to pick me up.

"Mr. Weintraub, can I go see her?" Melinda asked as the conversation wound up.

"You can, but you must realize she has lots of tubes and is on a respirator. It's pretty shocking, so be prepared. I'll walk with you over there, but the visit must be short."

As they entered the ICU and saw me, Melinda couldn't help but gasp. Her mother stood by her side as Melinda burst out in tears and had to leave. The Hans and Dad joined her in the waiting room to find comfort in one another.

Melinda felt a weird guilt inside, as if she shouldn't have left me alone in Mexico. Maybe if she hadn't, I wouldn't have been on that particular bus, or she would have been on the bus too and we both would have been in the wreck. Her emotions were in turmoil, leaving her confused and depressed.

Mrs. Han worked for one of the doctors in the hospital and needed to get back to her desk. "Melinda, I'll check on her regularly and keep you posted. You go home, take care of yourself; this is quite a shock." Shirley hugged her daughter a little tighter than usual. Mr. Han put his arm around Melinda and led her out to the car to take her home.

Dad decided to walk home and tell Mom the news in person. On the walk home he thought about the complications, the IUD especially. "How could she have done that? How dare she act so immorally? Haven't I taught her better than that? Out of wedlock ... where have I gone so wrong, God, where?" The thoughts went round and round in his head and his emotions were a rollercoaster, changing from anger to sadness to confusion to worry to exhaustion and back to anger.

The family sat around the kitchen table to hear about the doctor conference and the complications. Everyone was numb and just couldn't absorb any more shock. Mom had taken her sedative with breakfast and was remaining calm throughout the conversation.

They decided to visit in shifts so someone would always be close at hand if any decisions needed to be made. Rick and Pat were eager to see me and get out of the house for some fresh air, so they walked to the hospital. Mom would go with Doug and Howard later.

* * *

Mom sat at the kitchen table in a daze. Too much information. The sedative made her feel as if she were millions of miles away, which helped. Dad was resting in his favorite chair but had a frown on his face, even though his eyes were closed. Mom's thoughts circled. *Nan, why did you have to be such a rebel? Now you've upset your father even more, getting an IUD. We taught you better than that. I hope you can still have children, my grandchildren.*

Suddenly, Mom heard her own mother in her thoughts. "Oh child, your daughter carries our Hebrew blood and blood of our family. We are survivors and carry the spirit of Jewish history in our blood. Be proud of who you are and where you came from. Teach your daughter who she is, then she will make better decisions when she too is filled with her soul whisperings. Remember, we are with you always. You are not alone. I love you. Be truthful to your own spirit and learn the beauty of your own heart."

Mom was stunned. It had been over ten years since she heard her mother's wisdom breathe into her. "Mother ..." Mom cried softly, hoping to speak with her again, hold her, and be loved by her. As she spoke, she felt an embracing force around her heart, giving the warmth of love. She knew it was her mother and that the presence had always been there, just neglected. "Thank you, Mother, I will nurture my soul and rely on your presence of love to get me through this." Mom was strengthened and felt more peaceful. She was tired and dozed off with the murmurs of her mother leading her to dreams.

* * *

Dr. Lindberg was in his office, thinking about Dad and me. It reaffirmed his commitment to be there for this family. He began calling his colleagues from his alma mater, Harvard, to see what anyone knew of this strain of salmonella and what might help.

Rick and Pat sat by my bedside.

Rick was nodding off when he felt a hand on his shoulder. "Hey bro, long time no see." Howard had arrived. They embraced and Howard's eyes turned to me. "Has there been any change?" Rick shook his head.

"Hey, sis, can you hear me, it's Howard." Silence. Howard stroked my arm and talked softly. "Hey you, it's good to see you. We need you, Nancy. Hang in there. I know you have it in you. Remember, you are Dad's little jock, stronger than all of us put together. Remember the time Doug and I put a lizard under your covers and how you jumped? That was sure funny. Remember the time we went camping in the Jemez and it rained so hard we had to spend the night in the front of the truck? You were so mad at me, because I was farting all night! How about all the times we sat on the edge of the mesa and watched the sun rise and the moon set? Sis, we have so many more good times to share, come back ..." Tears rolled down his face.

"Whew, she's worse than I thought," he said when he joined his brothers in the waiting area.

"Yeah, I know, we feel the same way." Rick needed to go home, get fresh air and some perspective. "Howard, get your blood tested. She needs lots of AB positive. We're heading out—see you guys at home."

The twins proposed bringing home some chicken so no one would have to cook. By the time they all gathered around the table, the mood had lightened somewhat. Mom and Dad were both happy to have Howard home. He had been the only child to take after Dad's interest in science. No matter how Dad tried to inspire the others, none of us responded the same way. Dad was very proud of him; Howard was smart and had received many scholarships. He was working at the scientific laboratories in Livermore, California with a scientist on an AIDS project worthy of a Nobel Prize. Also, Howard was always making everyone laugh, acting a bit like a nutty professor. He was full of crazy ideas and lived his life with gusto; a little comic relief would help right about now.

They all broke into the bucket of chicken and ate heartily, nothing like salty grease to help with tough times. Howard told story after story and had everyone cracking up to the point of tears. These tears verged on insane relief combined with insane grief but helped boost morale. 'Just like the old times' was the unspoken thought of everyone.

After dinner, Dad and Howard headed to the hospital. Mom would wait until tomorrow.

Luckily Dr. Lindberg was at the ICU when the two arrived. "Mr. Weintraub, I was just going to call you. After researching this form of salmonella, we've identified a drug I think will do the job. We were just about to give it to her. We should know in a couple of days if it's working."

"I'll put my prayers in for success. Thank you." Dad introduced his son and beamed when he told Dr. Lindberg Howard was working on AIDS research. They stood by me and talked science while the nurse administered the first dose of the drug via the IV.

"I spoke with Dr. Eilert about an hour ago. He reported her blood pressure has gone up a few points, which is a great sign. She might be starting to respond. Other than that, everything is the same. I have to run. Nice meeting you, Howard. You have an amazing father and I know he needed you here. Talk to you tomorrow, Mr. Weintraub."

"Call me Larry, please …"

"Talk to you tomorrow, Larry." And Dr. Lindberg left.

Dad sat with Howard by the bedside as the sun set outside the hospital window, overlooking the canyon and mountains. Dad told Howard about his trip to Mexico and how chaotic it was. Howard saw a side of his dad he'd never seen before; his dad needed him. It was dark when they left. I hadn't moved since being admitted into the ICU. Dad said a prayer before turning to leave.

At home, they all sat outside, having ice cream. Dad spoke up, "You don't know how much you all mean to me. Your mother and I really miss having you here at home and it helps that you're here now. I love you." This was a new father.

* * *

Early the next morning Dad walked to the hospital to see me. I was the same. Mrs. Han came in early to visit; she'd been able to find a few more people to donate blood. "Shirley, you are a blessing, thank you so much," Dad told her as she left to go back to work. Unknown to me, the community was pulling together for the Weintraub family—the rabbi visited, people brought meals to our home, even high school friends called to see if they could help. The answer was the same to all—we're still waiting.

Mom decided to visit me with Howard and Doug. She'd had her sedative so was relatively calm. It still wrecked her to see her baby in this ICU environment, so she made it fast. Mom bent over to lightly kiss me on the cheek, "Nan, darling, come home to Mom. I need you." She turned to leave before she broke out sobbing. Doug and Howard stood beside her and led her out.

Monday morning, three days since the surgeries, and still no response. Dad arrived at his usual seven-thirty a.m. just in time to see the doctors as they were doing their rounds.

"Mr. Weintraub, Nancy's blood pressure is showing signs of improvement. I think getting some of the PID infection under control is helping. The salmonella medication isn't showing any indications of improvement yet, though. We'll give it two more days and if we don't see any change, Dr. Lindberg will have to find a different medication. We'll keep you posted." The two doctors walked away, leaving Dad feeling a tiny bit encouraged.

He came to my bedside and gave a little pep talk. "Well, Nan, sounds like you are hopefully turning the corner. Keep it up, baby; we are with you the whole way." When he stroked my cheek, he could have sworn he saw my eye move under the eyelid, but it was too subtle to know for sure.

"Love you, baby, see you later."

Mrs. Han did her usual check-in followed by Rick and Pat's morning visit. "She looks a little different today, don't you think?" Rick commented. Everyone was trying so hard to see improvement, but it was difficult.

Chapter 16

Awakening

Why can't I swallow? There's something in my throat. Argh, what is it? I opened my eyes.

"Nancy! Nancy! She's awake! Call the doctors," the nurse called excitedly. "Hi baby, how are you?"

Something is down my throat deep. It hurts. Nothing registered but pain.

"Don't try to talk, Nancy, there is a respirator down your throat. Nod or shake your head. Do you know where you are?"

I remained motionless as I became conscious.

"Be still. You are in the ICU at Los Alamos Medical Center."

What is going on and why do I have so much pain down my entire esophagus. It even hurts to moan. My eyes closed and I went back to sleep.

"Nancy! ... Nancy! ... Wake up Nancy! Nancy wake up!" In the distance I heard a voice.

I can't open my eyes ... I'm trying but they won't cooperate. Finally, after much effort, they opened to see a group of people staring at me. *Damn, get this thing out of my throat.*

"Well, hello young lady. We are very happy to see you. I am Dr. Eilert and this is Dr. Neuman. Don't try to move; we have a respirator down your throat to help you breathe. I'm going to ask some questions. Blink one time for yes and two times for no, okay?"

I blinked once and everyone smiled. *Hmmm, what is going on? Who are these people and why am I here?*

"Good, Nancy. Do you know where you are?"

Two blinks.

"You are in ICU in Los Alamos. Do you know why you are here?"
Two blinks.

"You were in an accident. Do you remember that?"

Two blinks. *Pain, pain everywhere, help!*

"She's getting agitated. Nurse, when was the last time she had morphine?"

"She's due, Dr. Eilert."

"Give it to her."

The nurse put something in the IV drip. A tingling relief started at my toes and fingers and slowly filled my entire body and brain with euphoria. *Ahhh, sleep.*

* * *

Dr. Eilert phoned. "Good news, Nancy woke up!"

Rick repeated his words and the doctor heard yells and screams of joy in the background.

"We just gave her morphine, but if you come in around three o'clock, I'm going to try waking her again, so you might want to be here."

"Thank you, we will!" The family was yelling, crying, and hugging.

Dad was at his desk and worried the call was bad news when Rick phoned.

"The doctor called to tell us Nancy just woke up, Dad. She woke up!" Rick was joyous to deliver the news. "Be at the hospital at three. She'll be between her morphine shots and they want to try waking her." Dad couldn't help but sob, "I'll be there! Let me talk to Mom."

"She's awake Keppe, she's alive! I love you and I'll see you at the hospital at three!"

"You did it Lar, you got her home!" Mom was also ecstatic with tears.

* * *

"Nancy! ... Nancy! ... wake up, Nancy ... Nancy ... she's blinking." Dr. Eilert smiled.

I hear my name far, far away. They keep calling me. I'm trying to open my eyes. They are so heavy. Okay, they are looking at me again. My throat, why can't I swallow? What is that pain? My struggle was intense.

"Hi, Nancy, remember me? You can't talk because you have a

respirator in your throat. Do you remember to blink one time for yes and two times for no?" Dr. Eilert asked.

Oh yeah, the respirator. I hate this.

"Your family is here." Behind Dr. Eilert, the family came in closer so I could see them.

Mom! Dad! Howard! Doug! Rick! Pat! My eyes smiled. Everyone took turns to say hello briefly.

Please stay with me, no don't go! Help me with this pain down my throat and pain throbbing everywhere!

"She's getting agitated again. It's time for her morphine. I'm sorry but you'll have to go, we don't want her getting more agitated," Dr. Eilert said.

Ah yes, the nurse is putting something in that tube again. MMMMM, tingles of euphoria taking me away to a peaceful place.

* * *

Everyone congregated around the doctor in the waiting room with smiles across all faces.

"The first step; she woke up. This is a critical sign. She's responding to the surgeries and finding equilibrium. There is a fever, which is not unusual after such a trauma and surgeries, but we need to control it. Hopefully, the PID infection is starting to diminish and that's possibly why she finally woke. We still have a very long road ahead before we know if she will survive all that has happened. Feel free to try and talk to her, the more she wakes up, the better. But, don't overdo it." Dr. Eilert had a smile on his face for the first time.

The family hugged, cried, and soared with joy. Melinda and Mrs. Han came and the good news filled them with hope. Melinda went in and tried to get used to seeing me in this condition.

"Hey you, I just missed your waking up. Glad to have you back, girl. Keep it up, and I'll be visiting again."

"She's going to make it fine, Melinda. I just know it." Mrs. Han was so positive and confident, it was hard to not be encouraged by her attitude. The two mothers embraced. "You be strong, Annette. Take care of yourself so you can deal with this, and if you need anything, please let me know." The two women looked each other in the eyes and shared a soft smile and nod.

The next two days were mirrors of the last. I woke momentarily and blinked to communicate. I woke more often and my blood pressure continued to rise. The PID infection improved, but the salmonella was not responding to the drug so Dr. Lindberg went back to researching.

Pain was my world. I had three drainage tubes in my abdomen, four IVs were sewn into veins on my arms and chest, tubes went in my nasal passage and collapsed lung, and a catheter. In all, fourteen tubes invaded my body. Jaundice made the whites of my eyes and my skin yellow as a banana. The fever continued and weakened my already frail body. When the pain medication wore off, I stirred, moaned, and opened my eyes. I became aware of where I was and recognized my family. Howard spent time by my bedside and worked on communicating with me.

The nurse gave me a pencil and paper to communicate by writing. I would scribble a few unintelligible words and then fall asleep or lose concentration and leave a line dropping off the page.

Howard and Doug had to get back to their jobs and came in for one more visit before they left. They stopped to tell me they would stay in touch.

I needed my brothers close and squirmed in discomfort. *Don't leave! I have so much to tell you. Pain always … help!*

"Nurse, I think she needs her morphine," Howard told the nurse as they left the ICU. They administered it and let me rest in peace.

Together, the three doctors discussed the salmonella problem in a conference room. Tests revealed infection invading the liver and another surgery was necessary to clean out an abscess. Dr. Lindberg was frantically researching potential drugs and had a new one to try. They reported the unwanted news to my family.

The surgery would be early the next morning. The respirator would remain until after the next operation.

Rick and Pat were going back to Albuquerque, but after the news, decided to stay to support Mom and Dad.

The fever made me despondent, so I didn't realize I was being prepped for surgery. Before I knew it, I was waking up afterward. The doctors had cleaned out the massive abscess, and started a new drug Dr. Lindberg found.

He took a chance with one of the drugs he had researched. It had been taken off the market and didn't have FDA approval, but there was no choice; they had to try it or the salmonella infection would kill me. The doctors and the Weintraubs discussed the dangers, but all agreed something had to be done, so the decision was made to use the illegal drug. Dr. Lindberg obtained special clearance for its use and began treatment immediately upon receiving it. Two days passed before the infection declined and an improvement was perceived. Once the post-op pain lessened, I finally began waking more regularly to blink my yesses and nos without prompting.

Finally, after ten days, they removed the respirator. Everyone was nervous but the doctors were confident I would do fine. Removing the long tube down my throat was, of course, painful, but the relief of having it removed was immediate.

"Throat hurts," I croaked. Thankful to not have that contraption in my raw esophagus, I continued with much effort to say "Hi" to the nurse and doctor. Every attempt to talk hurt, so it was kept it to a minimum. "Pain." Once they dosed the morphine, the warming bliss alleviated the constant horrible pain throughout.

* * *

"Cheney! Nan! Your mom and dad are here. Wake up ... wake up." Mom was anxious to hear her baby's voice.

I slowly awoke from a distant slumber. "Mom?" I moaned.

"Darling, it's so good to hear your sweet voice again. Don't talk too much if it hurts."

"Nan, it is so good to hear your voice." Dad was almost crying from relief.

"Dad!" Again it was raspy, but I was so happy to speak. "I love you."

In unison, Mom and Dad said, "We love you too."

Pain rumbled like a storm over my body. "Pain medicine," came the choked request. Before I knew it, I fell into a peaceful morphine bliss. Mom and Dad smiled as my eyes closed.

I began to stay awake longer, which was a double-edged sword. On one side, I started rejoining the world; on the other, the pain increased. Every day, the doctor started withdrawing the drainage tubes by an inch. The tubes had been in for so long, they'd adhered to my skin, inside and out. I felt my flesh rip after each session and counted on the morphine to ease the staggering pain. I loathed the entrance of the doctors because it assured an inevitable painful event. At least the throat pain had subsided and talking became less difficult.

Rick and Pat stopped by to say they needed to get back to Albuquerque but would be back soon. They told me Melinda was waiting to see me.

"Melinda is here? I haven't seen her since Mexico. I was living in Mexico. Hmmm …" Confusion filled me as the pain began its brutal descent.

Almost the moment she entered, I requested more medication, and before I got two sentences out I'd faded into sleep again. She joined my parents and her mom in the waiting room.

"The nurse told me she speaks Spanish all the time in her sleep and sometimes when she's awake!"

"Yeah, that's how she was in the Mexican hospital. In fact, she barely uttered a word of English the whole time I was there." It was the first time in a while that everyone was a little more relaxed. I still had a low grade fever, but the new medicine made an impact. My being able to talk encouraged everyone.

* * *

"It's Dr. Eilert. Wake up … hello, how are you today?"

Fear shot through me, hearing his voice, because I knew there would be pain. Slowly my eyes opened. "Good."

"Today I have to remove the tube from your lung. It won't be done slowly, like the drainage tube. This one will be a rapid removal and it's going to be difficult. I will do it quickly and I want you to hold on to the nurse's hand and yell if you need to. As soon as we get it out, we will dress it and give you your morphine."

"I'm scared. No more pain, pleeeease!" I panicked.

"I'm sorry, it has to be done. Now grab her hand, that's right … okay, one, two, three," and he yanked out a tube about ten inches long.

I screamed. The pain felt as if someone was tearing my lung out. I cried and cried then felt the morphine and disappeared.

"One more time, and we will be all done taking out the drainage tubes." The next day Dr. Eilert pulled the last one out with no less pain than any of the others.

I screamed, cried, got morphine and finally peace. This had become my daily routine for the last month, ever since the respirator was removed.

"I have no more tubes to pull," said the doctor. "The IVs, catheter, and drip lines are going to remain in, so the good news is, we can get you up! Would you like that?"

I nodded yes but was full of fear. I felt safe where I was. Would there be more pain? "Do I get pain medication before I try?"

"Well, we want you steady, so I don't want to administer it before, but we will immediately after."

I wasn't convinced but didn't seem to have any choice in the matter. They lowered the bed rails and began moving my legs around to the side of the bed. The pain was excruciating. "Let me just stay here a minute to stop the pain." I felt like fainting but managed to stay conscious. I reflected on how easy it was for everyone to tell me what to do, but they didn't have to pay the consequences like I did.

"Okay, nurse, that's good for today. I want you to do that three times a day at first, then increase to six, and at that point we can get you in a wheelchair. And, once you get in a wheelchair, maybe you can go outside and look at the canyon and mountains." Dr. Eilert was trying to entice me to be onboard, and he used the right temptation, because I would love to go outside.

After three weeks in the ICU, I gained enough strength to enjoy outings to the balcony overlooking the canyon, accompanied by mobile IV setups and family. The salmonella medication made a significant improvement in the infection fight, although yellow was still my predominate skin and eye color.

Three times a day, the nurses changed the extensive wound dressings. My abdomen was cut from below the sternum all the way to the pubic hair. It was left open to heal so the infection wouldn't breed in a closed environment, as it might if stitched together. Twelve one-inch pearl buttons held my stomach together, connected with wire underneath the incision; my abdomen resembled a man's suit coat. The wound was packed with abundant gauze that adhered to the flesh and was painful to remove, especially three times a day.

I existed in a primal world of bodily function. Even though I talked and acknowledged the world around me, morphine and pain was where I lived. One day, crying from pain, I watched the nurses change the dressing and looked down at my belly for the first time. Shocked from what I witnessed, I gasped in disbelief, "Oh my god, my belly looks like steak. It is marbled with fat and looks like a cut of meat from Mom's kitchen."

Moments like that would haunt me regularly—in my dreams and in my future life.

Day by day I began to return to my body and notice the needles and holes invading my flesh. Fear of pain brought immediate tears as soon as a tech, nurse, or doctor approached to take blood, remove a stitch, or take the obligatory blood sample. Coming around was a double-edged sword.

Finally, the doctors felt they had controlled the salmonella infection and I was moved from ICU into a private room for the next leg of recuperation. I had lost more than thirty pounds and was to start on solid food to gain weight. The goal was one hundred and fifteen pounds. Presently, I weighed ninety-eight.

My hair had fallen out in handfuls from all the medication and trauma. Just a thin amount remained and was pulled into a bun atop my head. Someone gave me a stuffed puppy that became my security, and I wouldn't let it out of my hands. The nurse's aide gave me the usual sponge bath and handed me a mirror for the first time.

"That's me?? My eyes are yellow, I look like a monster. My face is so thin. My hair is so thin. *I'm* so thin." For the first time since the hospitalization, I met the new me, a survivor.

I had to be strong before they would let me out of bed to walk. They removed the catheter and now I used a bed pan until I could get up to the bathroom. The wounds were still dressed three times a day with the same daily trauma, but without morphine, much to my chagrin. The doctors were concerned about addiction, so they started to change the pain medication to Percodan. I begged for the morphine, but only got it occasionally. The wound was beginning to close from the inside bottom up, but was still mostly open.

I had no appetite and vomited most food. Sometimes I kept light items down; protein was necessary, yet far too heavy and rich for my weakened system. I began feeling the same way toward my food tray as I did the vampire, or blood tech, fearful and resistant. The staff cut out pictures of delicious food from magazines and posted them on the wall in front of me in hopes of tempting my hunger. It didn't work. They just made me queasy. The doctors told Dad the true cause was that I still fought a low-grade fever which kept me unable to eat.

The fever continued and the doctors feared the salmonella was not completely gone; they started the salmonella medication again, which didn't help my appetite. Around the same time, I complained of pain in my side by the liver incision. Upon examination, an abscess was discovered growing on my liver. Another surgery would be needed to evacuate it.

"Another surgery? Am I ever going to get out of the hospital?" My depression grew.

It was now six weeks since the accident.

The surgery was performed and an abscess the size of a grapefruit was removed from the once split liver. A drainage tube was placed to evacuate the steadily dripping pus and would stay in, even after I went home. The salmonella medication was increased.

Finally, the fever abated and I began to have an appetite and was able to keep food down. A dry hamburger on a bun with ketchup was the only thing I craved—breakfast, lunch, and dinner. Everyone was delighted to accommodate. At last, the infection was under control.

I feel as if I'm at the end of a tunnel looking out at the world. I feel so very far away, but I'm right here. As much as I try to get closer I remain deep in a cave at the end of an endless black corridor. I thought to myself. I struggled to show a smile to everyone else, but inside I felt lost and depressed. *I just want to get out of here and back to my life.*

* * *

Dad and Shirley visited daily, but Mom came infrequently. I asked to see her regularly, but was always told she was unable. What I didn't know was that Mom had taken a leave of absence from her hospital job because she was on sedatives. My hospitalization undid her and she was challenged to cope.

Melinda had also been an infrequent visitor, as it was also very difficult for her to handle my situation. Melinda broke up with Brian after the accident. Unknown to me, she started hanging out with my old boyfriend, Bob, to find comfort. They both cared about me and that shared sentiment made a natural connection. Melinda's guilt also kept her away.

I felt like a newborn baby. I had to learn to eat, go to the bathroom, walk—and I had to be taught to do these things. *So disappointing.* I needed assistance to do *everything.* Standing up, walking to the bathroom, squatting on the toilet, and getting back to bed was the height of my life. I didn't think about much outside of my hospital existence and felt safe there.

Nights were always bad. After dinner, my anxiety increased in preparation for nightmares. I was plagued with visions of doctors running after me with knives, bleeding that wouldn't stop, and flying amidst broken bodies. I'd wake up screaming and the nurse on duty would come in and comfort me until I could doze off peacefully. They became my most trusted friends.

After two months in the hospital, I had reached one hundred and eight pounds, lost the yellow hue, and used the bathroom with assistance. The painful abscess on my liver continued to return. It was regularly incised and yellow pus drained out. By then my pain level was quite high and I managed these regular evacuations without much fear, knowing the relief that followed. My fever was low-grade and the doctors were confident the salmonella medication was doing its work; it was just going to take time.

Dr. Eilert entered the room with Dr. Lindberg. "If you continue improving this way, you'll be out in a few weeks. Keep eating, walking, and getting strong."

I nodded with anticipation and a little bit of fear. *I feel safe here. If anything happens, someone is here to help. The nurses comfort me at night too. I'll be all alone at home, maybe it's better here.* As each day improved, my fear to leave this nest of care increased.

Finally, after three months in the hospital, my doctors gave the permission to go home. I hadn't quite reached the weight they wanted, but they felt I was strong enough to go. The abscess would need to be regularly evacuated at outpatient visits and a drainage tube would remain until it was completely gone.

I cried and hugged the staff as if they were my family. I would miss them terribly. They loaded me into a wheelchair, and I went out the front door of the hospital with Mom and Dad to start my life over.

Outdoors for the First Time

My Security Puppy in Hospital Bed

Chapter 17

Euphoric

The car pulled up in front of the house.

"We're home, darling!" Mom was smiling from ear to ear. Finally, life could go back to normal with her cherished baby home.

"I can't believe it. I was beginning to wonder if I'd ever get out of there. I'm going to miss the staff; they were so good to me." To myself, I thought, *I'm scared, what if something happens here and Dad or Mom can't help?*

"You take it slow and easy, Nan. Take your time." Dad assisted me into the wheelchair.

"Dad, the doctors want me to walk."

"You will. Let's just get you in the house then you can walk, little by little. Get accustomed to using the wheelchair for when you are tired or hurting."

"I know." I responded with irritation. I knew my physical limits better than he did. "This is the first time I've seen the house since I left for Mexico. Everything looks the same—except me."

"You are beautiful, Cheney. So slender now. See if you can keep it that way and not get chubby like before." Mom held the door as everyone entered.

I flinched at the unintended criticism. "I have to work on my appetite, but moving around will help. The doctors want me to gain five more pounds. Never had that problem in my life!" I looked around inside the house. It was so familiar, yet felt so distant. I hadn't thought about my life outside of the hospital for months and it was going to take some time to adapt.

Melinda had spoken about Mexico a time or two in the hospital, but when I entered the bedroom and saw my backpack leaning against the wall, suddenly the reality of what had happened hit me. *I was living in Mexico, going to school... decided to travel. Melinda left. I was heading home ... the bus, my journal and sketch pad...* Stunned by the realization, I needed to lie down.

After resting, I went over to my backpack and started unpacking it. Memories, some vivid and others vague, flooded me as each item was removed. *Where are my journal and sketchbook? I need those to help me remember my travels. They aren't here. Dad and Mom must have them.* Uneasiness ignited deep within. This one was not physical, but deeply intangible and embedded in my core. Not knowing exactly what had occurred during the last three months in the hospital, and feeling distant to the previous year in Mexico made me feel like an outsider in my own life. Subtle panic quivered subconsciously.

That night at dinner I asked about my things, but Dad informed me they were not included in my personal items at the accident site. The news disappointed me beyond belief. The journal and sketchbook were the maps to my former life. I was inquisitive about the accident, but Dad was hesitant to talk about any of it, for both Mom's and my sake.

"This weekend we will sit down and I'll tell you what you want to know, but for now, let's just get you settled into your routine." Dad dished out bowls of ice cream and set them in front of Mom and me. "This is a night to celebrate!" Everyone agreed and dug in. We watched a movie and went to bed.

I woke in the middle of the night, in a sweat from a nightmare, but didn't want to bother my parents. I shed a few tears and thought about my nurse friends in the hospital. *I miss them already. How am I going to get through this? It's weird being home; it doesn't feel like my home anymore, I've changed so much, I feel like a stranger in my own skin.*

* * *

Over the next few days, Mom and I spent time establishing a routine. A visiting nurse taught Mom how to change my wound dressing. Only an inch remained before it was totally closed; it required another month's care. The drainage tube slowly dripped yellow pus and got cleaned at the same time. Hopefully, that would also be removed within the month. I walked with a cane until I was hurting or tired and then used the wheelchair. It was great having mom's homemade food and my appetite picked up.

The family was in a state of euphoria to have the hospitalization over and me alive.

"You mean I almost *died*?" I was shocked to hear Dad explain. Never once had I thought or felt that. "Why didn't anyone tell me?"

"The doctors felt you were too fragile and the information might make you unconsciously worse, so they told me to tell you only after you were home."

I repeatedly pondered, *I can't believe I almost DIED. All this time I thought everyone was needlessly worrying, but I almost died. Wow. I'm a miracle. I'm alive, back from almost being dead.*

This knowledge rocked my very core. Somehow, it changed everything in a profound yet subtle shift. I was unaware how significantly this shift would develop in the years to come. Now, I was just euphoric I had survived.

Dad answered my questions, but was unsure how much to tell me. I seemed so easily overwhelmed. I would ask a question, but upon hearing the answer, seemed to go blank and change the subject entirely. He decided to let me be the initiator for more information about the accident. One night out of the blue, I asked about Dad's trip to get me and he unraveled the story. I remembered very little and was shocked to hear the details. I repeated it over and over in my thoughts and began having nightmares, then became shy of the subject and avoided it completely.

Days passed slowly, with recognizable improvement at the same rate. Mom did the wound changes carefully, thankful to have her daughter home. Weekly visits to the doctor were met with rave reviews, and they decided to remove the drainage tube to see if it would finally heal. Dad returned to his work routine, and all seemed to be falling back into some type of order.

"You are pushing yourself too fast, Nan. Slow down and take your time. You are not ready to go out to the movies yet. Give it another month."

"But, Dad, I *am* up to it. I know my body and I'm ready. I'll just go and come back. What's so different from watching a movie here?" Cabin fever increased as I improved.

"I will not argue with you. You cannot go. Invite some friends over here."

"All my friends have gone back to college."

"Listen, Cheney, this is going to require patience. You've been out of the hospital only a month. The doctors said for every day in bed you will require two days to get your old strength back—that means six months. This is hard for us too, having to watch our child go through this." Mom saw an old pattern emerging and fell into her role as referee, trying to provide a bit of reason.

"I know, Mom. I'm just tired of all this and I want my life back. I guess the euphoria of getting out of the hospital is over and reality is sinking in. I'm twenty and living at home with my parents when I should be off living my own life."

"Give it time, darling, give it time."

"I'll try." Frustration grew as I faced my predicament. *But I won't be happy about it. My body is ready for more activity, I can tell. They aren't in here with me.*

Dad offered an option. "Nan, let's start walking around the block to see how far you can get."

I happily took it. Over the course of a week, we walked around the entire block. It was encouraging to everyone. I started feeling stronger, got fresh air, and released the tension from being cooped up. Dad was a good walking partner, and we both loved the beauty of the mountains and onset of fall colors. By this point, Mom decided it was time to return to work and was content to leave me home alone.

I gained momentum physically, but my heart and mind were a confused mess. I couldn't figure out why I felt so distant within. *What is going on with me? I see or touch a beautiful flower or feel a passing breeze and it is a million miles away, as if I'm not even in the same place. I feel like a stranger amongst my own family and friends. I don't even know myself anymore. I live with pain every day as my body heals. I feel like a newborn in a twenty year old body, with someone else's history. I only have darkness in my deepest soul and no one sees it but me. Who could possibly understand?*

I found myself wanting to leave and get away from these dark feelings. A deep yearning for something else grew. My past history didn't fit in this new skin I found myself in. Everything was different now—everything. I started to realize there was no getting back to normal. It was gone. There wasn't a normal and I would never be the same person again.

Everyone around me wanted me to be the old Nancy, but I was finding she no longer existed and I didn't fit in any longer. The more I tried to be like I was before, the worse the gap became.

"Darling, just try. You can do it. Go a term at the community college here until you are back to your old self, and then go back to Albuquerque to school." Mom saw the unrest in my eyes and worried at what she saw.

"I don't think my old self is around anymore, Mom. She's gone—I mean really gone. And what's left is an empty shell."

"Nan, listen to me. You've been through a lot, but you are strong and a survivor. The thing you lack is patience. It's going to take time to get back to your old rhythm."

"I'm trying, Mom, but I don't know or feel the old rhythm anymore. I don't feel *any* rhythm. It's like I'm living in a void."

"Don't talk like that, Nan. Try, just try. Your father and I are here to help, and we won't give up on this. I know you are the same young woman as before all this. You just have to accept the delay and go forward with your plans. We have all been through a lot, but now our routines are getting back to normal, and life can resume where we left off. Try for us, Nan. We have all been affected by this and we have done all we can to pull you through it."

"You just don't understand. But, I'll try." Inwardly, I thought, *I have put them through a lot and they have literally saved my life, so I owe them my life, really. I can get back to my old self … somehow.*

"Good girl, now come help me get dinner ready."

* * *

Disconnectedness grew inside. As much as I tried, the darkness within intensified no matter how good an attitude I mustered or how many routines we established. Luckily, the wound finally closed, and no more dressing changes were needed. The abscess appeared to finally be gone. My strength improved along with my appetite. I reached the goal weight and had to be more mindful of calories because I didn't want to get chubby ever again.

Dad watched my progress and also noted my unrest. He wished I had more patience, but that had never been my forte. He also fell back into his old strict ways and was more critical of my behavior whenever I wanted to do something he didn't want me to. I was much more fragile and sensitive than before the accident and didn't take his advice well. Continually upset and in tears, I couldn't figure out how to deal with anything or anyone. The household dynamic impeded progress toward my mental and emotional recovery. My mental state was equally, if not more, traumatized than the physical, but because it was invisible, that aspect was discounted.

I continued to take walks with Dad and was now managing two miles along the road by the canyon. Walking helped me feel connected to my body and released the angst I felt within. Although I still felt like a newborn inside, I was able to hide behind my twenty year old body when interacting with the world. No one understood how fragile I really was.

"Nan, there's something I have to say ..." Dad hesitated as we walked along the open road one day.

His tone alerted me and made me tense immediately. "Okay, Dad ... what?"

"I know about your IUD. The doctors told me that was the reason for your PID," Dad said angrily. He had been holding this inside for months.

Shock permeated me. I was speechless and stopped in my tracks with my mouth open.

"How could you, Nan? How could you act like such a slut? I taught you better than that. No daughter of mine would act like a whore. Loose morals and unseemly behavior, I can never forgive you. You've risked having children, my grandchildren, with what you have done." He went on and on, demeaning me for more than a half hour.

I was dumbstruck and said nothing, but my thoughts roiled relentlessly. *I have just finally gotten up, after all this trauma, and he is slamming me back down. A slut? A whore? This is what he thinks of me, and I'm just trying to remember life again and my feelings for this man as being my father. What kind of father would say this to someone he loves?*

He doesn't understand how wiped out I am. I will never talk to him again, never. I'm gone, I'm out of here, and I will find another life. I can't live with someone who thinks this of me. I'm too fragile to deal with this.

I have not acted like a slut or a whore, but maybe I'll start trying it out so at least I'll deserve what he's accusing me of. I need love, encouragement, understanding, not hateful anger and accusations.

My decision was made; I would leave as soon as I got a job and some money.

Interaction with Dad went blank after that walk. I became focused on one thing—leaving. I became withdrawn and didn't care about anything except getting away. Mom pressed until I told her about the walk with Dad. She became upset and depressed, and nothing could be said or done to change the dynamic between us. Against my parents' wishes, I got a job waitressing and saved every penny.

* * *

Anna was an old friend from high school. She had heard about my accident and had come over for a visit. "My sister lives in Seattle, and I'm going to move up there and live with her."

"Wow, that's neat. When are you going?" I had *always* wanted to go to the northwest.

"Well, sometime after the new year. Do you want to go with me? I'm taking the bus and wanted to visit a few friends in California and Oregon on the way. I was thinking about taking two weeks to make my way up there."

A bus trip? I felt a bolt of fear, but curiosity and yearning piqued my interest. "Could I stay with you and your sister in Seattle?"

"I think she has plenty of room, but I would have to ask her."

"Ask, and I'll think about it; I've always wanted to go to that region. I've only heard good things about it." Anna promised to get back to me when she found out her sister's answer.

This could be the perfect opportunity to start anew. I could go explore a region I've always been curious about, and it's perfect that I have a friend from here I can stay with. Maybe we could stop and see Doug in Los Angeles and Howard in Berkeley on our way. If it's okay with her sister, I'm going. I can work through the holidays and save enough. And if I like it as much as I think I will, I'll get a new job in Seattle and stay. My wounds are healed, so nothing medically keeps me here. I like Anna, I could live with her.

Anna called the next day to tell me it would be fine. There was more than a month to set an itinerary for visiting friends and family along the way. Both Doug and Howard happily agreed to see me, plus Anna had two friends to visit. We picked a few more places to stop along the way and found a good deal on bus tickets.

I got everything arranged before dropping the news on Mom and Dad. I had withdrawn immediately after Dad's talk and both parents knew something was brewing. When I told them, they tried to talk me out of it, but knew I would do what I wanted. I had done it before. At least I was going to be in the United States and living with Anna, whose parents they knew well.

Mom fought depression around losing her daughter one more time and focused her energy on work, as did Dad. They were mostly worried about my health, because it had been only three months since I left the hospital. The doctors consulted on my leaving and didn't see a problem since my tests came back clear.

My decision provided the hope I needed to get back on the path of life. I felt badly about leaving Mom, but I knew it was time. My body was always sore, due to the extensive ongoing healing, but I was becoming accustomed to a certain level of chronic pain. Enduring it was part of my new self and life.

I thought about the upcoming bus trip. Traveling in motorized vehicles was now a deeply rooted fear, but my flight mode was stronger. I could do this.

One more time, I was saying goodbye to my parents. I was fleeing from something invisible and hoped to find safety by moving toward a new future and place. An adventure and settling somewhere else carried the promise of getting back to normal. I hadn't thought about my gypsy spirit for a long time, but it seemed to have me tucked underneath its wing without my even realizing it.

Chapter 18

Finding a New Home

Mr. Han always told me I needed to get back on a horse if it bucked me off. The bus ride felt something like that. It was a long ride, with me trying but failing to completely overcome my fear, when we arrived in Los Angeles to visit Doug. He worked at Hughes Aircraft and met us at a beachfront restaurant after work. He couldn't believe how thin I was and seemed surprised I was already on the road again. We got caught up on all the hospitalization stories and my time with the parents over dinner and a few beers.

Doug sensed something very different about me, but couldn't put his finger on it. I seemed like I was millions of miles away, with a blank look in my eyes, even though I appeared happy on the outside. He knew me better than anyone, other than Mom, and was worried about me moving away so suddenly. I just didn't seem my old self.

"You can live here with me if you want, sis. Seattle is kind of far, don't you think, especially after what you've been through?"

"Are you kidding? I hate Los Angeles. I'd go crazy here. I'm fine, bro. I'm looking forward to starting a new life. Everything will come together once I settle in. Please come visit me." *He's worried about me too. Nice for him to offer, but I need to figure out who I am first and not have someone trying to make me be who I was before.*

Since Doug was busy with work, we continued our journey north after two days in smoggy, crowded, chaotic Los Angeles. I was happy to see Doug but felt so different and distant from anything in my past. Actually, everything—past, present and future—felt uncomfortable and strange. Moving forward seemed to be the only thing that relieved the internal pressure.

Next stop, Santa Cruz. Pat's mother had a beach house and gave us a place to stay for two nights so we could save our cash. We also knew a few people from high school attending the university here, but they were too busy with classes to see us. I was disappointed and relieved at the same time. Would seeing my friends stimulate the distance I felt, or connect me more? That would be left unanswered.

A few more days were spent sipping coffee in coffee houses and taking in the hippie scene of downtown Santa Cruz. I loved the Bohemian and beach lifestyle. Chatting with Anna, I examined the benefits of Santa Cruz: I knew some people here; it would be close to Doug and Howard; and I liked the alternative lifestyle. But Bob, my old boyfriend lived here now and Melinda talked like she might move here too. That would be awkward. Besides, I was feeling more and more like establishing a new life, clear of my past.

Howard welcomed me at his Berkeley home with open arms. Anna and I took in the local scene during the day and went clubbing with Howard at night when he got in from his research job. I noted changes in Howard; he'd been away from home for two years now and seemed to be growing into a man I didn't really know anymore. He felt the same way about me so the visit was fun, but both of us were eager to get on with our own lives.

One of Melinda's sisters, Lee, lived in San Francisco and wanted us to stop by for a night or two. Lee hadn't seen me since she visited Mexico. Lee was a lawyer and took us out to dinner.

"You are so skinny! You look great!" She gave me a big hug. Both Lee and I had always struggled with a weight problem.

"Thanks, but I wouldn't recommend the diet I was on!" I always felt Lee was the older sister I didn't have; I enjoyed our friendship. We caught up on the most important stories, but I was getting tired of repeating the trauma and wanted to talk about other things.

"I have to work tomorrow but I can meet you after. What do you want to do? How about the ferry to Sausalito, that's lots of fun."

"Great idea!" We both agreed.

Anna had brought a bag of psychedelic mushrooms for the trip and it was decided our first dose would be for the excursion to Sausalito. I wanted to try mushrooms and hoped for something like my peyote trip in Puerto Vallarta, but I was also hesitant. I had just spent so much time 'out of body' and on drugs in the hospital that I really needed to stay grounded and work on being connected. But, it sounded fun.

We were on the ferry heading toward Sausalito when we started coming on to the mushrooms. The boat was crowded which made me very uncomfortable. *This is so different from peyote. The patterns and colors are making me dizzy. All these people are looking at me.* "Anna, I feel like hiding, I don't like this."

"This is great, just chill out. Check out the tracks when you move your hand."

I became more and more paranoid. We finally disembarked and I went immediately to a patch of grass in the middle of a busy tourist park, lay down, and closed my eyes. I wished I hadn't done the mushrooms, but it was too late. Anna joined me, enjoying her hallucinating experience.

"You girls are stoned out your minds, aren't you?"

A tall black man with a big smile was standing over us, looking down at the two horizontal girls. "Do you need any help?"

Astounded at what we opened our eyes to, Anna sat up and struck up a conversation with the guy. I felt even more paranoia, touched with humiliation, as I realized how stoned we must look. He offered to show us around, which Anna was on board with. I just wanted to disappear but tagged along for fear of being left alone in this condition.

After getting some food, I felt a little more in control and was able to relax and enjoy the journey by the time we were heading back to San Francisco to meet Lee for dinner.

"Sounds like you two really got high." Lee laughed as we shared our day over Chinese food.

"Well, I did have a good time, I just don't like being high around a lot of people." *Actually, I really didn't like feeling so out of control, makes me think about my accident, but they don't need to know that.*

I was happy to be sober again and wanted to head to bed. Anna and Lee stayed up, laughing and telling stories. In the middle of the night, I woke up with food poisoning from the dinner and threw up until dawn. The illness triggered memories of the hospitalization and I withdrew. For some reason Anna and Lee were fine. I felt like a wet rag for the remainder of the day, so Anna ventured off on her own. We would leave the next day.

When it came time to part, Lee could tell I wasn't my usual self. She told me to take care, and hoped time would take me back to my usual gregarious self.

Why don't I feel more connected to her? Why am I always disconnected these days? Just go forward and don't look back.

Eureka, California, appealed to me. It was on the water, had a university and maybe it could be a potential home. We stayed with Anna's aunt for two nights and explored the area during the day. My scars were feeling sore, so I was happy to spend quiet time alone resting, while Anna visited her family. *I can't let anyone know I hurt or else they will tell me I shouldn't be doing this, and I don't want to go back.*

We didn't know anyone in Oregon so we picked two places to stop, Brookings and Eugene, before landing in Seattle. I was finding it challenging to be around so many people all the time. It was hard enough managing my own internal chaos. I craved alone time; it seemed to be the only time I wasn't reeling from too much input. Yet, at the same time I was desperately lonely, created by feelings of disconnect. This vicious cycle only grew as time went on. I was in the throes of post-traumatic stress disorder, but no one knew it.

Brookings was a small coastal town based on tourism, logging, and fishing. We spent the day walking on the beach amongst the huge boulders which sat majestically on the shoreline. It was wonderful to spend the day in nature, taking in the fresh air. It was beautiful, but I didn't see a prospective home here; it seemed tourist-transient and very conservative in attitude. We enjoyed the visit, but were ready to hit the road to Eugene, after calling home. I did it for Mom.

"Don't worry, Mom, I'm fine. We are having a great time, don't worry about me. I feel good physically and mentally, no problems." *What a liar I am. Mom is worrying too much though and I've got to protect her. She's so vulnerable.*

"It's so good to hear your voice, darling. I miss you already. If you feel anything odd, come home, okay?"

"Sure will, Mom, but I'm fine, really. You take care of yourself too. You deserve some peace. I love you and will call again soon." *It's hard enough trying to be strong for myself, but I need to be strong for her too. I've really messed up her hope, but I just can't be someone I'm not.*

The first thing I noted about Eugene, Oregon, was how emerald green everything was. The ride in from the coast meandered through beautiful rainforests, along rivers full of cut logs to be floated to mills. It was wet everywhere. This was definitely logging country. The scenery reminded me of *Sometimes a Great Notion*, a story about a logging family on a river. This was the opposite of the southwest with its brown, dust, and dryness. Here everything was green, muddy, and wet. I was intrigued and drawn to the differences in this land of vegetative riches.

Eugene was a small university town a little bit bigger than Los Alamos. I liked that, the size felt manageable and familiar. Anna suggested we walk around the University of Oregon campus and check out the scene. We found a hotel and were able to walk easily to the campus. We passed many coffee houses brimming with people who were studying, talking, visiting, and playing music. Food co-ops, vegetarian restaurants, and vendors selling handmade arts lined the avenue to the university. The rain didn't stop anyone.

Lively music was coming out of a hole-in-the-wall joint called Mama's Home Fried Truck Stop. Hippie types were everywhere and we decided it would be a great place for a meal. I loved what I saw—interesting and alternative people everywhere. The community board was full of fliers advertising rooms for rent, yoga classes, nutritional vegetarianism, herbal medicine classes, solar and wind energy products, and many things we had never heard of before. People shared tables, were open and friendly without being pushy. A trio played lively Irish tunes and cracked jokes to the appreciative crowd.

"This is great, Anna. I feel really comfortable here. How about if we stay one more day to explore?"

"Sure. I like this place too. Maybe we can take another dose of mushrooms tomorrow and wander around town."

"Yeah, let's do it." *I'm scared but maybe if I take less and have space around me it will be fun. I like this place, it's a good size for me, has a great vibe and the university is here too.*

We walked through the university campus and were impressed with the beautiful enormous trees, vibrant flowers and old stone buildings surrounded by emerald green grass everywhere. The green relaxed me, and I could envision enjoying this campus. Compared to the University of New Mexico campus, the University of Oregon was like a national park or botanical garden.

We went to a popular tavern frequented by students, had a few beers and watched the scene unfold into the evening. After joining a dart game, we had a sandwich and headed back to the hotel.

The next day we shopped at a food co-op and found bins and bins of local dried fruit, granola, baked goods, and vegetarian fare for a picnic. "I love this style of shopping: healthy, fresh, delicious, and inexpensive too. Look at this fruit section; we never see this fruit or berries in New Mexico." I felt excited for the first time in a long time; maybe this type of life is what I needed.

We ate another dose of mushrooms and I decided I would do half as much, hoping this time would be more enjoyable. We walked toward campus and started to feel high when we arrived. I wanted to stay near some large spruce trees off the beaten track where I could maintain privacy, but still watch the world walk by.

This time I enjoyed the mushrooms; the effect was far less intense. I still combated feelings of paranoia, but the private location helped. Occasionally, we would take a walk to explore, but would return to our spot by the spruce trees. We nibbled picnic goodies all day and were very contently high. The colors and patterns were there, but not like the hallucinations in Sausalito. I felt relieved and enjoyed myself. I noticed after both times taking mushrooms my liver area ached and I was very exhausted, but I just chalked it up to my new normal.

The next day, we took off for our final destination, Seattle. I had a good feeling about Eugene, but wanted to go to Seattle first. If life was going to start over, I preferred living around someone familiar. Anna and her sister, Donna, would provide a place to stay, perhaps job connections, safety and a thread connecting me to home, just in case. I traveled well with Anna and liked her grounded nature. We could share expenses and travel or explore together. It made more sense to move to Seattle.

Upon arriving, I thought the city was immense but amazingly beautiful. Seattle looked like an amusement park with waterways, highways, the Space Needle, and rambling developments lining every open spot. The Northwest greenery tied it all together: vines, flowers, trees, grass, and the water framed it into a masterpiece. It was awesome, but huge.

We found Donna's house and fell in love with the neighborhood. The Victorian-style houses were multi-level with wrap-around porches, balconies and tiered gardens abundantly growing flowers and vegetables.

"Welcome to the Northwest!" Donna greeted us at the door. She gave us the tour and showed the bedrooms we could choose from. There was plenty of room for two families in Donna's house. I chose the room upstairs overlooking the back yard and counted my blessings for the opportunity that came my way. I knew I'd made the right decision coming to the Northwest.

Over the next two weeks, Anna and I explored Seattle. Every day started at a new coffee shop called Starbucks. We would try a different coffee drink daily, along with a pastry. Coffee shops were popular in this region since it rained so much; they acted as community meeting places. *I could really get use to this lifestyle. It feels much more like a community and would help me meet people, because this place is huge.*

We were both astounded as we walked through the Pike Street Market, gawking at all the homemade and homegrown goods of every sort, from fish to fruit to fashion. Donna bought fresh flowers every week, a practice which was usually reserved for special occasions back home where flowers weren't so available. *It feels like people really appreciate and enjoy life here, everything is so bountiful.*

We both were interested in going back to school, so we visited the University of Washington. It was ten times bigger than UNM and nowhere near as cozy or pretty as the University of Oregon. They had better programing though.

On the weekend, Donna took us on a ferry to Bainbridge Island and then to a shoreline spot for a picnic. Water sports of every type were done in this area which appealed to me; I'd always loved swimming and anything to do with water. Nature was a part of life here, was protected and valued. Environmental awareness was emphasized and built into most every aspect of living.

I keep thinking about Eugene. Seattle is so big. I'm battling being overwhelmed every time I go out the door; too many people, cars, activity. Same with the university here. It would be easier with Anna and Donna and I'd save money. I need to be in a smaller town; it feels more manageable and safe. Decision made, Eugene is my new home.

Chapter 19

The Emerald City

As I boarded the bus, Anna promised to visit me in Eugene.

"It will be fun to visit each other. I'll come up to Seattle, too, and if it doesn't work out there, I'll come back up here and live with you. I'll see you soon."

My first bus ride alone, my first time living alone, since … I tamped down the fear. *I hope I'm making the right decision.*

I watched the beautiful scenery along the route lined by tall spruce trees, framed by the Cascades in the distance. Green, every form and shade of it, covered the earth like a quilted comforter. It was soothing to the eye and spirit. The clouds hung like a blanket over everything, a little claustrophobic after the endless vistas of New Mexico, but there was a majestic presence here in the Northwest that drew me. The ominous overcast sky mirrored how I felt, a mixture of fear and excitement for the future. Mom and Dad were not happy to hear of my decision to be in a place where I know no one, but what could they do? It's my life.

I made plans—I would stay at a hotel and start looking for a place to rent. Maybe the coffee houses or university would have postings on their community boards. I'd to have to find something real cheap and get a job fast, because my money was low, and I *would not* ask Mom and Dad for one more penny.

I was looking at a poster at the university when a young man approached me.

"I see you are looking at the roommates board. Do you need a place to stay?"

After talking to him I learned he lived at the Newman Center, an off-campus house for Christians. He convinced me I could stay there for a week with meals for free. The free part appealed to me and I hesitantly accepted. *Maybe something is leading me this way. There is safety in numbers and I've never tried Christianity; maybe I should be open and see what happens.*

The members of the house welcomed me. They immediately began trying to convince me to be saved by Jesus, through classes, discussions, and evening lectures. I tried to be open, but it didn't work. I was raised Jewish, and I actually didn't feel there was a God anymore after what I'd just been through. The free week of housing gave me time to find another room in a house not far from campus. It was affordable for a month or two until I could find a job.

The house was a three-story Victorian that had been divided into thirteen single rooms, with each floor sharing a bathroom. I was on the top floor. Slowly, I met the residents and struck up friendships with Mike, a teacher and divorcee, Dale, a working gay man, Beth, a student, and Kathy, on disability.

Even though the accident is at the root of everything I think and feel, I don't want anyone to know how crazy I feel inside. I will just ignore that chaotic distress within.

Unconsciously, questions about God and why this happened affected me twenty-four hours a day. A blatant disconnectedness plagued every waking moment. My dreams left me desperately seeking peace within and running from it in the outside world.

I see life differently now ... life doesn't align with what I feel now and causes conflict. It feels like a channel of wisdom is flooding my deepest soul where no words could describe. If I tried to explain this to most people they would just roll their eyes at me like I should be locked up. To me, it's very real and confusing to mesh with the 'supposed reality' of what I had known and what most of society follows. I need to talk to someone who understands ...

The drizzling rain and hanging clouds were new to me and magical in many ways. I would walk the neighborhoods lined with flowers and trees that dripped with raindrops and get lost in deep thought. When the clouds would lighten periodically, everything turned into glistening rainbows, reflecting shadows of moisture. No one used umbrellas, which I found fascinating; they just had their hooded rain jackets and would walk in this liquid sunshine as if it wasn't there.

I miss the sun, but it should come out soon ... these hanging clouds intensify my depression.

Beth, Mike, and Dale started sharing meals and evenings together. Everyone seemed to be between life-moments and looking for a more settled home. Beth was a free spirit with intelligence, looking for a place to apply it. She loved to dance and would crank the music and get me to join her in the living area. Mike had a broken heart from his recent divorce and was one of the nicest men I had met. He was an elementary school teacher and a caring listener. Dale was working as a waiter and looking for love, but still uncomfortable in his recently proclaimed gay lifestyle. He was a clean-freak to almost a fault. One night we four decided to rent a house together to save money and enjoy a more comfortable home life.

Kathy and her husband were the only ones not joining us because they wanted their own home. Kathy and I recognized something in each other related to handicaps. Kathy had a degenerative eye disease and one day would go blind. I did share my accident story with her, and we spent a lot of time together discussing spiritual matters, which loss can stimulate. Our losses helped us recognize and honor each other's special sensitivity, which created a foundation of empathy and acceptance we both needed. We each felt we found a friend of true understanding.

Our foursome found an affordable and nice house in a totally different part of town. Once we settled in, I bought a bike to get around. Despite the bus rides to the coast, I still feared most motorized vehicles so was thrilled to know a bike would take care of the transportation problem. Eugene had an excellent bike path system throughout the city and it was a popular transportation method. Every main street had a wide lane for bikes, and cars actually respected the cyclists sharing the road. I loved biking—it was simple and kept me in touch with nature. The exercise helped my body feel better, too.

"I'll wait until the rain stops, and then start looking for work," I commented. Beth laughed, "I hope you can get through to July, because it won't stop until then!" The rain had been nonstop since my arrival, so I bought rain gear to bike in and started looking for a job, knowing I would not melt and would dry eventually!

Eugene's job market was sparse, since it was so small and a college town. The type of work I was looking for was the same type everyone else wanted, too. I was beginning to get worried when finally a recycle plant hired me. The job was sorting recyclable trash like newspapers, plastics and cardboard. That is all I did, but it paid the rent and gave me a sense of accomplishment and belonging to something.

In a rainy climate, coffee houses were a place to visit and catch up with news. When the clouds hang low and rain drizzles for weeks at a time, seeing other people in a cozy, warm, aromatic coffee house provided me time to people watch and feel a part of something.

I craved being rooted because most of the time I felt like a balloon, floating above reality. Even though I liked going to the 5th Street Public Market, I also liked that I could remain anonymous and observe from afar. I needed people, but was also afraid of them. *These conflicts are making me crazy.*

Weekly, I would also visit the Saturday Market, a fair where vendors sold their homemade foods and new product lines. Eugene was full of hippies and environmentalists, perfect for me. I loved the open minded, common sense, and progressive ideas shared in this community, where people felt safe and trusting. Creativity saturated every aspect of life whether it was making a homemade item, sponsoring a cause, lobbying in politics or designing a utopic neighborhood, everyone was inspired.

I can leave behind this person inside, choking me with her doubts, fears, confusion, pain and bewildered lack of ideas. I hate myself and all I have to deal with.

I was trying to get used to living with pain since my accident. My 'innards' ached often but I worked to adapt and accept it as part of the healing phase, yet it was an ongoing battle. My period had stopped for months after the accident and was just now starting to return, which the doctors told me would probably happen. The periods were very painful and I chalked it up to cramps. I started to learn about herbs from my roommate, Beth, who suggested a chiropractor that specialized in products based on real tissues designed to stimulate the problematic organs. I decided to try ovaries and adrenal supplements to help my periods regulate, but the period pain remained as well as the overall pain I was accustomed to living with.

Digestion was another big problem or, more accurately, lack of it.

I decided to eat simple and natural foods, avoiding packaged and convenience products. The food co-ops carried rows and rows of bulk items such as beans, grains, dried fruit, and nuts, most locally grown. I was quickly becoming a granola groupie with the varieties of homemade granola I was finding, and I experimented with yogurt, tofu, moche, and tempeh. Kathy and her sister said they would teach me some new recipes and introduce me to vegetarianism. I didn't have much choice—the old foods were affecting me 24-7 with blocked bowels and bloating.

Sometimes my tummy liked it but most times it didn't. I knew I had to learn what foods I could eat to support my new system since I lacked a gallbladder, had a compromised liver and extensive internal scar tissue. It took trial and error to learn that foods high in fat and density irritated my system. All animal flesh was eliminated and, over time, dairy and wheat were also. Nuts had to be limited, but I could still enjoy some. The more simply foods were prepared, the better. Beans, grains, and veggies became my staples.

Finding the right foods was frustrating and sometimes I just wanted to give up.

Chapter 20

Spontaneous

I was still deeply lonely and wanted a relationship. My friends were nice, but I really wanted a man to love me and need me, a husband and children—that's what would make me feel whole and connected to myself and to life. At age twenty, I still felt like an infant in some ways. Yet, at the same time, I felt like an eighty year old because of all I'd been through.

I went to coffee houses and tried to meet young men, but no one seemed interested, or they were not interesting to me. I was looking for someone who had depth and perhaps had known loss and trauma, or at least understood it.

Spring was in the air and one day I was at the university, people watching from a favorite bench under a cedar tree surrounded by blossoming rhododendron bushes. I went there often to watch life from a safe distance yet feel a part of something.

The spot was a hangout for transients circulating all day long, hauling bags, pushing grocery carts, and tending to their stray pet dogs. Someone was always bumming change for a beer or sharing scraps they had found. Sometimes they were quiet, other times yelling and often laughing. *For some reason I feel akin to those people … they seem as rootless and lost as I do.*

The last few days, I had noted a charismatic black man running his game with the group. He was full of laughter and had a gregarious nature. Occasionally, he noticed me and smiled but went back to his activities of bumming change or socializing with the others. This day, he walked toward me.

"Hi, beautiful, how are you today?"

I felt nervous but was drawn to this man's energy for some reason. "I'm fine, how about you?" *He seems fun, I like that, and I need to laugh.*

"I'm Ron."

Ron asked to sit on the bench with me and I agreed. I was cautiously enjoying an opportunity to meet a new person. He was courteous, told jokes, and had a depth that attracted me. He was good at bullshit too, and I couldn't always tell if what he said was true or a joke, but I laughed anyway. The laughing felt like healing balm to my soul and drew me to his energy.

He said he lived in Salem, Oregon, and was down for his regular visit to Eugene. He did something in Salem he didn't want to share so I left it alone. He boasted of having many great friends everywhere and knew I would like them. I shared a bare minimum and let Ron take the lead on most of the conversation.

"Well, I have to get going; I have some business to take care of. Maybe I'll see you later, or tomorrow." Ron got up after about an hour, took my hand to shake, then gave it a light kiss and walked off.

I was astounded at this and knew I would return tomorrow in hopes of seeing him again. *There is something about this guy. I think he likes me, unlike everyone else I meet. It's nice to feel liked by a man for a change.*

The next day was a repeat of the day before and I made this a part of my routine for the next week. I started letting my guard down, but still kept my stories to myself and mostly listened to Ron.

The next week Ron approached me with a grin. "Hey, beautiful, I have some great people in Eureka, California, I have to go visit. Do you want to go with me? I will hitchhike down there and stay about five days before returning here."

"Hitchhike?"

"I do it all the time. I'll take care of you and protect you. Really, you would love these people."

I was hesitant to go off with this guy, but also curious to do some hitchhiking. I wanted to see Eureka again, and maybe these people would bring me a new opportunity. *Am I being crazy to go? So far he hasn't pushed me to do anything physical, so maybe I'll go just for the friendship and liven up my life.*

"Meet me here at eight a.m. with a sleeping bag and whatever else you need for a few days. If you aren't here, I'm leaving because I have an appointment to keep in Eureka." Ron was straightforward with me, but noted my hesitation. "It's fine if you don't want to go, I just think you will really like my friends."

"Well, I'll sleep on it and if I'm here I'll go, if not, go on."

I arrived at 7:30 the next morning to make sure I didn't miss him. Luckily, I had some days off from work and only had to trade out one day. After informing my very worried roommates and going against their advice, I took my new blue backpack and sleeping bag packed with some clothing and food and sat on my bench to wait. At 7:45 he arrived. We walked to a main avenue heading out of town and he stuck out his thumb.

A pickup truck pulled over within five minutes. We jumped in the back and enjoyed the incredible scenery and fresh air to Florence, on the coast, where we would find another ride south. Luckily, the rain had let up and sun shone through the clouds, which I took as a good omen. *Look at me, I've done it. Maybe this will help me get over my chronic fear of life.*

Ron was moody at first, but after the first fifty miles he changed and started cracking jokes and offered me some of his sandwiches. I pulled out some fruit and we had a pickup truck picnic. I was starting to relax and feel happy with my decision by the time we were let out at the visitor center in Florence.

After a bit, we found a ride and headed back down the highway.

"Thanks for the ride, dude," Ron and the driver high-fived as the two of us were left at the entrance to a state park. "Hey, beautiful, this place has an incredible cliff overlooking the ocean. Let's stash our packs in these bushes and go for a walk. You'll love this place." We sat, looking at an amazing view overlooking the Pacific Ocean from a high cliff with craggy rocks and wind-blown trees. Ron was quiet most of the time, seeming moody again. We finally decided to get back to hitchhiking southward.

"Fuck! Where's our packs!" Ron yelled and cursed. After searching everywhere, we realized someone had taken our packs with everything we owned. I'd even left my wallet in the backpack; we were penniless, with nothing except the clothes on our backs.

"What are we going to do? This is your fault, I didn't want to leave our packs, and here we are!" I cried, blinded with anger. Ron yelled and screamed back. Finally, we realized there was nothing to be done about it and went to the road to hitchhike. Ron knew it would be harder and harder to find a ride on this stretch of road so late in the afternoon. A black man and white woman without backpacks was another strike against us for getting a ride.

I was furious and scared out of my wits. Darkness came and we still hadn't gotten a ride so we went back to the park to sleep. Ron made a small fire, but we were cold, wet, and in bad moods.

Finally, the sun rose but it was still drizzling. Cold and achy, we walked to the road, put our thumbs out, and got a ride in the back of a pickup destined for Eureka. Luckily, the people had a blanket they offered the two shivering travelers. I felt awful and was determined to return to Eugene. Now I didn't have any money and didn't know what I'd do.

"I'll hitchhike, I don't care," I told him.

"It's too dangerous. Just hold on until we get to my friends—they'll help us, you'll see." Ron started being very sweet and considerate, so I lightened up and went along.

"Well, this is it!" Ron was swelling with pride as he pointed to an old vacant apartment building, boarded up and falling apart. "Just you wait and see. This is great, and my friends ... the best."

I was dumbstruck. *We are going in here? Why? This is abandoned, maybe we just pass through here to get where we are going, what is going on?*

Ron led me through a boarded up doorway that wasn't nailed down and picked up speed. I had a hard time keeping up with him as we ascended several flights of stairs. People were going in and out of empty rooms and dilapidated halls. Slowly, I realized these were homeless people living in an abandoned building.

On the fifth floor, I heard someone yell, "Ron, where've you been?" A big fat, unkempt man in his twenties embraced Ron and looked at me. "Who've you got here, you old dog, she's a pretty one."

Ron beamed with pride as he introduced me to his friends in a sparsely furnished, dilapidated apartment. "This is Mike and Kim. These are my other friends, Sam, Jeff, and Deb, they live down the hall. I have some business to do with my buddies here, so you hang out and get acquainted."

"I'd rather stay with you." I was very uncomfortable and scared being left here.

"Listen, beautiful, I got things to do. I'll send my good friend, Sara, to take you around and show you the sights then we'll hook up later." With that, he turned and left me in the company of Mike and Kim and he walked out with the others.

Mike and Kim asked me about my trip, and I told them about losing our backpacks and wanting to get back to Eugene. They assured me Ron was a good man and he'd take care of things, but the two of them seemed to be high on something.

Before I could fret too much, a young girl entered the room with a confident stride and put her hand out to me, "Hi, I'm Sara. Ron told me to entertain you for the day." I was surprised and relieved. *This is just a young girl, I can handle that. She's the first person I've met I'm not scared of.*

Sara took me out of the building, and we walked toward the center of town. She seemed to know everyone along the way and acted like a thirty-year-old but looked about ten. "How old are you, anyway?" I asked as we ate a free sandwich Sara scored from a restaurant.

"Nine."

"Nine? Wow!"

"Yeah, I don't have a family. They abandoned me years ago and I've lived here since I was six. Good people here, they've always kept an eye out for me at the hotel."

"Hotel?"

"Oh yeah, that's what we call the apartments. It used to be an old hotel but has been abandoned for years and years. Luckily the city lets us stay; cuz there is nowhere else for us to live."

"You act older than me. I can't believe you are nine!"

Sara assured me she didn't take shit from anyone and would watch out for me. With no other options, I stuck by her. "I've got to go home. I think I'll try hitchhiking." I was desperate to leave.

"Ron said to not let you. He's trying to take care of his business today so he can go with you. Just wait. He said to meet him at the hotel at four p.m. You'll like the harbor." Sara convinced me to stay.

I spent the day with Sara at the harbor. I relaxed only slightly. When we returned to the building, I came into the living room and saw Ron with his back to me by the fireplace. I asked if I could borrow money from someone to catch the bus back to Eugene. Request denied—no one had that kind of money, he said.

"Ron, I want to go home NOW!" I was firm and angry.

He turned around. Blue paint was all over his mouth and nose. His eyes were glazed beyond recognition. A can of spray paint was in his hand and a sloppy smile greeted me. "Want some?"

No wonder he's not all there and getting so moody. He's destroying his brain. A million thoughts raced through my mind. *What am I going to do? What am I going to do? I can't call for money from mom or dad. Maybe Kathy would wire me some money for a bus ticket. I probably would be fine hitchhiking if I just stay on main roads and do it during the day.*

Mike and Kim entered the apartment and informed me Ron would hitchhike home with me in the morning. I curled up on an old mattress, just to get through the night.

I had nothing to say to him all the way home; I was exhausted and traumatized by the trip. My roommates had been worried about me and were going to call the police if I didn't get back that day. I pretended everything went great and I had a good time, because I was far too humiliated and embarrassed to tell them the truth. None of my roommates liked Ron, so I didn't want to confirm their suspicions. I did tell them the backpacks were stolen but that was all I shared of the adventure.

It was great to be home with the good people I knew.

Chapter 21

Changes

May, 1978

Kathy and her husband, Dennis, sat with me over a cup of coffee watching the rain pour down the window at the 5th Street Public Market.

"We found a four-bedroom house on Friendly Street. Would you be interested in moving in with us and my sister, Connie? The house is in a quiet part of town, less expensive than what you pay now, by a community swimming pool, and we think the street name is a good sign."

I accepted the offer and when I told my roommates, they understood and supported the decision.

I was looking forward to living with Kathy. She understood health issues and would help me build a connection toward healing. Kathy's entire family lived in Eugene and had extensive roots in the community. Her parents owned an old-style vitamin store and were knowledgeable in vegetarian eating, which would become a daily part of the new arrangement.

Kathy had three sisters: Carolyn, Connie, and Karen, and each had an unusual story. Carolyn was the oldest and had been a nun until she was excommunicated because she had an affair with a priest. Connie, the second oldest, was a masseuse and found she had the gift of channeling spirits. Karen was the youngest, into Wiccan beliefs, and was a witch. Kathy seemed to be the most normal of them all yet her eye disease also set her apart. Dennis was a hippie and did incredibly artistic construction jobs. I was most comfortable around Kathy and Dennis, so I concentrated on that friendship. I found her sisters fascinating and nice, but weird.

I started preparing for the move, set for two weeks away.

Another move, more disorder. I craved stability and normalcy, but my family and old friends didn't seem linked to my heart or soul now. Between the blood transfusions and the time in unconsciousness, I felt as though I had died and come back as a new soul, one without roots. But no one would believe that, so I kept it to myself.

Aside from the mental anguish, there was the physical. Pain began increasing in my abdomen, but my high threshold allowed me to work and continue daily routines. A chiropractor, recommended by Beth, started me on doses of ovarian and adrenal tissue to see if it would help regulate my periods better, but they continued to get worse.

I started my period out of sequence, and this time the flow was heavier than ever. Beth convinced me to go see her gynecologist immediately.

After hearing my recent history and about the pills Beth's chiropractor had given me, the doctor examined me. She was shocked.

"You have an abscess the size of a grapefruit on your ovary. We need to schedule surgery immediately."

"Oh my God, not again. Please, is there any other way? Why has this happened?"

"I think those pills have been stimulating your ovaries, combined with the scarring from the Pelvic Inflammatory Disease, but we can't be sure until we get in there."

The shock felt so familiar to me. Instantly, I fell backwards into the place I profoundly struggled daily to get out of … a place that felt like a gluey hole. *What am I going to do now? I can't even think straight.*

The worst was that I would have to tell my parents. Damn it to hell.

This was Friday and the surgery was scheduled for Monday morning. Mom would fly up to Eugene and be with me. It happened to be the time I was supposed to move too, so the old and new roommates offered to assist in the move, the surgery, and the recuperation. Succumbing to despondency and depression, I was committed to bedrest until the surgery. After the operation, I would move right into the new house on Friendly Street and recuperate there.

Mom arrived late Saturday night, also overcome with stress and depression. She came in to see her girl in bed and broke out in tears. I could barely hold it together myself. *I wanted Mom to see me doing well after the choices I've made ... I've screwed up again.*

Maybe dying would have been better because this living is hell.

"I'm so sorry Mom, I'm soooo sorry. I'll be fine though. Don't you worry." I was overtaken with guilt mixed with despair and frustration. I hoped Mom would get along with my roommates, who would carry the burden of caring for me. *I don't have anything in me to give her. I need it for myself, to survive.*

Monday morning arrived and Mom and I went to the hospital to check in. They were prepping me for surgery, which required an iodine dye test to help see the internal organs. As they injected it into my bloodstream, I went into cardiac arrest.

Everything is constricting! I can't breathe ... I can't breathe ... everyone is yelling in the distance ... ah, here comes that familiar darkness.

The nurse gave me a shot of adrenalin and, immediately, I started breathing again. When I became conscious, Mom was out of her mind, upset and yelling at the staff. Far in the distance I heard bits and pieces of what just happened but was confused and contentedly fell into the sedation. *Why is Mom so upset? It's okay Mom, I'll be just fine.*

"Allergic to the iodine dye? Why didn't you know? I'm not going to let you do surgery on my daughter. I want to talk to the head surgeon—NOW!" Mom was beside herself.

"It's impossible to know, Mrs. Weintraub, but we are always prepared for these types of surprises. She is fine now, but her condition is too dangerous; we must go forward with the plan." After discussing the situation with the head surgeon, Mom calmed down and allowed the surgery to proceed.

Kathy and Beth stayed with Mom throughout. Finally, the doctor came out to report.

"Mrs. Weintraub, I'm sorry, but there was much more internal damage than expected. The abdomen was full of infection. We think her past internal bleeding left blood pooled in her body cavity, and it was not removed entirely. The PID and salmonella infections bred in the sitting blood and caused extensive damage. All her intestines had adhered together, which is what infection will cause. We had to remove all her intestines, cut them apart and replace them. But, that's not the worst. The uterus and ovaries were destroyed by the infection. It was a huge mass we could barely identify. We had to give her a total hysterectomy."

Mom gasped and cried uncontrollably.

Once I was moved into my hospital room after recovery, Mom

wanted to wait for me to wake up, but the doctor suggested they go home and rest. It was decided she would return in the morning and be present when the doctor broke the news to me. Kathy and Beth did what they could to comfort Mom and took her back to the Friendly Street house, where she stayed in my new room.

The next day, I woke up to find Mom and the doctor talking at the foot of the bed.

"Hi guys, how's it going?" I halfway smiled. The doctor proceeded to tell me the news.

"Wow," I calmly replied. The news didn't sink in. I knew it was serious, but my response was lost in medication and shock. I left my body again and it would take even longer this time to understand and come to terms with the consequences of this surgery.

Mom stayed at my bedside. "The doctor said you will probably be in the hospital four or five days before they discharge you. I'm taking a week off work. I think we should make arrangements for you to come home with me."

"Mom, I want to stay here. You've met my roommates and seen where I live. I want to stay."

Mom had known there would be this difference of opinion. In the phone conversation with Dad the night before, it was clear; he was angry at me and was ready to get on with his own life. His greatest disappointment was realized; he would not have grandchildren from me. He told Mom if I fought the idea to come home, leave it alone, I would have to deal with the consequences of my actions. The attitude devastated Mom, but her husband was her partner in life and she had to live with him. She was very worried about me, but didn't know how to help. Luckily, she did like my roommates and where I lived, so that helped.

"I won't argue, darling. I'll stay until you go home, then I'll go back to work. Kathy said she would assist you in your recuperation."

In the hospital, I was back to wound dressings, but this one was sewn up and nowhere near as big as the previous one. In fact, the doctor had cut along the lower half of the old scar that extended from the bottom of the sternum to the pubic area. He made it look cosmetically better than the upper half. The other surgery had totally removed my belly button and this doctor boasted that he put one back. Sure enough, when I looked at my abdomen, there it was. It did make me happy because it made me feel I looked more normal, even though there was still the long, hideous scar.

This surgery was a breeze compared to what I'd gone through before and I was ready to go home after five days. Bedrest was ordered for two full weeks, with walking only around the house, and then slow increases from there. Also, no work for six months; the hospital social worker got me on disability for that time, which relieved me immensely. After that, I could resume my normal life, whatever that was.

Mom was worried and depressed, but did what she could for me. Kathy, Beth, and Dale took turns entertaining her when she wasn't at the hospital, and everyone enjoyed each other's company. Mom filled them in on the whole story about my accident which surprised them, because I had kept most of it to myself. It gave them a deeper understanding of my situation and enabled them to be more supportive. Mom was grateful and more peaceful about leaving her darling in Oregon with this group of friends. They would let her know if there was trouble and would take good care of me.

I had only seen the Friendly Street house once before and was happy to come home to this new space. Mom and Kathy ushered me into my bedroom, which they had set up for me. A beautiful bouquet of flowers was set by the bed. It was great. A window looked over the back yard to two big cherry trees in bloom.

"I love it. Thank you two so much for making my room cozy. I'm ready to christen my bed. Can you help?" I leaned between the two, hobbled to the bed, and grunted as I climbed in. Being discharged and getting home was tiring, but luckily they gave me strong pain medication. "I think I'll take a nap. Love you, Mom."

"Love you, darling. We'll have dinner together tonight and then Dale said he'd get me to the airport tomorrow." Mom's eyes were brimming with tears, knowing she was leaving the next day. She knew she had to accept this, and the sooner she could return to her routine the better.

Kathy and Beth made a beautiful vegetarian dinner, and all the roommates from the old and new houses were there to welcome me home and bid Mom goodbye. It was a bittersweet evening.

Mom and I lovingly embraced and pecked each other on the cheek as she got in the car with Dale. Never once was Dad brought up; it was unspoken knowledge he was angry. I was relieved to have Mom go so she could get on with her own life, and I could be without the guilt and worry I felt when she was around.

"Darling stay in touch. I think you should watch this vegetarian thing, you need protein, okay?"

"Mom, my gut doesn't like meat; it's very hard for me to digest. Anyway, I can get protein by combining grains and beans ... don't worry, I'll be fine."

"I don't know, it just seems like you'll get weak."

"Really, Mom, I'll keep an eye on it all."

After Mom left, Kathy took charge. She was the only one who didn't work, due to her eye disease, so it was quite fortuitous she was available. I needed assistance with everything and felt comfortable with Kathy attending to my private and personal needs. The doctor set an appointment for me to return in three weeks for a checkup, at which point they would discuss and start the required hormone replacement. I was overwhelmed.

I loved the new house and spent most mornings on the porch in the backyard watching the cherries grow and hearing the birds tweet. There were two trees: a Bing cherry with huge juicy garnet gems and the other a Queen Anne cherry that were also huge and juicy, yellow with a red blush. They had a bumper crop and Kathy did everything she could think of with those cherries. I also learned that too many cherries were hard on the gut, so I had to cut back, which was okay—I had eaten my fill.

Kathy was a great companion. I could be honest and tell her my deep, dark feelings. We would discuss spiritual matters, emotions, healing, and laugh–it all provided me a sense of desperately needed connection. She turned me on to all types of new music to soothe my tortured soul. She also loved nature and took me to sit by the river or go to Mt. Piscah for picnics. Kathy was very sensitive; she saw dark emotional changes in me since the hysterectomy, which worried her, but she didn't know how to help.

I've been neutered, my fate sealed against ever being a mother. I really don't think I can do this life thing ...

I had been home one week when I awoke to sharp pain high up in my vaginal channel. There had been regular blood discharge, which the doctor told me to expect. This acute pain was new though. My immediate fear was more surgery.

We called the doctor, who told us to come in immediately. It turns out they hadn't warned me that there was packing gauze deep in the vaginal channel that was supposed to have been removed after the surgery. A safety pin was attached to it for easy removal, but it hadn't been, and now it had opened up deep inside me. After anesthetizing the region the doctor removed it with as much delicacy as possible. He sincerely apologized and sent us home, dazed.

"Kathy, it's always something. I'm so sorry for bringing you into all this …" A storm of tears and sadness was brewing within and washing over me like a raging tide.

"Don't worry. I'm glad I have you as my friend; that is my reward." Kathy hugged me, which helped lessen my distress.

I felt so lucky to have met Kathy. She understood me better than anyone. After months of dealing with pain and disappointment, I now had to start on hormones like a menopausal woman. I had been neutered in my prime. *No man is going to want to be with me now. I'm so scarred up and look like I belong in a circus. What's next? Maybe death would be easier than this craziness. What is the point of life … of me?*

My self-talk was kept private, but my depression was growing more obvious daily. The doctors started me on an estrogen hormone that made my mood swings even worse. I felt like a chalk board someone is scratching twenty-four hours a day, screeching to the depths of my being. Anger, depression, anxiety—I wanted to escape my body but felt like a prisoner to these tortuous feelings and thoughts. *HHHEEEEELLLLLPPPPP!!!!!!!!!* The hormones were horrible, but I had to take them or the doctors said I would age faster. I was on an emotional rollercoaster.

* * *

After two months on the hormones, I returned to the doctor with my complaints, and she decided to try a new hormone, Premarin, manufactured from pregnant mare urine. Supposedly, it was more natural than the Ogen I was on. *Ugh, now I'm adding horse products to the mix, perhaps I'll start neighing soon.* The mood swings were there, but not as intense, so I continued with them and tried to adjust to the incessant moodiness. It felt futile.

Even though everyone was being so nice to me, I felt like biting their heads off. It was a constant struggle to maintain a pleasant disposition, so I started isolating. It was easier to deal with my own craziness without being under the magnifying glass of others trying to help. It was up to me, and no one else, to feel better.

I was fearful of everything, especially men. Since it was my sexual organs that suffered the trauma, men automatically and subconsciously were targeted as the enemy. Any man looking at me sent a shock of fear through my mind and body, and I was compelled to look away toward escape. One day on the bus, a man who simply smiled at me sent a sharp pain through my abdomen and scars. The last surprise surgery left me feeling as though I had been raped with a knife by the doctors, with everyone watching. Now, this sentiment infiltrated my subconscious and triggered fearful responses to otherwise harmless situations.

Isolated in my room, my thoughts went in an endless loop. *This hysterectomy has left more emotional scars than all the other surgeries. This is my sexual identity. A woman is supposed to meet a man and have babies, a family ... What is the point of sex now? What good am I now? I'm neutralized, neutered, a blank. Men want a sexual partner, but with me they'll get only trauma and hurt. I'm on a crabby emotional roller coaster all the time, oversensitive to everything. I'm twenty and going through menopause. No one understands, not even older women who've already gone through this. They, at least, have gotten the chance to have family and children. Me ... I'm already an old woman inside.*

It's complicated though, because another part of me is wiped clean of historical emotions and self. It's been a year since the accident, and now I feel like a one year old now trying to live the history of my twenty years. This is all so confusing and no one understands me.

I decided I should go to a counselor.

Through disability services I found a counselor who would see me six times. He worked at the University of Oregon as a psychology professor, and his clients agreed to be part of his research. It was nice, walking on campus again to his office; I craved the stability and continuity school offered. Maybe I would look into a grant.

The psychologist was shocked at what I had been through, but knew I would need more than six sessions. He was very worried about my state of mind and provided comfort for the short amount of time we had. When I mentioned I was thinking about going back to school, he was very supportive and added that, as a student, there were free counseling sessions at student health.

For the first time, I felt the kindness and understanding I needed to start unraveling my complicated emotions. The problem was, as soon as I started opening up, the six sessions were over. I plummeted back into the confusion but did make the decision to go back to school at the University of Oregon. I was accepted into the School of Community Service and Public Affairs, CSPA, something I was very interested in. The focus helped me take steps forward, at least in my external world.

Financial Aid provided a grant that would allow me to attend school, and I would need just a part-time job for my other expenses. I lived frugally with minimal rent and food stamps. I needed something stable to help the dust settle from the past storms.

Chapter 22

More?

It was now a year and a half since the accident and, in my external world, life with my roommates on Friendly Street was good. I was learning about vegetarian eating and herbs. Daily, I drank a cleansing herbal liver tonic and other herbs to support my hormone system. Digestion was a continual daily struggle. I still felt deep swelling internally, but knew the lack of a gall bladder, my scarred intestines and split liver affected the enzyme balance. It was a constant work in progress. I was also starting to get low grade headaches and backaches but chalked it up to the other imbalances caused since the accident. Chronic discomfort was my normal.

I started my first semester at the U of O but struggled to keep up with classes. I was exhausted all the time and my concentration for assignments felt like a rubber ball bouncing off the wall. I loved being a student on campus again, for the routine and sense of belonging to something, but the crowds and busyness were overwhelming.

One day Kathy and Dennis informed me they had found a house to buy and had decided to leave the Friendly Street house. I would miss them, but knew they would still be in my life. Beth moved in, which was great, because she was also a student at U of O, which might help my focus. Connie also decided to leave, but was replaced by her youngest sister, Karen, the witch.

Karen had a boyfriend, Kenny, who believed he really was a warlock. They belonged to a coven and met regularly to place spells and study. Kenny's aggressive attitude and abusive language toward Karen scared me from the first encounter. The couple was very sexual, frequently going at it in plain sight of others. The behavior triggered all my sexual fear issues. I vowed to avoid them as much as possible.

I started swimming at the nearby community pool every morning at six a.m. to expend some of my angst. I was extremely shy to show the red angry scars covering my abdomen. The reason for them was not a topic I liked to talk about, so I avoided talking to anyone and dressed where no one would see me.

The water relaxed me and was something I had always been drawn to. Connie had taught me about chakras, the energy centers of the body in the Yogic tradition. When I swam laps, I meditated and did color cleansings intended to strengthen my chakras and energy. I would mentally wash each wound and chakra with liquid white light and the color related to that specific energy center. If the center was too pale or dark, I would wash it with a richer, deep watery color, until it changed to the color intended, and then do the same for each one. After each was done, I did an entire rainbow cleanse from the root to the crown chakra.

This, combined with the circulation of swimming, purified and washed away the darkness within, and I felt energized for the remainder of the day. It became a necessary activity. I had put on weight again and hoped it would help me trim back down. Without swimming, I felt congested, clogged, and confused. It also improved my digestion.

One day after swimming, I came home and found Karen and Kenny naked in the backyard, having sex. Only a broken-down fence surrounded the yard, and all the neighbors could view the show. I went blank with anger. I had a class to get to, so left the two entangled with each other and vowed it was time to address the couple's behavior.

Beth and I sat across from Karen at the dinner table and brought up the subject. Karen seemed oblivious, apologizing for offending us. Their coven encouraged free and open behavior, she said. We set down some house rules about closed doors and keeping their activities private. She agreed, but the next day Kenny didn't take it so well. He yelled at Karen then stormed across the hall to confront me in my bedroom.

The confrontation unnerved me, and I burst into tears and ordered him out. He adopted his warlock glare and told me he could cast a spell on me so I'd better watch out.

Finally, after circling me two times, he harrumphed and turned away. "Watch yourself. I'm a very powerful warlock and I don't like you." Karen led him out the door looking back at me with eyes full of worry.

Once they were gone, I took off walking. My mental fog was so great I found myself miles from home before realizing where I was, near the campus. *How did I get here?* I had a raging headache and felt terrible. I decided to lie down on campus and take a nap.

The sun was setting when I woke up under the same tree where Anna and I had spent time together when we first arrived in Eugene. Blinking my eyes, I slowly remembered the event with Kenny.

Somehow, I had blacked out. My head felt like it would burst; pain ripped down my back. I called Kathy, and she was able to get me home. She promised to talk to Karen about Kenny's behavior; all I wanted was peace and darkness for awhile.

Karen and Kenny stayed away from the house, which suited me just fine. I attempted to attend classes, but couldn't do my part-time job, filing at the CSPA administrative office. The low grade headache and backache I'd had for months was now a blizzard of pain. Unable to work or go to school for two days, I decided to go by the Student Health Center. The doctor there delivered another bombshell.

"Miss, I'm afraid we need to do some tests on you. I think you may have spinal meningitis, which is very serious. We need to admit you to the hospital for a spinal tap and find out if it's viral or bacterial. The bacterial can be life threatening."

"What? I don't understand … are you sure?" My headache had gotten so bad, talking even hurt. *I don't even care anymore, just take away the pain and if I die, so be it.*

Once again, a shot to make me sleep, then searing pain as the needle entered my spine. After that, they wheeled me into a dark room until the diagnosis was confirmed for viral meningitis. The treatment was a full week in the hospital, with darkness and rest. I spent most of the time sedated.

Kathy and Dennis had been visiting, but I never knew what was dream and what was real. They came to take me home at the end of the week and filled me in. She had called my mother. The doctor didn't feel it necessary for Mom to make the trip; Kathy and Dennis could keep an eye on me until I returned in a week's time for another spinal tap to be sure the meningitis was gone.

"What more can happen to me, Kathy? I don't think I'm supposed to be here in this world …" My depression reached a new depth and I retreated within, feeling as if I were suspended in a gluey glop of nothingness at the bottom of an endless pit.

The spinal tap came up negative, so I was released to slowly return to normal life … whatever that was. *So many gaps in my head, I can't seem to track or cope very well. My internal life is too much, I can't handle things anymore.*

I got behind in school, although I somehow managed to return to classes. Professors gave extensions on everything, which allowed me to survive the first semester.

The winter holiday season arrived, but I didn't care. Most of the time was spent catching up with studies, as I felt safer and in more control being alone with books. The furious inner undercurrent had consumed me and I lived two lives; one was focused on trying to function in the outside world and the other was surviving the inner disarray and madness.

Friends were very worried but had no idea how to reach me. "Why don't you go to the Student Health Center and sign up for counseling— it's free. Talking to a professional might help." Beth wanted to call my parents, but suggested this route first.

"I guess." I was desperate for something.

Dr. Edwards was a middle-aged psychiatrist who thought she had seen it all, but she was taken aback to hear my story. She was very compassionate, wise, and a good listener. I felt safe with her and was able to slowly open up and attempt to address what lurked within. I shared issues related to my family, the accident, the hysterectomy, fear, and pain, but she was most interested when I talked about God.

"I'm mad at God and don't believe there is one anymore. Why would God let this happen? I'm a good person and try to not hurt people. Maybe I'm being punished for going against Mom and Dad. Maybe it's true what Connie and some others have said, we create our own reality and I created the accident. That's so scary to think I brought all this on myself, it has all felt out of my control."

Dr. Edwards put perspective on the topic and I agreed with her; there is an X factor out there that is uncontrollable and everyone is subject to it. I was at the wrong place at the wrong time. It happens. How could it be possible for me to cause the bus to go off the road in Mexico? The concept gave me some peace, but I still felt there wasn't a God. I didn't like talking about Mexico or the accident either; it made me feel as if I was falling off a cliff.

"Why don't I feel an emotional connection to my history and family anymore?" I asked her. "I truly feel I died and a new spirit entered my body. I'm so different now; I don't even relate to the old me. She was happy, funny, carefree and together. I'm now depressed, angry, lost and dark. The accident sobered me up and turned me into a completely serious old soul. Then the hysterectomy neutered me and took away any dreams of children, which is the one thing that would complete my purpose in life."

Dr. Edwards believed the old was still there and tried to help me see that, but I felt differently. The old was dead, there was no pulse whatsoever. Only the dark remained and I did not feel anything but loneliness, pain and loss.

I was able to see Dr. Edwards for the entire semester. My studies plodded along, giving me focus and a period to relearn how to function in the 'real' world. I studied at coffeehouses, the library, and quiet university locations—anyplace to stay away from home, Karen and Kenny. Even though I still felt numb, at least no new traumas inflicted my life.

One session, Dr. Edwards broke the news to me that she was moving after the end of the term. I was devastated and became fearful. Even though recommendations were made, I didn't feel like starting over again and having to tell my story one more time, to teach another therapist about whom I was. I decided to see how things went without it.

It was time to visit Anna and see someone who knew me. I caught the train to Seattle and spent a long weekend traipsing around Anna's haunts in Seattle. It was fun and comfortable, but even Anna's humor couldn't break through my despair. I was anxious to get home to slow-moving Eugene.

Occasionally, the two of us would visit each other and talk about New Mexico and how we were tired of all the rain. Twice, we went to the San Juan Islands and stayed with some friends who were homesteading, a tough lifestyle only for the strong and independent. The two of us loved taking the ferries around the region and witnessing the great Orca whales emerge in the straits as they passed through. Being surrounded by water was always calming and a good escape for me.

Anna was a student at the University of Washington, a Husky, so she was up to her eyeballs in studies also and had limited time for visits. It was always nice to see each other, but our lives had diverged. Anna seemed to have no problem getting boyfriends; it was just finding the right one. Anna thought after graduation she would move back to Albuquerque, but time would tell. *If only I was as grounded as Anna, I too would have boyfriends and a feel for my future.*

Caught On Camera –
This photo partly reveals my state of mental fog
during the Oregon years.

Chapter 23

Another New Start and a Step Forward

Entering the third year of coursework, I finally completed the CSPA prerequisites. It had been a challenge in concentration and grueling to adhere to the rigid format of classes. That combined with my mental, physical, and emotional unrest made me think I would never succeed. At last I reached the part of my education where I could choose electives for my major. Community Service and Public Affairs partnered with the City of Eugene to provide progressive opportunities.

They worked together with communities to build neighborhood gardens, food and apartment co-ops, teach environmental safety practices and alternative energy incentives. For the first time in my studies I was excited and motivated to learn about this commonsense and creative approach. I loved that it provided growth that directed me away from my unyielding past. Besides, I loved being a U of O Fighting Duck, another unique identity different from everything I'd known! I was starting to get a handle on how to study, and that—combined with inspiring progressive subjects—meant I might just succeed and survive college.

In one university class, a group project brought a new friend to my world, Claudia Tots. Claudia was very skinny, had loads of freckles and laughed easily. She wasn't particularly pretty, but something about her made guys love her. She joined the program at the same time I did, so we shared many core classes. The two of us hit it off immediately.

I loved her down-to-earth and very deep spirit. Claudia had worked for the Forest Service for years before returning to school. She had no pretenses and spoke exactly how she felt. Such honesty was refreshing to me. We became inseparable and studied, biked, and picnicked together often.

Nature was our mutual love. Claudia had a car and started taking me out of town on weekends to visit some of her old Forest Service buddies and to see the stunning scenery of Oregon—the coast, the Cascades, clear blue rivers, and farmland. Claudia adored me and couldn't believe how much I had been through. She said I was still 'a sweetie-pie.' When Claudia's lease was up, she asked if I wanted to get a house together, just the two of us. She had heard the stories about Karen and thought the change would be good for me. I agreed.

Claudia was a rock for me. She helped with studies, emotional problems, and sexual issues and introduced me to the alternative-energy world of Eugene. She had done projects in the community related to solar and wind, and she had friends I was comfortable with. Claudia had more male than female friends; she was like one of the guys. Most of them were tree planters, fire fighters, or forest service workers who were ruggedly handsome and down-to-earth. Several of them were past lovers who were still after her. I couldn't figure it out, because she definitely wasn't sexy or attractive, but the guys loved her.

Claudia's diversions helped me ignore the clamor inside myself, and for the first time since the accident I trusted someone entirely. I loved my other friends but shared the same interests and approach to life as Claudia. She would spend hours talking out complicated feelings with me, and maybe we wouldn't resolve an issue, but it became clearer. Claudia accepted me as I was. The new home was a small two-bedroom off a busy street. It was five miles from U of O, and we often biked there and back together. Claudia also loved swimming and running, which further inspired our friendship. Meals were shared, as were movies, concerts, festivals, studies. We were inseparable.

Physically, I still struggled with hormone and digestive issues, but pain and illness diminished. Exercise made me stronger, but I still fought a weight problem. Emotions, on the other hand, continued to be a roller coaster, but I was learning to live that way and hide much of it.

Mom and Dad were happy I'd found Claudia and was staying in school. They only knew what I wrote or called to tell them, which was only the good things. I felt so guilty about what I had put them through and didn't want to worry them. I hadn't been home in two years. Occasionally, I spoke on the phone with my three brothers, but it always felt so distant.

Mom and Dad were working and trying to get on with their lives. They traveled to Europe, Hawaii, and planned to go to Vancouver, British Columbia. They wanted me to join them at the end of my spring term. I hesitantly agreed.

"Darling, oh how I've missed you so!" Mom hugged me for a long time. Then Dad did the same.

"You two look great! Good to see you!" I was nervous but happy to see them. It had been a long time. We met at the Portland Airport, where we would rent a car and head for Seattle. The next day we would drive to Vancouver for four days, and then back to Portland. There was no time to go to Eugene because they had to get back to their jobs.

Dr. Edwards had told me I had a lot of work to do to repair my relationship with my parents, but I just wanted to avoid it all. This trip would be the first attempt to start reconciling. Everyone was on their best behavior and we were able to focus on the travels and vacation instead of the emotional cauldron brewing beneath it all. I was happy to avoid charged issues and just enjoy the trip. We went to museums, stores, Granville Island, Stanley Park, and happened upon a street fair.

There were a few tense moments. I still felt resentment from Dad's accusations and kept a safe emotional distance from him. Mom remarked on my weight gain several times, which was a sore spot. All in all, Mom and Dad were happy to see me doing so well and staying in school. They wanted me to come home for the holidays this year and would pay for the ticket home. I was curious to go home to see how I felt, so I agreed.

After the Vancouver trip, I reflected. Although I still felt very different and distanced, we didn't argue and say mean things to each other this time. I owed much to the parents; they had done so much for me. I had two years left on my BA, then maybe I would go back to New Mexico. *The rain here does get tiresome.*

The fall term passed quickly. By now I had established a study routine and followed it religiously because that was the only way I could concentrate. Diversions wrecked my attention, and it took real effort to apply myself to my classes.

I went home for the holiday but felt out of sorts and uncomfortable. The first thing when I walked in the door, Mom commented, "Nan, you are getting fat!"

I lost my temper and yelled. "Mom, can you at least say hi, I love you, first? This is why I don't come home; you always criticize me! Is that all that matters to you?"

Immediately we started yelling back and forth, then Mom said, "STOP! I'm sorry, Cheney, can we start over? Look at me, Nan. I'm sorry. We fell immediately back into old history. I'm past that; you are too … Can we start over and work on our friendship?" She was so sincere and honest; it stunned me and stopped the emotional rollercoaster in its tracks.

"Thank you, thank you, thank you, Mom. You broke this horrible pattern and have led us where we both need to be." I looked at Mom and we embraced.

From that moment on, our relationship changed and we became best girlfriends. I was amazed how quickly and completely the shift happened. For the remainder of the vacation, we spoke honestly and more candidly than ever before. I was able to share feelings about my hysterectomy, hormones, men, and my emotional chaos. Mom was a great listener and tried to give what advice she could; it often surprised me how appropriate it was. *For the first time, an inkling of a mature mother-daughter bond has emerged, allowing our love to grow… and help me reconnect to my family… feel my family… introduce them to the new me.*

Dad remained friendly but aloof; it was not our time to reconcile.

Mom wanted me to go to a respected internist, related to my hormones. I had nothing to lose, so I went.

"So, do you have a boyfriend?" Dr. Miller asked.

Why is he asking me that? "No."

"Why not? You're a young, attractive woman. Most girls your age have one."

"Uh, I'm too messed up inside and scared."

"I'm asking you these questions because I'm used to working with diabetics, and when you have blood sugar that's off, the first symptom is moodiness. So I understand about emotions, and I discuss moods first because I understand that has a lot to do with health."

"Wow, that's so unusual. No doctor has ever asked me about my feelings or moods."

I opened up and explained my situation to Dr. Miller, told him about the hormone doses, my fear of men, my loneliness. "I fight feelings of … of suicide all the time. I may look fine on the outside, but inside is an unruly mess of depression and hopelessness." *I haven't even told Dr. Edwards of my suicidal thoughts.* He leaned back against the counter, listening attentively to every word I said. I couldn't believe it.

"Well, I don't think any new hormone will change what you have told me. This all comes with the territory. Only your attitude and mind can make a difference at this point. But, what I *can* say is you have two choices—either you try or you don't. What do you want to do?"

He made it so simple. The fog vanished and I saw the problem clearly. I thought a moment on the two options, and the answer came to me, "I want to try."

That simple statement and conversation was a turning point in my life.

Suddenly, I understood. *I want to try to make my life and emotions better. I want a boyfriend. I want peace. I want internal stability. Trying one more time is a choice I do have and one I will make.* Having it presented as two options made the choice very simple.

Mom noticed the difference. "Nan, you have become a wise young lady. Everyone asks about you and respects you so much. I love you, darling. Please write and call. I know you can do it. Your Dad and I are so proud of you. Be strong and know you are an amazing young woman."

It's nice to know people from my past still care about me and don't see me as a loser. I hugged both parents and felt better having come for the visit. "I will stay in touch. I love you and thanks for everything. Have fun you two!" I blew them a kiss as I walked toward the airport gate and boarded the plane back to Eugene with a new confidence—to try.

Claudia immediately saw the new, upbeat, open energy in me when I returned. I told her about the visit and my new attitude, to try.

"Claudia, you are so comfortable with guys … I want to be that way. I'm just so terrified. But I'm also lonely." *I just don't want to act or feel like a slut and regret what I do.*

"Take it slow. Get some male friends and start there. No relationship or physical contact other than a friendly hug. It takes time, don't rush."

"Yeah. I don't even know how to meet anyone. I think I scare everyone since I have so many issues."

"You know some of my friends; just keep it that way. We can have a few small dinners and have them over so you can practice."

"But what about if I feel attracted? As soon as I do, I get scared and shy."

"That's okay. Take your time. Notice it, then remember, only friends."

"Sounds hard."

"The key is to go slow, and try."

I liked the idea but was nervous. The first dinner made me tense and I felt like a babbling fool, along with the second, third, and fourth dinners. When I opened up, the guys either didn't respond or changed the subject. It was obvious I wasn't comfortable, and the guys felt it. Claudia had a great time and actually started dating one of the young men.

Sadly, the dinner plan backfired. I found myself jealous of Claudia's time with the new guy and myself in the role of third wheel. I withdrew again. It was easier to be alone. Claudia wasn't around as much and decided to move in with her boyfriend. We saw each other in classes, but now her boyfriend occupied the place she used to have for me. There was no one to take Claudia's place in my life. Now what?

Going Backwards Fast

Chapter 24

Alone

Five moves in two years—geez. I don't want to look for a new roommate—I'm tired of it. Maybe it's time to just deal with myself.

I couldn't afford the house on my own, but a classmate had very cute studio in the old part of town by the river bike path. They were moving out and I moved in. It was very small, very cheap, very secluded, and very old; I loved it. At last, my space and my time were my own.

I had one more year to graduate. As a senior, an alternative option became available called University Year in Action, or UYA, sponsored by the Peace Corp. A student committed their last year to working in a community program, attending school seminars with a professor, doing a final project, and would then graduate with a BA in their field.

I continued struggling with my studies, so, the UYA program appealed to me for its hands-on approach and real world experience. They paid a small monthly stipend and covered my school grant, so I wouldn't have to work a part-time job. My placement was with Headstart, a preschool classroom for under privileged children at an environmental preschool farm. They had animals, a garden, alternative energy projects, and worked with the parents and community to learn ways to save money using these methods. I thought it would be good to be around children, to help me through my own feelings of lost motherhood, plus I loved the progressive nature of it. Unfortunately, once I was spending time with the kids, it only brought home to me the fact that I would never have my own.

In addition, the program was much more vigorous than I'd expected.

I commuted out of town to work three days a week, teaching and caretaking the farm. The other two days, I attended seminars with my professor and a group of twelve other UYA students.

My professor was Satsuki Komeni, a caring Japanese woman with incredible sensitivity and warmth. She noticed I was withdrawing and my studies were suffering after the first six months. Finally, she had to bring it up because her employers at the farm had shown concern as to my mental status—how embarrassing. I shared my story, including the effect it was having on me to work with children, and she began counseling me twice a week.

Through UYA, I met a new group of people. Linda, Felice, Lon, and Don worked at a shelter for women. They were very tight and had a bond I was drawn to. No one knew my history, but they accepted me into their circle with ease and included me in most of their extra-curricular activities.

We often met for Sunday breakfast at Mama's Home Fried Truck Stop, to eat and listen to music. I was feeling particularly out of sorts this day and, suddenly, decided I wanted a new name, to help me escape the old misfit self. The decision was final.

"Anybody have any ideas? I'm serious, I don't feel like Nancy anymore. I'm different, and I want a new name. The old me died in the accident and it's time to be the real me."

Everyone was surprised by this declaration, but they started offering up ideas.

After batting ideas around for fifteen minutes, Lon said, "How about Eli, a takeoff of Elaine, your middle name?"

Everyone stopped, smiled and liked the name, especially me.

"That fits. It's short and sweet, just like you!" Linda nodded her head.

"But it's a guy's name," Felice argued.

"I don't care—I like it. I'm neutered anyway. I feel like an Eli. Hello everyone, I'm Eli!" Immediately Nancy became Eli, and a noticeable calm came over me. Everyone noticed.

I loved my new name. It freed me from my previous history and gave me a clean start. From that moment on, my new name, Eli, was adapted by everyone except my parents, who didn't like it at all.

"We named you Nancy. That is who you are to us and always will be. We love that name. Anyway, Eli is a boy's name." My parents were in agreement on this one, refusing to use my new name.

At first, I tried to force the issue but finally backed off and understood how it would be hard for them. It was fine if they didn't want to call me Eli, but everyone else would know me that way. UYA and the university officially changed my name to Eli Nancy Weintraub, and the shift was complete.

I graduated the UYA program and U of O with a BA in Community Service and Public Affairs in 1982, five years after my accident. I wasn't sure how I pulled it off, considering there were entire weeks I didn't remember, but it was graduation and Mom and Dad were coming.

I needed to make some decisions about my future. I was ready to leave Eugene, but didn't feel ready to return home to New Mexico. With an offer for a place to live in Portland, I headed that way, hoping to work during the non-rainy summer; after that, I would decide whether to stay in the Northwest or head back to the desert.

I quickly found a job waitressing. The hours were flexible and tips were great. Then one day I arrived at work to find the restaurant locked up, with an 'Out of Business' sign hanging on the front door. I hadn't received my paycheck for the past two weeks either. The owner was nowhere to be found. I tried to learn what happened, but got nothing except hearsay from the local business owners.

Well, I guess this means my decision is made for me; my time is up in this rainy climate, and I'm going back to New Mexico. It is time.

Chapter 25

From Mold to Dust

Wide open views, blue sky, bright sun—chapped lips, dry skin. I was back in New Mexico. I was happy but nervous to be home and didn't trust myself around Dad, now that I was back. Would he verbally slam me down again? Would I find peace here?

After spending a few uneventful weeks at home in Los Alamos, I moved to Albuquerque to find work. I was feeling very out of sorts around my old life and felt anxious to get out on my own. My brother, Rick, and his wife Pat let me stay with them until I found my own place. Three years ago, while I was in Oregon, they had a baby boy, Corey. I loved the idea of being an aunt. I knew it would be difficult, but maybe this time being around a baby would be different since he was my nephew.

Corey and I bonded immediately and played nonstop. For the time at Rick's house, I didn't get too depressed, although I still fought off relentless feelings of my childless destiny. I couldn't let anyone know how hard it was to hold this child, especially this child who was such a blessing for Mom and Dad.

They would need a blessing after the news Doug and I got from Howard. On my way back from Oregon, I had stopped in Berkley for a few days together with my twin brothers. That's when Howard dropped the news that he was gay. Doug, especially, was in shock. I knew this would devastate my parents—another chance for grandchildren gone—but Howard didn't seem worried. He felt they would accept him and his new lifestyle.

"Aren't you worried about AIDS?" I couldn't help but ask about the elephant in the room.

"No." That was all he said.

I was terrified because AIDS was rampant in this community, and I could only feel fear for Howard's life. The ironic part was that he was doing scientific research, looking for a cure for AIDS.

Now, I daydreamed while I watched Corey play in the grass. *The reality of not having children is sinking in the older I get. Watching Rick and Pat with Corey is something I will never get to experience. I can babysit, but will always have to leave the child with their parents. I won't ever hear anyone say, they look so much like you, or I love you Mommy, or be able to talk proudly about what my child is doing now, or know someone will be there for me when I get old. A child creates purpose for its parent and I will never get that. I look at couples with babies, and I feel pain and loss instead of joy. What is my purpose? It will just be me, as the final period in my life's sentence.* These thoughts cycled relentlessly in my heart and soul, but the only thing others saw was my attempt to hide depression.

I found a roommate and a place near UNM, and got another job waitressing at an upscale New Mexican restaurant. I also enrolled at UNM to take a few classes and gain access to the Olympic-sized swimming pool on campus. Among the classes was Spanish. I discovered I was a bit rusty, but I liked reconnecting with this old skill. I also got certified to substitute teach for the Albuquerque Public Schools. Substitute teaching was rough—a different school every day, different levels of need among the special education kids … and mainly the pain of being around children. I soon quit and took on extra waitressing shifts.

There was still no man in my life. Apparently, I still put off vibes that scared guys away. They liked me as long as I was a friend, but nothing more happened. If they did show interest, it was usually only about sex, but even then, once I mentioned scars or hysterectomy, they lost interest and disappeared. I couldn't stand being around my friends who were happily dating or in relationships.

I remembered a counselor telling me that the relationship with Dad needed to be repaired before any romantic relationship would be possible. I decided to talk to Dad about the event that had motivated my leaving Los Alamos after the accident. My self-esteem suffered from that and I wanted an apology, so I decided to visit Los Alamos for the weekend.

I invited Dad to walk up a canyon we often visited. After making small talk, I changed the subject to the accident as a lead-in and then got the courage to bring up the topic. "Dad, I have to talk to you about something very difficult. I need to talk to you about the conversation we had that provoked my decision to leave home ..."

"I don't remember, refresh my memory." Dad was curious but clueless.

"Well, remember when you found out about my IUD and you told me ... actually got really angry at me and called me a slut and a whore and all sorts of other ugly things?"

Dad looked stunned. "I never said anything like that to you."

"What? Yes you did! You told me over and over how terrible I was and how I was acting like a slut and a whore."

"I don't remember ever saying anything like that to you ..." Dad was genuinely oblivious to the incident. After a few more attempts to refresh his memory, I realized he had really forgotten. "If I ever said anything like that to you, I am sorry, but I do not remember doing that."

I shook my head in disbelief. *Oh My God. All these years I've been carrying this horrible hurt inside, letting it run my heart and mind ragged ... and he doesn't even remember ... why am I torturing myself then? What a waste of ... me.*

I turned to Dad. We both looked into each other's eyes, and I asked, "Friends?" And he replied, "Friends." We embraced and I felt the same as when Mom changed our relationship direction. I could move ahead with my life. *These keys are so subtle, how will I ever find them all?*

* * *

I'd been back in New Mexico almost a year, but still felt cut off and out of place. I missed Eugene and the progressive lifestyle, but I didn't miss the rain. An idea came to me: travel for awhile and see what happens. I'd saved quite a bit; I could afford this. I could leave in May with the idea of deciding where to live before the winter. I could slow down to nature's pace, catch up with myself inside, and if I found a place I liked I would stop there, just like I did with Eugene.

I decided quickly that was my next step. Of course everyone was surprised by the sudden decision and tried to talk me out of it, especially Mom.

"But darling, you just got back. Give yourself some time. This floating around is not good; please settle down. And, you want to go alone ... not again ..."

But no one could talk me out of it and I became convinced this was the right thing to do.

Chapter 26

The Rhythm of the Seasons

The Amtrak made its way through the stark desert of Arizona, with me smashed between the inside wall of the car and a huge woman who didn't seem to know I was there. The train was full. I had no option and I prayed Los Angeles would appear soon. The ride was long, stinky, sweaty, and torturous on this beautiful May morning.

On the verge of screaming and going ballistic, I was overcome with relief when we finally pulled into the Los Angeles train station.

I spent a week with my brother, Doug, where we took in the sights of Venice Beach, museums, restaurants, and movies. We talked about Howard

I knew our parents hadn't been told of his lifestyle yet.

"I go visit him occasionally, but now that he lives in the Castro, his roommate doesn't like him having visitors that aren't gay, so I don't stay long. Howard has really changed."

"I'm supposed to stay with him when I visit; he said his roommate would be out of town. I'm okay with people being gay, but I worry about his risky lifestyle."

Doug said I seemed to be doing better, and I filled him in, a little. It was too complicated. "Well, I'm always here for you, sis, no matter what. I mean it."

"Thanks, bro. I love you. It means a lot to have you in my life." I was ready to leave crowded, smoggy Los Angeles, but cherished reestablishing our bond.

My next stop included a few days at Pat's mother's beach house at

Santa Cruz, where I watched surfers and seals, and loved feeling the sand between my toes. A group of my old high school clique was here, attending UCSC. The group included Melinda and my ex-boyfriend Bob, who were still a couple. Deep down, I felt jealous because they got together while I was in the hospital. There was nothing rational about those feelings, and I decided to get together with the group and see how it felt.

First contact with Melinda was awkward, but I was invited to dinner at the log house six of them shared in the nearby woods. Everyone was excited; most hadn't seen me since I left for Mexico. They still felt I was a dear friend and wanted to catch up. Again, at dinner, Melinda seemed distant; Bob made the effort to be friendly; the others were curious as to how I was doing. I gave a brief synopsis, but mostly tried to show I was good, even though it was a lie. It became crystal clear that I didn't fit in anymore and this wasn't an option for my new life. I left the next day, feeling despondent.

* * *

I met Howard at a San Francisco coffee house in the Castro district. He was energized and happy, and immediately took to calling me Eli. At first, I thought it odd that his roommate didn't like visitors, but after seeing the Castro District—deemed the gay neighborhood—and inside the apartment, I understood. The apartment was full of nude male art. Statues, posters and paintings of explicit sex and male genitals filled every room.

I was in shock. I tried to act cool with it all, but was deeply overwhelmed and uncomfortable. Howard apologized because he saw that I was reacting, but this was him now and nothing was going to make him change; everyone, if they wanted to see him, would have to adapt. After a while, I relaxed and tried to be more accepting. *I'm trying not to blank out, but this definitely triggers my sexual issues, even if I am straight.*

That night he took me out for Chinese food and then to a gay disco bar. I tried to enjoy it, but found myself disgusted watching the obscene moves and flamboyance in the multiple-partner gay nightclub scene. *It's one thing to live a quiet gay life with a partner, but this having multiple partners is dangerous.*

I was exhausted from the dancing and the spectacle, so went outside for fresh air. Howard had been drinking and dancing for five hours without stopping when he emerged soaked in sweat and high as a kite.

After spending the weekend walking around the Castro district and attending a festival with him, I asked Howard if he was afraid of getting AIDS. He said he tried to use protection, but didn't think he would get infected. Then he changed the subject.

We had a good talk about life and death, and I felt closer to Howard on that level than I ever had. He was a deep thinker and seeker, so he was able to discuss the issues I struggled with and provide relevant insights. But I left San Francisco with a deep worry in my heart for the lifestyle he had chosen.

* * *

I spent the next two weeks in the Eugene area, where I caught up with many old friends and even attended Linda's wedding. It seemed the thing—everyone was pairing up and many getting married. As much as I felt happy for them, I was also jealous. Everyone was finding love but me.

I told them about my very loose travel plans. Nearly everyone wished they had the flexibility to travel for so many months, but everyone had jobs and responsibilities. I left Eugene, knowing the rest of the journey was all mine. On to Seattle, then to Orcas Island, where I knew a place for camping.

I had bought a one-person tent and was ready to live as simply as possible. Also, a small propane burner was going to help me cook basic meals. I was learning that the more simple and natural my food and life was, the better my belly worked.

I gained confidence, being able to travel alone.

Orcas Island was a perfect place for me. The people were friendly, slow-paced and progressive. My campsite was beautifully located on a point overlooking the water and other islands, with community showers and bathrooms available. I was happy in my pup tent. There were many other travelers around, but I wasn't ready to meet them, I wanted time to hear my own thoughts.

Days passed quietly and the weather was perfect. The area was heavily populated by deer. They came out in the morning and evening to graze, while I sat quietly watching them and the wonderful sea life abundant on the shores. Orca whales swam in the distant water passages, blowing water spouts as they passed. Nights were lit with a universe of stars twinkling over my head as I laid quietly in the sleeping bag, looking out the tent.

I didn't have much to say, even to myself; I just listened and watched the world around me. The commotion within began to slow down and a shimmer of peace grew.

One particularly brilliant starry night, I lay watching the enormous showing of the universe. Suddenly, a sensation deep within burbled to the surface of my consciousness. As a falling star whipped across the sky, I remembered. I remembered the gypsy spirit that inhabited me so very long ago. It descended on me quickly and completely, with the impact of a sonic boom.

Everything shifted in that moment. Something changed within the post-accident chaotic blur. It felt like a kaleidoscope turning and clicking to display a masterpiece of design and well-being. Deep spiritual connection and understanding flashed through my heart and mind. It was fleeting, but thorough.

I gasped and held my breath. Looking around to see if anyone was around, I sat up, wondering what had just happened. *That was amazing! What a rush! My gypsy ... my gypsy spirit has returned. What total contentment. I lost her in Mexico and finally she is back! I knew something was there; I've just been too overwhelmed and lost.*

The remainder of the night was magical. I got up and made a cup of hot tea and sat looking into the deep midnight dark of the cosmos and slowly remembered the time on the mesa in New Mexico when I was first visited by my guardian spirit. I felt an authentic smile spring forth from a place rich in timeless knowing.

Finally, the first puzzle piece of self provided a place to start. To start over, this time aligned with a life I felt a part of and able to take the lead—a life I wanted to be a part of instead of run from. A self that chose instead of followed. A path forged not of history or of other's desires. A deep intuition filled my soul and accessed the wisdom and knowledge of all my painful experiences, presenting them as lessons to be learned from. The work now would be to see the lessons and learn their gifts, instead of their being rocks to be continually stumbled over.

The last thing I remembered before falling asleep was the gift of my gypsy friend in Taxco, the man who read my palm. *It happened just as he said. There would be a life changing event, but I would survive. I didn't believe him, but my gypsy spirit knew better and I didn't listen. From now on, my intuition is my guide, no matter what ... I hope this isn't another fleeting moment of courage and insight that doesn't last. I need this one to remain as permanent as it feels on this enchanted evening. I feel I am no longer alone.* As I closed my eyes to sleep, another star fell, but this one was in slow motion and flickered blue, as if to say sweet dreams and good night. I mumbled good night, friend, and drifted into sweet dreams for the first time in many years.

The next morning, I woke up happy. Imagine that! Everything from the night before had happened and wasn't just a passing dream. I felt different. Something deep within had come into alignment. *Maybe I still don't know where I'm going, but at least I have a place to start.*

During the next few days, I met other campers and joined them occasionally around their nightly campfire. One man, Glen, was very spiritual. I opened up about my past, and I hung out with Glen more than anyone. He was very non-threatening and was good company for spiritual discussions.

Stopping on Orcas Island had been the happiest time of my second life. To live at my own pace in such a remote, fantastic environment, rich in beauty and life without others' constant interruptions had been the gift I needed. All my spinning parts finally stopped and I could see. Like a snow globe, shake it and there is a blizzard, but if you let it alone, it all settles. Well, my snow finally settled and I could see clearly … at least for the time being. It seemed I was always on the lookout for the next cataclysmic change.

* * *

It was now the final week of August, and I had one more month before I had promised Felice and Lon to be back in Eugene for their wedding. I planned two weeks for my train adventure to Vancouver and Banff, and another two getting back. Money was lasting longer than I expected since I was living so frugally, but I would have to get a job soon after finding a place to live.

It was hard leaving the island and returning to the 'real world.' Everything sped up and came at me much faster. Even though Vancouver was beautiful, I was happy to get out of the congested city and head toward the majestic Canadian Rockies. I ignored the partying contingent aboard the train, settling in to enjoy the magnificent views. This was the same Rocky Mountain chain that extended all the way southward to my home in Los Alamos but, here, the mountains, trees, rocks, and plants all seemed five times bigger and wilder.

A naturalist talked about the sights; he kept repeating how many bears were out there and to be careful when hiking. I filed that for future reference because I did hope to do some wilderness hiking. This train trip was even better than I had hoped.

We finally reached Banff around four in the afternoon. After a quick call home, I opened my torn guidebook to youth hostels. There was one about five miles out of town.

After hiking for about an hour, dusk was descending and I realized I had just been walking in a big circle. I had to get to this youth hostel so I tried again, but it was getting dark and starting to drizzle.

I found where I'd taken the wrong path and went straight this time. By now it was dark, and I couldn't think about anything but bears. My flashlight led the way, but not one person was on the trail to give me courage, and the once-comforting pine forest felt like tall, enclosing predators. By now, I was too far in to stop and the rain had increased. I was scared.

I needed to get under shelter, so I hiked up the hill a few hundred yards and set up my tent between trees on the inclined hillside. It was miserable in my soaked tent, and the whole time I waited for a bear to show up. I had just dozed off when I heard voices. *There's nothing else up this path so they must be heading to the youth hostel.* I didn't want them to see me, just in case they were trouble, so I waited until they passed, then followed at a distance. It must have been midnight when I approached lights in the distance. The youth hostel cabins appeared and I wandered bleary-eyed into camp. Several people saw me.

"Are you okay? You look like something was chasing you. You didn't get chased by a bear did you? Are you alone? Come this way, we'll get you set up." A young man ran up to me and helped me take off my pack.

Still paralyzed by fear, I gave them the story and was immediately led to a cabin and put to bed. It was the second-scariest thing I'd ever been through.

I spent the rest of my time there hanging out with other travelers, visiting Lake Louise, and taking a few side trips. I realized I might never have another opportunity like this, once I settled back into a job. I felt as if I'd gotten to really know myself out here in nature. I didn't want the trek to end, but winter was on its way. Eugene felt like the place to go—I could work at the Saturday Market, continue my counseling, and pursue my spiritual quest very easily there.

Once I made the decision to move back to Eugene, contentment filled my heart and I was able to peacefully take in another week in the mountains. It was easier to be around the other travelers and I started to feel I didn't need as much time alone.

The time to leave arrived, and I boarded the train back to Vancouver. It was very sad and difficult to know my destination had been reached and had to return to life in so-called 'reality.' Reality was the incredible untamed nature I had witnessed. This trip proved there were so many other options on how to live, and I wasn't about ready to follow the script which society said had to be followed.

The key is to keep it simple and not let the material world own me. Nature has been here longer than all of us, and that is going to be the most precious way to evaluate and assess my desired goals. If it fits into that framework, I will follow it, if not, I won't. Nature will be my priority for self-care, because this trip has proven to me that's what works and brings me peace.

I was learning to trust my intuition and listen to my gypsy spirit.

These thoughts surged through my mind as the scenery passed, during the return train journey. Going the opposite direction, it all looked different and felt like a new experience. Also, my serenity provided a new perspective on everything.

I spent two more weeks, ferry hopping through the Gulf and San Juan Islands. Orcas Island campground was just as I'd left it, but the nights were getting colder, which encouraged a quick return to Eugene before the rains set in.

I feel so blessed to have done this journey. My spirit has slowed to the pace of the seasons and recalibrated my being. I feel more encouraged to join life now, on my terms.

Chapter 27

Return to the Emerald City

Once Felice and Lon's wedding hubbub settled, I started looking for an apartment. I found an inexpensive studio and moved in immediately. It was perfect, with its own little patio covered in morning glory vines, and located off a private alleyway.

I started job searching and found temporary work helping a couple at the Saturday Market. Dorothy and Omar sold chicken wraps and needed help preparing and serving. Dorothy was a big-boned woman with a jolly outlook on life, and her husband Omar was a large Vietnam vet who looked scary but was a teddy bear at heart.

Everyone told me to watch out for Omar because he wasn't very friendly, but I got along with him perfectly. We both recognized in one another the pain carried deep down within. Omar wanted to protect me and took me under his wing.

Happily, they included me in all aspects of the business. I shopped and prepped two days during the week and then helped at the booth on Saturdays. Dorothy and I became fast buddies. Dorothy also worked at a binding company and got me on for another couple days a week. The work was tedious, but it paid the bills. So, between the two jobs, I was set for the time being.

One day I was wandering through the Saturday Market and slowly recognized a familiar face walking toward me, his mouth open in surprise.

"*César?*"

"Nancy?"

He came forward to embrace me. Both of us were absolutely in shock as we pulled apart and looked in disbelief at one another.

"What are you doing *here*?" He had put on weight but still dressed in denim and had that killer smile and sweet energy.

"Nancy? Oh my goodness, I can't believe this. I live here with my wife ..." César spoke nervously.

My heart panged at the news, and we spoke only briefly because he had a booth to attend, selling Guatemalan weavings. "I would like to see you, but my wife can't know; she is very jealous."

We met about a week later for a brief visit. I told him all about my accident and he spoke of how he came to be married to an American. Emotions ran high, but the writing was on the wall. He was married and wouldn't risk his status. I had no interest in being 'the other woman' anyway. We parted as friends. I would see him occasionally at a distance with his wife, but I stayed away. The coincidence of our meeting replayed in my mind over and over, leaving me feeling lonelier than ever.

All my prior friends had either left town or were in new lives, so I was happy to have met Dorothy and their circle of friends.

For the first time since Mexico I felt excited about life. I was still getting accustomed to my health issues, but at least there were no new ones. *Maybe the worst is over—I hope.*

Dorothy had been born in Eugene and had friends everywhere. The couple stayed home most of the time when they weren't working, and I would go hang out if I wanted company. Local blues musicians often came over to jam. It was quite the mix of people. Their place was the local haunt where I was introduced to the local black population. There weren't many, but they all knew Dorothy and Omar and were always coming and going. Omar had a contingent of Vietnam vets who gathered at their home regularly to smoke joints and shoot the bull. I was very shy and mostly just smiled and nodded when everyone was around. Omar always made sure I was 'okie dokie' as he would say. They all welcomed me without hesitation.

Sometimes, we would go dancing and listen to a local group, The Robert Cray Band, at the Eugene Hotel. The music was amazing, and I became a dance addict to their fantastic tunes. I was still shy around guys, so I usually danced with the other women, which was perfectly acceptable in free-spirited Eugene.

I started going to a local jazz bar offering good music. I was used to being alone so it wasn't an issue to sit and enjoy the music. A few guys were there doing the same routine, but it seemed evident everyone was happy being solo.

The binding job was very monotonous and didn't pay much, so I started looking for waitress work and found a position quickly. The restaurant was upscale, trendy, and owned by a gay man. I liked the place and thought I would meet interesting people, along with making good money.

Fall was a busy time for the Saturday Market, so I stayed busy helping at the booth. An annual street fair was held at the University of Oregon, and I looked forward to being back on campus, helping Dorothy and Omar on this very busy day.

I was sautéing chicken when I noticed Dorothy talking to a black man I had seen around town at the jazz bar. I felt an attraction—the first time in years. I stood at a distance regarding him when Dorothy called me over. "Eli, this is my good friend, Smokey. I've known him and his ex forever. This guy plays a mean harmonica; one day you'll have to hear him."

"Hey, nice to meet you." His big smile flustered me, and I mumbled a hello back. Smokey seemed preoccupied, exchanged a few words, and then took off.

"What do ya think? He's a sweet guy and a longtime friend." It almost seemed like Dorothy was trying to set me up.

"He's so handsome … yeah, he does seem nice. You say he plays the harmonica?"

"Not just *the* harmonica, but a *smoking* blues harmonica. That's where he got his name, Smokey! I'll take you to hear him; he jams with Robert Cray sometimes and other blues bands. He broke up with his wife a few years ago and has just been lost since then. I wish he'd get a break; he deserves it." Just then Omar walked up and we got so busy I didn't look up one more time the whole day.

That night as I dropped from exhaustion, I couldn't figure out why this man, Smokey, left such an impression on my heart. When I'd seen him around, I'd wanted to meet him. It was an undeniable attraction toward him, physically and also emotionally. *I feel his deep spirit, like he's seen a lot.*

I became obsessed to see him again, but didn't want to get Dorothy involved. I needed my choices to be on my own terms and timing. Luckily, he came by the Saturday Market booth weekly for a free wrap from Dorothy, but he never spent much time once he got it. Smokey always smiled and said hi, but seemed preoccupied and flighty.

Over the next few weeks, I saw him at the jazz club on occasion and he was always alone, like me. I was too shy to go up to him, and he didn't seem to even notice me, but that didn't deter the attraction I felt. I didn't know what to think about that.

The holiday season had arrived and I decided to go to the Christmas fair at the university to look for gifts and listen to music. There he was, grooving to the band and flitting from one person to another with that big handsome smile of his. I summoned my courage and walked up to him.

"Hey Smokey, remember me?"

He didn't seem to recognize me immediately, then broke into a smile and said, "Dorothy's friend, right?"

"Yeah, mind if I hang out?" *I can't believe I'm being so forward.*

He looked confused at first, looking around to see if I was really talking to him. Once he realized I was, he finally responded, "Uh, sure. I got to go pretty soon though."

The music was loud, so we couldn't talk very well and just stood next to each other swaying to the tunes.

"Man, I wish I had my harmonicas here. I'd be jammin' with this group."

"Dorothy told me you were amazing and she'd take me to hear you play."

"Yeah, Dorothy, good woman. She helped me out a lot. I'm glad you've gotten to know her. Well, I got to go; nice to meet you again." He started to leave, then turned to me, "What are you up to now—want to take a walk with me? I've got some business to take care of." I was caught off guard, but happily accepted his offer.

We talked nonstop. Smokey kept looking at me. "You are so different than the women I usually hang out with. I think you are way too nice to be hanging around someone like me."

I thought that was an odd thing to say, but considered it before replying, "I've been through a lot more than it looks. But what do you mean ... 'someone like me'?"

"Well, uh ... let's say I've had my share of trouble. In fact, right now I am going to go score some cocaine—are you interested?"

"Well, I've never done it before, but I'll go with you to get it."

"You sure? You sure you want to be seen with me?"

"Why do you say that?"

"A lot of people are mad at me right now. You see, I pawned my harmonicas and a friend bought them back, but he's holding on to them until I can come up with the money to pay him back. He's a good friend, but is angry I let my shit get so bad, that I let my babies, my harmonicas, go. He loves my music but won't give them back unless I give him a hundred dollars."

I pondered his answer. "Can I lend you the money to get your harmonicas back?"

Smokey stopped dead in his tracks and looked me in the eyes. "For reals? Nobody has ever offered me anything like that. I would pay you back as soon as I find some work … I can't find a job either."

"How do you get by?"

"I have a friend who lets me stay at her house, and I do little odd jobs here and there to get food money."

He seemed honest and in need of a hand. Dorothy had said he'd been down on his luck. *So many have helped me, I want to pass it on.* "After we're done here, we can go to my apartment. I'll get the money, and we can go get your harmonicas. What do you think?"

Smokey couldn't believe what he was hearing, but he was so excited I was willing to do this for him. "I'll take you to the club tonight so you can hear me play. No one will believe I've gotten them back. I'll blow them away. You are a guardian angel!" He quickly kissed me on the cheek and grabbed my hand, leading me up a road where he 'had business' to attend to.

"We need to celebrate this. It's been six months since I've played and I'm hurting to get it on. I'll share my cocaine with you after we get the harps."

"What are harps?" I wasn't too sure about the cocaine, but I wanted to hear him play.

"Oh, that's what I call my harmonicas." He smiled that killer smile, and I was ecstatic to follow along.

Smokey wouldn't let go of my hand as we hurried back to my apartment after getting the cocaine. *I'm so happy he isn't ashamed to hold my hand even though we have just met. We fit together easily.*

We kept looking at one another, wondering about this surprising connection. Smokey talked nonstop about my 'guardian angel' status and with each minute became more and more interested in this woman at his side. I got the hundred dollars and we walked to his friend's house. He wanted to go in alone, and came out beaming, holding a shoebox filled with his harps.

He gave me a big hug, a kiss, and almost started crying. "No one has ever done anything like this for me. You are a good, good woman and I thank you from the bottom of my heart. I will pay you back after I do a few gigs, I promise. You are the first bit of luck I've had in a long time."

"I'm so glad to help you, Smokey. Dorothy has been talking about your playing, so I know this is your gift. But Smokey, don't let it happen again. Respect your gift and don't let anything take it away from you ever again … agreed?"

"This will never happen again. I've been given a second chance and I'm no dummy." Smokey was delighted; he started skipping and dancing around with me in the middle of the street. I was embarrassed, since I wasn't used to drawing attention, but no one was around, so I joined in the spontaneous, joyful celebration. For the first time, my heart felt alive.

We returned to the apartment where Smokey wanted to share a few lines of cocaine before heading out to jam. It was the first time I'd tried it and was hesitant; drugs seemed to untie me. I'd spent so much time struggling to not feel spacey and disconnected. Getting high is opposite to what I really needed, but I was curious and hoped 'this time' would be different.

It wasn't as intense as I thought it would be. Usually, cocaine speeds people up but with Smokey it had the opposite effect. I noticed he tended to be high strung, so I liked the calmer version of him. Smokey took my hand, his harps, and we walked to the bar.

Smokey was right, everyone knew him and immediately insisted he get up front to play. I felt like an intruder. The women sure let me know I was not welcomed, and the men looked at me like, who the hell is she?

I had never seen this dark, smoky dive. It was crowded to the walls, with a loud blues band playing on the stage. Smokey was a celebrity and everyone came up to him, congratulating him on his getting his harps back. Evidently, his troubles were common knowledge, but they just wanted to hear him play again.

"Eli?"

I turned to see Dorothy and Omar. "Hey! I'm so glad to see you!"

"I was so surprised to see you walk in with Smokey! Come sit with us, okay?" The noise was so loud that I just nodded happily. Smokey was also happy I could sit with his friends; he felt my angst and was feeling very protective of me.

"Friends, we would like to invite our good friend and amazing musician, Smokey, to come sit in with us for a few songs. Smokey?" The lead singer looked out over the crowd, shading his eyes from the lights.

"Well, babe, this one's for you!" Smokey bent over to kiss me in front of everyone and joined the band on the stage. Dorothy and Omar smiled at each other, then over to me. I nodded back. I was glad it was dark, because I knew I was red as a beet.

"Hi, everyone. It's been awhile since I've been able to play for you all, but this is all possible because of my guardian angel, Eli. Thanks again, and tonight I dedicate all my songs to you!"

Everyone turned to see who he was talking to, and I died of embarrassment to be the center of attention. That was *so* not me. Then, the most amazing music flowed out of Smokey and overtook the crowd.

I broke into a big smile as I watched him play. Smokey became a force, a force of sound and movement, that whirled melodically in a deep wild soulful sound. He moved his hands from his center to where the breath formed, then high above his head, as if he were tickling the notes emerging from his mouth; then he'd dance and strut as if possessed by an unseen force. He filled the bar with music that had everyone dancing and partying with a profound release of joy, with every note emerging from the depths of Smokey.

Now I understood what everyone was talking about. Smokey looked my way most of the time and sang right to me. I was touched to the bone, and there was no going back. The night continued that way until closing, when we finally peeled ourselves away from the crowd and walked, or actually floated, to my apartment.

"Smokey, I can't believe your music. You should never, ever lose those harps again. They carry your soul."

He stopped suddenly, looking into my eyes. "You are right; I never thought about it like that before. Thank you so much, I owe so much to you."

"Just do the right thing, Smokey. Don't lose them again. And play ... play your music, it's your gift."

He nodded quietly, took my hand. We felt bonded, as if we had always been together, not for just one day. "Well, uh ... I should get back to my place. Can I see you again?"

"Yeah, I have two jobs tomorrow. I work for Dorothy until three, and then I'm waitressing until ten. Do you want to meet me after work?"

"I'll be waiting for you across the street. Thanks again, Eli. You changed my life today."

"Well, I don't know about that, but it has been quite the day. See you tomorrow …" He bent over and kissed me, then took off down the street.

* * *

The next day was a blur of happiness mixed with fear and doubt. Was it love at first sight? Could I trust him? It felt as if he was being genuine and honest about his problems. Dorothy wanted all the details and assured me she hadn't seen Smokey act the way he did toward anyone, ever.

"Eli, he really is taken with you. He's a good guy, just makes bad decisions, so watch out for that. Whatever it is, I haven't seen him this happy in years."

"Dorothy, I've never felt this way either. I think we both feel this energy exchange, like our souls are meshing. It's scary, but at the same time, healing."

"Eli you deserve good things. Try it, if it doesn't work out, at least you will have tried, right?"

I thought about it for a minute and was reminded of the doctor all those years ago. It was my choice whether to try or not. "You're right, I'm ready to try. If it doesn't work out, at least I'm stronger now and can move on. Thanks for the talk, Dorothy; see you tomorrow."

Just as Smokey promised, he was waiting outside the restaurant at the end of my shift. I was very tired and dirty, and just wanted to go home and shower. I had a bike, but he didn't, so we doubled up on my bike and maneuvered to the apartment. It was great to be near him again, and the two of us giggled like a couple of kids the whole way home.

"Hey, do you have a radio? I usually listen to the blues show that comes on in a half hour. We could just hang out and listen to the show if you want." Smokey saw I was tired.

"That would be perfect, Smokey. I can make us a snack…"

I didn't have much furniture yet, so we lounged on a pillow in front of the radio while Smokey told me all about the blues artists and songs playing. He knew them all and their history too. I was impressed with his musical knowledge and eager to learn more about what made this man who he was—it was the blues.

We saw each other daily, and Smokey always left at the end of the evening. We would sit, holding each other but he never tried more. I was hesitant to take the next step. It had been so long since I last had sex, and I was afraid.

We had been getting to know each other's life stories. Smokey was very sensitive about my accident and traumas, which helped me feel more comfortable as I told him about the craziness of my life. His compassion was tangible. It was incredibly healing to me, to be unconditionally cared for.

Smokey had his own share of trauma, which came in the form of physical and sexual abuse growing up. No wonder he related to the blues. Both of us were full of pain and loss. *This is a man I can be myself with and not have to hide in embarrassment or pretend to be someone I'm not.*

One night after listening to the blues show, I wanted to stay up and listen to the upcoming soul program. The two of us were more passionate on this eve, and I decided to ask Smokey to stay the night.

"Are you sure, Eli? I don't want to push you into anything you aren't ready for." Smokey was surprised at my offer.

"I'm sure, Smokey."

"Well, in that case, hell yeah!" He took my hand and led me to the mattress on the floor, as soul tunes filled the room.

Stevie Wonder came on the radio and sang "My Cherie Amour" as we moved together in perfect harmony and satisfaction. Making love to Smokey was so beautiful and intense, not scary at all. I had never felt anything so profound and special before. A stream of tears flooded from my eyes. When I looked to Smokey, his eyes were also filled with tears.

"I have never cried from making love before, Eli. You touch me so deep in my soul, that was the most healing lovemaking I've ever had."

"Me too, Smokey. I feel the same way. It's as if there is a highway of energy back and forth between us … do you feel it?"

"You are very special to me, woman."

"And you are most special to me too. I am so glad you feel the same way." The two of us wiped each other's tears away.

Chapter 28

Love Blooms and Moves in 1984

It was mid-February, with the skies hanging low and drizzling nonstop. I worked, and Smokey started playing again. He paid me back the hundred dollars, which proved to me he was sincere. The two of us became an inseparable couple. Smokey was proud to have me on his arm and I was proud to be there. He was such a blessing for my heart. He made me laugh all the time and was a force of joy. He was like a gregarious puppy who approached life with a spontaneous smile and a pounce.

"Let's go get a sandwich. Wait here, I'll be right back." Smokey darted into a deli and came out with a long sub. He carried a menu and handed it to me. "This is a great place to eat; do you see anything on here you want? I know the guy in there, and he gave me this for free. He loves my music, and he said he'll give you one too."

After finding something on the menu, I handed it back and pointed at the one I wanted.

"What does it say?" Smokey asked.

"Right here, this one ..." I was confused as to why he was asking.

"Uh, Eli ... I can't read ..." Smokey hung his head with embarrassment.

I was dumbfounded; I'd never caught on. "How is this possible, Smokey? I've been with you almost two months now, and you get along fine. Are you joking with me?"

"For reals, Eli. I can't read. I use my eyes and memory to note markings, ask questions and use all my senses. It's actually better than reading, because you would be shocked at what everyone misses that I pick up on. I have common sense and I'd take that over reading any day. Look at all these smart people who can read but screw up the world with their stupidity …"

"But reading opens so many doors—like jobs, school, travel … everything." I was having a hard time conceptualizing this because he had hidden it so well. "*Why* don't you read?"

Smokey got very quiet and pensive. "I tried, I really did. When I was little, if I made a mistake my mom would whip me with the extension cord. She beat the 'want' out of me … and when I've tried again, I can't get past the memories. I just freeze up. It's like it bounces off me." His voice changed and became very somber.

"Maybe I can teach you. Can we try?"

"No, I don't want to put you through that. Now I suppose you don't want to be with me anymore …" He sounded as if he was going to cry.

I reached over and held him. "I love you Smokey, just the way you are. Maybe sometime down the road we can try … we'll see. Don't worry." I took his hand and led him under a tree to share the sandwich. It took the remainder of the day for him to perk up again.

Once I found out this information, so many other things started making sense. *So that's why finding a job is so hard, why he can't drive, why I'm the one to always read street signs and books* … I only felt empathy for him and a new appreciation for his ability to survive. This also made sense about the importance of his music. It's his breadwinner and without his harps, he's lost.

Smokey made good money gigging at least four nights a week. Robert Cray was an old friend he used to play with, but when he lost his harps and got into cocaine, Smokey owed him money. Luckily, playing helped lower the debt and he was able to continue playing with the local groups. But, Smokey had burned too many bridges and his friends weren't as forgiving as they once were.

I had never been in this position before. I felt his authentic love, but didn't like the responses of his friends. Dorothy and Omar were the only ones supportive of our relationship.

Also, I was from a different sort of people. Most of his crowd were smokers and drinkers; I didn't do either. Few had more than a high school diploma, and not many had ever left Eugene; the small town mindset for gossip and their small world was all they knew. I did the best I could to keep my dignity and stay focused on Smokey.

I rarely saw my old group of friends anymore either. When I introduced Smokey, they got quiet and exchanged glances like ... *really?* They were friendly, but also saw the extreme differences between the two of us and most couldn't see beyond that.

Since there were not many people of color in Eugene, being with a black man drew disapproving stares. I was surprised to see discrimination alive and well in liberal Eugene. Smokey definitely got treated differently than I, which incensed my moral code. In New Mexico, Hispanics, Anglos, and Native Americans all got along well, although my Jewish upbringing had not exactly been a great fit in Los Alamos. Feeling like an outsider was nothing new to me.

"Babe, what would you think of moving?" One night as we lay in each other's arms, Smokey brought up the subject.

"Well, I just got back here and planned to settle in for a while. Why do you want to move?"

"I'm tired of how everyone treats us in this town. I want to see more of life. Get a fresh start. I think my music could make it big if I was somewhere new. A lot of the musicians talk about Austin. It's rockin' with music and opportunity. I've always wanted to try out my skill there."

"I don't know anything about Austin. I really like the northwest."

"I think it would be good for us. Think about it, okay?" I agreed to ponder the thought.

We started investigating Austin. We asked questions, got books and learned about the thriving music scene. We would have to put away some money, because the cost of living was much higher there. I balked because what I knew of Texas was the endless plains of west Texas and a certain bubba mentality.

Smokey continued to encourage the move, but I felt conflicted over making a new start—again. On the other hand, friends here were not supportive of us, and it would be nice to see the sun more often. Smokey planned to go anyway because he was sure his music would succeed, while I worried it would be a cutthroat atmosphere. *It really is a dead end here for him ... and I can make it anywhere. Austin would be the place to find out if his music can give him a new direction...*

Then there was Mom and Dad. I imagined the conversation. *Hi guys, I'm moving again, to a place I know nothing about, and also, guess what, I'm going with a black harmonica player I met three months ago who doesn't have a dime and can't read. Great, I'm sure that will go over with a bang. But ... I love Smokey.*

"Babe, I'm going to move to Austin. I want you to go with me, *please*!!" Smokey had decided. "I'll make it work. Listen, I'll go first and find a job. Once I've gotten a job, a month's worth of rent and an apartment, I'll call you. Then you can join me. This way I will prove to you I can make it happen and you don't have to pull up roots until I have other roots set. What do you think?" Smokey looked at me with pleading eyes full of love.

"That can take months, Smokey ... What if you can't find a job?"

Smokey looked at me with hurt in his eyes. "Girl, I've taken care of myself for thirty years. I've survived hard times before and I can do it again. I'm going to play my harps and make a name for myself, I know I can do it."

I hadn't heard him talk like this before; I liked what I heard.

"Eli, you've changed my life and have given me a second chance. I don't want to mess up. You've helped me want to make myself a better person and use my gift."

I was impressed with his plan. It would give me the surety I needed to commit to the move. He would have to prove he could do it, without my having to take a fall if it failed. And, if it didn't work out, he could just return to Eugene. If it succeeded, his music abilities would grow.

I agreed to the plan.

I would pay for the bus fare to Austin and give him an extra couple hundred to start on. He would have to do the rest. Smokey would leave the first of April and hopefully, by late May, I would join him in Austin in our new apartment. It was heart-wrenching to say goodbye, but the smile on his face was huge. He carried a small bag of clothes and snacks, along with his box of harps, as he boarded the bus.

Now for the tough part—I called my parents. Initially, Mom sounded chipper; they had just returned from their new condo in San Diego. I had prepared them by sending a letter, and when that subject came up, the mood turned.

"Well, I know you won't listen to anything we say, so all I can say is please be careful. Your Dad and I are very unhappy about this."

I agreed to a short visit home on the way to Austin, but I was not looking forward to it.

They would be grilling me for information about Smokey. I was unsure of my decision too, but couldn't let them know. Moving to Austin wasn't really what I had in mind, but Smokey had landed a good job with the University of Texas, so I took that as a good omen for the change.

The job was as a full-time graveyard shift janitor, including benefits and a decent size check monthly. Working for the university came with all sorts of other side benefits, so I was elated he got in. Since he didn't have a car, it was difficult for him to get around and check out apartments, so we planned to look for one once I arrived, unless something came up before then.

He had been playing his music and was a hit on the 6th Street scene, the place where most musicians and crowds went. Until I arrived, he was staying for free with a co-worker from the job.

"Babe, you aren't going to believe this place. It's better than we could have imagined. There's a big river going through town, bike paths, and cold springs to swim in … you'll love that. People are crazy for my music too and are asking me to play everywhere I go. You are going to be proud of me, Eli. I did it! The only thing missing is you!"

"I hope all those Texas girls haven't taken your interest from me." I was feeling insecure about his popularity and good looks.

"Babe, don't you worry. I love you and only you. No one can touch what we got, for sure."

A friend had sold me a rusted old Datsun B210, but it was low mileage and cheap, and I could get all my stuff in it. Plus, we would have a car to get around in Austin. It would be my first time to drive since my accident. The road trip would be the test for how well I could get past that big fear.

Life. You never know what will happen. I hoped I was making the right decision. My intuition said yes, but doubts remained. My heart knew this love was real and he had already given me more happiness in these few months than I could ever remember. Smokey and I shared a kindred spirit forged from pain.

I believe this will be a healing chapter for both of us. I hope.

Chapter 29

The City of Music

The Datsun looked terrible. Originally, it was from Chicago where the streets were salted regularly, so most of the body was riddled with corrosion, and the previously white paint looked more like speckled rust. But, it ran great and the mechanic gave it a tune up for the long trek to Austin.

Not another object could fit in the small over-packed car; the only place open was the driver's seat. I planned to take four days to get to New Mexico. It was an intimidating undertaking, so I was going to take it slow and easy. The last time I drove was before my trip to Mexico, seven years ago.

Mostly, I was afraid of falling asleep at the wheel. For some reason, one of my lingering problems was dozing off in the middle of conversations, at a movie, reading, whatever ... exhaustion would overcome me and I would just rest my eyes. Then before I knew it someone was waking me up and I'd continue as if nothing had happened. *I can't trust myself when I blank out like that.* So, I planned for a few hours of driving followed by frequent rest stops.

Felice expressed the concerns of all my friends. "Are you sure about this move, Eli? It's awfully sudden and this guy, Smokey ... well, you hardly know him."

I knew my friends were suspicious of him. "I'll be fine. If it doesn't work out, I'll be back. He's good to me, and I really care for him." *On the road again … I am nervous about my decision. Please pull through for me, Smokey!* The road trip was fun. Taking it slowly and sticking to side roads took the pressure off. I made my way through Idaho, Utah, and southern Colorado, stopping at campgrounds along the way and sleeping in a small space I created for myself in the car. Good thing I'm short!

By the third day, I'd gained confidence in my driving, and the scenery kept my interest through the mountains. Arriving in Los Alamos brought back insecurities about my decision, and I hoped Mom and Dad wouldn't sense it.

It's been a month and a half since I saw Smokey … just long enough for doubts to set in. I hope he's been true to me. I have to go and find out, so I'll stay with my plan, no matter what the folks say.

Old issues cropped up briefly—Mom worrying about my vegetarian diet. Her brisket smelled heavenly, but I had to insist—I would not be able to digest it. Back home I was Nan again; they would not call me Eli, no matter how often I insisted. I finally decided to let it go. Dad scowled through the meal, finally voicing his opinion in the den after dinner.

"You just don't know how it can be, Nan. People will be mean and possibly hurt you if they see you with a black man. I, myself, am not prejudiced, but others are, especially in Texas, and they are proud of it!" Dad's voice was firm and emphatic. "Yes, I would prefer you were with a Jewish man because I believe a relationship has a better chance if there is a mutual foundation of understanding and upbringing. But, I know raising you here in New Mexico never gave you much of an option. I probably should have never come out here; it's kept my children so far from their heritage." He looked sullen and frustrated.

"Dad, I loved being raised here. It made us all independent and pioneers, which I am very proud of." I hated seeing Dad feel so regretful of his past decisions. "Listen, I know there is prejudice out there. There is a university in Austin, and usually there are more open-minded people from other places. If there is trouble, I will come back immediately."

Mom and Dad had their say and saw I wasn't going to budge, but at least they got it out. Dad even gave me a hug when he went to bed. Mom and I stayed up talking. Our relationship was better than ever, and I knew Mom was my best friend. She and Dad loved their condo in San Diego and she invited me to visit sometime.

I spent a few more days in Los Alamos, and then visited Rick's family in Albuquerque. Corey had grown and we played for hours. It was great to see everyone, but I was anxious to get to Austin, where my man awaited me.

* * *

I talked with Smokey on the phone. He expressed worry that my parents might have talked me out of coming, but I assured him I was on my way. "Once you get to town," he said, "ask someone where the university is and wait for me by a place called Duffy's. You can go in there and call me, and then I'll sneak out and get you."

"I can't believe this is really happening … I love you and I'll see you in a few …"

After a smooth two-day drive to Austin, I arrived exhausted and nervous in the dark of night. I followed his directions and waited in the car. *Will we still have the same connection? Has he been staying on track? Is Austin as good as Smokey says, or was it just a way to get me here?*

Those fears vanished when he came running up to me. We hugged and kissed; the connection was perhaps even stronger. He was thinner, but he assured me he had avoided drugs. He was walking a lot and eating little, he said. I told him we would soon get some food in him.

As we entered the student union of the University of Texas, I was overwhelmed at the size and affluence of the school. This town was opulent compared to Eugene. It was obvious there was oil money here and everything was Texas size, from the walls to the doorways to the couches. I felt like a country bumpkin entering a palace and was intimidated. I also wasn't prepared for how green and lush Austin was; I'd thought all of Texas would be flat. Green meant hot and humid—no wonder everyone went to Barton Springs to swim.

Smokey had gotten used to his surroundings. He led me to the third floor where I slept on a couch. His boss had said it was okay for a night or two. We had plans to go out and find an apartment in the morning. Meanwhile, he finished waxing and buffing the enormous halls that were his responsibility to maintain. For the entire shift, he had a grin from ear to ear with thoughts about his baby finally arriving to start our new life. Smokey was proud to show that he worked at such a nice place. This wouldn't have ever happened if we had stayed in Eugene, and he was going to make sure I saw that.

After a frustrating search, finally, we found an affordable one-bedroom in an apartment complex in an older neighborhood. We really liked the homey area, so we overlooked the 'not so perfect' apartment and were able to move in the next day.

That first night in the apartment was spent on a sleeping bag huddled together, until Smokey went to work at ten at night.

"I don't like this graveyard shift," I said. "I have to be home alone at night and when I work, you'll be sleeping. We'll never see each other. Can't you get a day shift?"

"It's going to take time, babe. I've been asking, but everyone wants day shifts, so I'm going to have to pay my dues."

"Well, maybe I'll look for graveyard work too. Then at least we are on the same schedule. I've never worked graveyard; I usually like sleeping at night. But, I'll try it out."

Down the street from the apartment was a twenty-four-hour deli named Katz's. It was on the way home from the 6th Street music scene, so it was popular with after-hour partiers who were hungry and drunk. I got a job immediately, since I wanted to work graveyards.

The tips were fantastic and I brought in seventy to a hundred dollars on weekend shifts. But, I worked my hide off. The crowds were obnoxious and sexist. Drunken guys would stand up in the middle of a packed diner, point at me and yell out, "I'll take that ass anytime!" I was humiliated, but we needed the money and I wanted to share the same work routine as Smokey.

The first night Smokey got off, he took me to his favorite bar for jamming. He had met a trio who loved to have him sit in with them and 'smoke' the crowds with his harmonica playing. It had been so long since I heard him play, and I was so proud when the crowd was on their feet, dancing and yelling for more after one of his rambunctious displays of raw harmonica talent.

He's right, they love his music here. Everywhere we go, people light up from his playing. It's opened so many doors for us. And his playing, oh my goodness, the guy is talented. Other musicians are lining up to invite him to play with them. I do love that man.

We were happy to be reunited. Smokey sincerely missed me and felt complete once I arrived. He held my hand tight wherever we went and made sure everyone knew I was his girlfriend. Sometimes women would do everything to get his attention, but he only had eyes for me. Smokey was proud of me which gave me confidence to overcome the tendency to feel threatened and jealous of these beautiful women throwing themselves at him. Never before in my life had a man chosen me over the temptations of other women.

We had established a routine and saved money. I cooked meals and worked on putting some weight back on Smokey, who greatly appreciated my effort. He played his music two or three times a week, depending on his schedule. He already had a reputation around the music scene and received offers to play all the time. We often went to Barton Springs to cool off in the hot summer heat and watch the people. Life was good. *I know Smokey loves me ... and it's mutual... it is so nice having someone there for me who really understands.*

One day, I was going to garage sales looking for household items while Smokey slept. I came upon a beautiful old-fashioned doctor's bag made out of alligator skin tinted brown. The owner had passed and his daughter was selling it for next to nothing. I thought it would be perfect to carry Smokey's harps, so I bought it as a surprise for his birthday, along with more harps he needed.

Smokey's eyes grew wide when he saw what he'd received. "This is perfect, I've been wanting something special to carry my harps in. Perfect, absolutely perfect ... Eli you know what I like!"

From that point on, I referred to him as Doctor Smokey; I even made a matching hat and shirt that said that. He would walk with authority into gigs carrying the doctor bag, which gave him an aura of mystery and someone not to be taken lightly. Pretty soon, everyone was calling him Doc.

Many famous blues and country musicians played the Austin music scene. Willie Nelson, Bonnie Raitt, and Stevie Ray Vaughn lived locally and helped create the music reputation. BB King, Albert Collins, Buddy Guy, and many other famous musicians played in the local bars and gave concerts. Often, the musicians would eat at Katz's after their gigs, and I would wait on them and receive great tips. Also, Smokey and I were attending most concerts for free, because Smokey always knew event staff who loved his music and would get us in.

Popularity was hard for me because of my private nature. I would accompany him, but once he was playing, I would sit on the fringe of the crowd and try to be inconspicuous. The bar scene was not my thing. The drunks, cigarette smoke, and bar drama turned me off, but I wanted to hear Smokey play and support his music. He wanted me there because he was also overwhelmed by all the attention, but he handled it better than I. On one level, Smokey had a very shy and private side, but he could be gregarious too. After playing, we usually left quickly and headed home, unlike most of the other musicians who wanted the 'after party' for a few more hours after the bars closed.

The graveyard shift was also not my thing. I already struggled with maintaining balance and my chemistry, so the odd sleep schedule jumbled me more. I started having more trouble with digestion and would fall asleep in some of the loudest crowds at the bars. Everything became a blur.

One night at Katz's, I did not feel like dealing with the offensive drunk customers and was more curt than usual with them. The owner, an equally offensive New Yorker, was all about money and didn't care too much about his staff other than his few pet flunkies. The place was not known for being squeaky clean and often had problems with the water and sewer pipes backing up. Well, this night in particular, in the middle of the after-bar rush, the sewer backed up and covered the kitchen floor. Instead of closing, the owner threw down a few wood pallets and told the staff to keep working.

"That's it, I quit!" I walked out. *I can't be part of this crazy unsanitary rude place anymore. I can't believe the owner would still serve food with sewage over the kitchen floor and look at me like I'm crazy to not want to serve it or go into the kitchen.* I would miss the great tips.

"It's okay, babe. I'm working, I'll take care of you. Besides, I don't think graveyards are good for you. Take a break." Smokey was proud to be able to take care of me; I had done so much for him.

"Well, I'll have to find something, your check won't be enough, but it will keep us covered until then." I felt like a failure for not being able to keep up with the graveyard shift because I wanted to stay in the same rhythm with Smokey.

"I'll talk to my boss. Maybe something will open up for the day shift. It's just a matter of time. I love you girl, don't worry, it will all work out."

It did work out, eventually. I found a new job at a restaurant downtown and worked breakfast and lunch. When I got off at two p.m., Smokey was just waking up and we would have the remainder of the day and evening until he went to work at ten p.m. We missed sleeping together but Smokey's boss said something was going to open soon for a day shift, so we knew it was temporary.

If Smokey could read, all sorts of opportunities were available to him through the university, so his boss and I worked together to get him into reading classes offered to employees. Smokey resisted, but eventually gave in and started attending classes. His prior negative experience was difficult to overcome and for every step forward, he'd take two back, but in due time started to make progress. I was very proud of him and encouraged him as much as possible. His self-esteem was totally wrapped up in this effort; some days he'd be very up and other days very down after his classes, but at least he was trying.

I loved my new job. The owner was from Colorado, thus the name of the restaurant, The Colorado Street Café. Most of the employees were artists, students, and down-to-earth people who all worked compatibly together. Customers were downtown professionals mixed with musicians. New friendships were made, which fashioned a new direction for our lives in Austin.

"I got it, Eli, I got it! I start my new day shift on Monday! I'll be working for the grounds crew over near Barton Springs!" After nine months of graveyard, the two of us were euphoric to get back into a 'normal' schedule together and settle into a comfortable routine of work, music, swimming, and hanging out with our new friends.

Smokey was always surprising me. I didn't know what to say when he walked in with an adorable cream-colored puppy one day after work. "This guy gave him to me for free at the park, and I couldn't resist. I got it for you, Eli!"

"He's cute, but babe, this apartment doesn't allow pets."

"We can hide him …"

"That will only work for a little while, but as soon as he grows, it won't."

"I didn't think about that. He's just so cute."

One thing I've learned about Smokey is that he's not real good about thinking ahead or thinking things through. I do love the spontaneity, but …

"If we want to keep him, we'll have to find a new place to live." The puppy was adorable and we both fell in love with him. We had already talked about moving, so this just made it happen sooner. A co-worker knew of a duplex with a yard in the same neighborhood, and we moved with our new pooch, Junior. We didn't want the puppy to be lonely, so we went to the pound and found Junior a girlfriend, Rosie. The four of us set up house.

* * *

A perfect storm hit us from a combination of directions. First, working in the brutal heat and humidity exhausted Smokey and made him not want to eat, thus making him cranky; he wasn't making good decisions. Second, I noticed a pattern in Smokey. As soon as he became successful, he would do something to sabotage himself to bring himself back to his previous comfort zone. His relationship, music, job, and reading were successes. Third, people in the music scene adored Smokey and often offered him free drugs, which to this point he had declined.

"I just did it this one time, Eli. I promise it won't happen again. I was so tired and these guys … Well, I didn't want to hurt their feelings …"

"You *what*? You didn't want to hurt *their* feelings? What about mine? I'm the one who feeds you, loves you, cares about you. I moved to Austin for you … on and on … and you wanted to protect *them*?" I was so angry I was seeing red. I thought we had beaten that cocaine problem.

Smokey begged and pleaded for forgiveness and finally convinced me it was a one-time mistake that wouldn't happen again.

But it did. Smokey fell off track and started sneaking around to get cocaine on his own. We began arguing more, and with that a quiet fear and depression reemerged in me.

"Smokey, I can't handle the drugs. You are going to lose me if you continue. I mean it. I love you and will do anything to help you stop." I prayed I could get through to him.

We had been together for almost two years now and established a wonderful life together in Austin. I wasn't about ready to give up after all I had done to create this life with him.

I finally got through to him, making sure he ate better, was well rested, and even chaperoned him at his gigs to keep an eye on those who were offering him the drugs. It took time to get back on track, but we finally did return to our previous stability.

"Eli, thanks for being here for me. No one has ever cared about me like you do. I was getting ready to go down again. Sometimes I think it's easier for me to fail than to succeed. Responsibility comes with success and I've always taken the easy way out."

"But living on the streets, down and out, is not easier, Smokey …"

"Well, it is if that is what you've always known. You are good with money, planning, budgeting. Me … well, I've never had money, I'm not educated and I run away instead of solving problems. You probably don't want to be with me anymore either …"

"That's not true! I'm here, aren't I? I want to see you and your gifts thrive. I'll start teaching you some things about living on a budget. You should take more time with your reading; it will only help you."

"Eli will you marry me?"

"Smokey, if you can prove to me that drugs are not more important than me, yes, I will marry you."

"Okay, it's a deal. No more drugs for me. I'll prove it to you!"

I was a nervous wreck. I'd never been around cocaine addiction or seen how it changes people, and I was embarrassed to tell anyone about the problem. I believed he wanted to quit, but drugs were so easy to get in the music scene. I hoped by learning to read he would start caring more about himself. He could get further with his music; everyone wanted him to sign papers but he needed to know what they said. When he was using, he became unpredictable and lost credibility and good music opportunities. Then he would get even more moody and we would fight more.

I'm starting to descend into my old depression. What to do? What to do? I love him and want this to work.

Chapter 30

Another Start

This place is perfect. The yard is bigger, it's more private, and less rent—let's take it!" Smokey walked around the yard, examining the house.

"It's right by the bike path and near a pool. The Magnolia Café is right here, we can have blueberry pancakes right out our back door!" I fell in love with the place and didn't need anyone convincing me to take it.

The move helped us start over to recreate the life we wanted.

Fall had come and the weather cooled, so Smokey was in better spirits and health. I took advantage of the bike path, walked the dogs by the river daily, and swam at the pool afterward. Smokey wanted me by his side when he played music and was diligent to stay away from temptation.

We had gotten caught up on finances, so when the little Datsun broke down, we sold it for five hundred dollars and put another five hundred in for a small pickup with a camper shell. The dogs rode comfortably in the back, and we started getting out of town to camp at Lake Travis.

The campouts were wonderful. Sitting around the campfire at night under the stars reminded me of my stay on Orcas Island and how important nature was to my well-being. The two of us slept in the back of the pickup, cooked meals over the fire pit, and swam in the refreshing lake with my co-workers who had become our new family.

One of the new family members was Lorraine. Each morning we would open the restaurant and gab over a cup of coffee. She was with a man from Argentina, so we shared the common relationship dynamic rooted in cultural differences. I usually didn't share personal history, especially the part about Smokey's drug problem.

One day at the end of the shift, Lorraine and I were eating lunch and somehow my accident came up in the conversation. No one knew about that piece of my recent past so Lorraine was surprised to hear a synopsis of the story.

"Oh my God, Eli. I can't believe what you went through. I'd never have guessed; you seem so normal. You know what is even crazier, I am reading a new book about Frida Kahlo—have you heard of her?"

"No."

"You have got to read this book. It's real popular right now, about this woman artist married to Diego Rivera, a famous Mexican muralist. The thing is, she was also in a bus wreck in Mexico, just like you!"

"Really?" To hear about someone with a similar situation perked my ears.

"I'll give the book to you when I'm done. This is really amazing; I think it will give you some ideas, because she used her art to help her through the traumas. The book is full of her paintings, and they are intense. It was meant to be that we talked today, Eli. This book may just change your life."

"That sounds so interesting. Art ... hmmm. I'd love to read it."

When Lorraine gave me the book *A Biography of Frida Kahlo* by Hayden Herrera, I couldn't put it down. I had so much in common with this woman. First, Frida was half Jewish from her father, a Hungarian Jew. Second, she was a rebel. Third, Frida was in a Mexican bus that wrecked. Fourth, Frida was 18 when it happened. Fifth, Frida lost her ability to have children from the injuries of the accident. Sixth, Frida was an artist in Mexico; I did art in Mexico. Seventh, Frida dressed like me, a gypsy with long skirts and jewelry.

Immediately, I felt I had found a kindred spirit and mentor. This woman used her art to portray the inexplicable feelings of pain, confusion, and loss.

I kept the book by my side until I bought my own copy. It was my new bible and I spent hours studying, rereading, and viewing the paintings in the book. On a deep level, something began to shift within my numbness.

Frida and Me

Smokey started playing regularly with the trio he met when he first came to Austin; he made good money on weekends with them. I liked the trio and knew they kept an eye on Smokey's cocaine temptation. I started feeling more confident he had it beaten.

"Babe, thanks for sticking by me through that last tumble. If it wasn't for you, I would have gone down. I got you a present." Smokey handed me a bag.

A pair of jade earrings lay in my hand. "They are beautiful, Smokey. You didn't have to do this …"

"I wanted to, babe. I walked by a street vendor and when I saw these, I knew I had to get them for you. You deserve much more, but I wanted something for my *cherie amour.*" He leaned over and drew me to him. "Please don't give up on me; we've got such a good thing going."

"I won't. I just want good things to happen for us. Our love is real, Smokey, but we have to take care of it and nurture it. Thank you so much for the gift."

I hope my love is enough to keep him on track. It's exhausting to ride the roller coaster of addiction and the behaviors it creates. I'm having a hard enough time managing my own emotions … frightening … very frightening.

* * *

The owner of The Colorado Street Café decided to sell the restaurant, so I applied for a job with the City of Austin Parks and Recreation

Department as an information attendant at their administrative office. I was elated to get it, but after nine months of an eight-to-five Monday through Friday job, with low wages and too much politics, I decided to look for something more flexible and less stressful.

I am just not built for a rigid professional life and schedules… I'm happier waitressing … and it's more lucrative. Crazy…

"I need help doing the books for the Magnolia Café. I can train you." Ann had been my friend since arriving in Austin. We met when Smokey was jamming with her boyfriend, another musician. We immediately became part of the same circle of friends. The office was conveniently located down the alley from our apartment. Ann let me have a flexible schedule, which worked with the waitressing shifts I picked up. I learned bookkeeping skills and became Ann's right hand woman.

Things were finally feeling stable again. Smokey and I were in good jobs now. I worried about the temptations around him in the music scene, but had to stay positive and do things that made me happy. That's when I noticed the old shed in our backyard, which reminded me of the batik room in Mexico. I could fix it up …

Fate was on my side. A batik class was offered as an eight-week course at a nearby school. When I found the box of batik supplies at a garage sale for two dollars, I knew it was meant to be. Smokey helped me get the shed fixed up and was excited to learn about batik. He was always supportive of anything creative.

At the first class, I realized I knew more than the teacher and could teach the class myself, but attended anyway. This was the first time I had done any art since Mexico, and it flooded me with memories and good feelings. *Remembering Mexico makes me feel spacey and disconnected and at the same time I'm drawn to it.*

The front living room became my art studio. The scent of heated wax filled the air, as simple white muslin cloth turned into colorful works of batik. Designs and images of Mexican and Mayan patterns were my favorite subject matter. Somehow it felt as if I was completing something lost long ago. I loved the quiet creative process, the flow that took me to a place of deep peace within.

"These are incredible, Eli! You could sell these! I am so proud of you and that you are my woman." He grabbed me and swung me around with enthusiasm.

"Thanks, babe. It feels great, like something lost has finally been found. All I want to do is art …"

"Go to it girl, you are good!"

Doing art again is stirring up something from long ago... I don't know what it is, but I am possessed by it. Part of it is exciting and part is threatening. I loved doing the coats of color and wax, then removing it to reveal a whole design. It was like gradually forming a mystery, then peeling it away slowly to find a hidden treasure. *Like layers of myself.*

I became infatuated with batiks and spent hours each day creating them. At first, I copied patterns from books but then challenged myself to find my own creative images and explored new designs from the recesses of my imagination. Once I tapped into my own creative eye, the batiks' subject matter took on a new life.

Anything of inspiration became batik. Smokey and I liked to listen and dance to Reggae and African music bands. Afterward, I would draw a scene from the concert and turn it into batik. One could almost hear the music playing when looking at the finished work. Each piece was better than the previous and they all fueled my creative desire. I was even impressing myself.

As images appeared, so did uncomfortable feelings. I wasn't sure what was going on, but something was getting stirred up. Frida Kahlo's work had given me the blessing to venture into new territory. One day, I created batik of two skeletons dancing joyously together, along the theme of Day of the Dead.

As I was drawn to this type of subject, depression surrounded the art making process. Instead of backing away from it, I was intrigued and delved further into it.

The feelings grew and began to control me. Smokey started to notice that I wasn't as patient; I was easily upset and would cry. I wondered if the feelings were related to him; I never fully trusted that he wouldn't go back to cocaine. But he swore he didn't want to lose me, that I was his reason for living.

Maybe it was my family. Howard had told the parents he was gay, Dad had disowned him ... it was a mess. *Maybe, I should go visit them ...*

Maybe I should get back into counseling ... Sometimes I feel life is too hard, and dying is easier ... that's where Smokey and I connect—I think we both have a death wish. His is more active and mine is more passive ...

* * *

I talked to Mom. The invitation to visit them in San Diego was still open, and she would send the money for my ticket, knowing our finances were tight. I cheered up, knowing I was going to visit. My intuition told me Smokey wouldn't like me going and proved to be right.

"Why are you going? I'm not invited? You are ashamed of me aren't you, because I can't read …" Smokey became more and more hostile. "You didn't even ask me. They are going to talk you out of being with me, I just know it …"

I tried to assure him this had nothing to do with him—it was a simple visit to my parents—but the argument took a dive, revisiting the old topics.

He flipped into one of his angry moods, getting louder as he stomped across the floor like a caged animal. "I'm going out to find somewhere to play, see you later."

"Don't leave like this, Smokey, please. Don't burn any bridges like you did in Oregon. We are doing so good …" The door slammed behind him. *This is exactly what will get him into the cocaine again.*

For the first time since we'd been together, Smokey didn't come home that night. I cried and hurt all night long, worrying and wondering where he was and what he was doing. He was due at work by seven a.m. and nonchalantly strolled in at six, changed into his work uniform and prepared to leave.

"Where have you been all night? I've been worried sick."

"Playing."

"And what else, Smokey, what else?"

"None of your business. I've got to get to work. See you later." He walked out calmly with his head down.

"Smokey, don't do this to us, please. I love you." I felt like I had been shot in the gut and left to bleed. I descended into that familiar numbness that washes over me whenever triggered.

Here we go, just when things are good and stable, he has to sabotage us. I can't live like this. That evening Smokey walked in from work, exhausted, with his tail between his legs. "I'm sorry Eli. I messed up. One of the guys at work has been on my ass all day for what I did, and I was wrong."

I was surprised at his response, which instantly soothed my aching heart and head. "Did you do cocaine, Smokey? Tell me the truth …"

"Almost … but no. I just hung out with Rusty at his place, talking. Look Eli, I got scared when you told me about your trip. I was jealous and hurt that I wasn't invited, but your parents need you too. I have to share you. Just don't forget me; I need you." He looked up at me with tears in his eyes.

"Wow, thank you, Smokey, for understanding … and for not doing cocaine. That was one rough night for me, though. Don't ever do that again, I can't take it. And, I don't deserve it. I am good to you and demand that same respect back. Promise?"

He nodded and we hugged each other and cried.

For the next month, the two of us clung to each other. That event had shaken both of us. I began accompanying him to his gigs again. His dreads were growing out, and he bragged to everyone that I was the person who did his hair. We talked about him joining a more stable band, but for the first time in his life he had a steady paycheck with his other job, and he was proud of it. We fit very well together and understood one another. He liked to talk and share feelings—where most men don't— and that's what I loved about him.

"Let's go get some ice cream and sit by the river!" Smokey smiled with his spontaneous idea, grabbed my hand, and we headed for the store.

Moving Easy   *Dancing Death*

Chapter 31

Trials and Tribulations

My parents' condo in San Diego was beautiful, with a lagoon in the courtyard outside their balcony. Dad could run on the beach every day, and Mom loved visiting the library. The only sore spot was when Dad brought up the subject of Howard. He was convinced that if he could only get my brother back to New Mexico, he could somehow 'repair' his gayness.

"Dad, I don't think he is going to change. I think we are going to have to accept this."

Dad exploded with anger, the conversation went nowhere, and the topic was avoided for the remainder of the trip. I just tried to be a good daughter and appreciate the opportunity they gave me. I didn't even talk about Smokey or much of my life in Austin. The trip was all about San Diego and enjoying each other's company, but I was anxious to get home.

Smokey seemed sullen when I walked in the door. "I missed you Smokey!"

His mood was distant. "I missed you more … how was your trip?"

Although I assured him I was happy to be back home with him, his old insecurities came up until I reassured him that I loved him. We settled into routine, but I noticed something 'off' with him, something I couldn't put my finger on. Maybe he was missing the old friends back in Eugene. I might suggest we take a trip back there soon.

Then one day the phone rang while I was home alone, working on my batik. The man said he had a package for Smokey. Would I give him the message? I said I would, but I was immediately suspicious.

When I brought it up with Smokey that night, he first tried the 'none of your business' tactic, but finally admitted he'd slipped up and done cocaine again. He slammed out the door and, for the second time in our relationship, didn't come home all night. I cried until I was wrung out.

"I can't do this anymore, Smokey. I won't live with drugs. We have to break up." My voice was flat and exhausted. I had never said I wanted to break up before, and Smokey's eyes softened. We stood silently looking at each.

Smokey lowered his eyes and became pensive. "I always fuck up a good thing. What is wrong with me?" Tears welled up in his eyes as he sat down and put his head in his hands. "I don't know what to do anymore, Eli. This monkey controls me. I finally get a good woman, a good job, good friends … and I fuck it up … I need help, Eli."

I didn't know what to say. My resolve to leave him was strong when he was belligerent, but as soon as he was truthful, it crumbled. I knew how many times my own issues consumed me, so I had empathy for him, with his history and makeup.

"So, what do we do?" I tried to rise above my raging emotions and think constructively.

We talked about it and I suggested a support group, but he was afraid of losing his job if his boss found out. When I told him the only way I would stay with him was if he went for help, he agreed, but only if I would go with him. I said I would—whatever it took.

I found a Narcotics Anonymous group that Smokey agreed to attend. After going to a few sessions together, I was told I should go to another group for partners called Nar Anon. The two of us diligently attended.

I started learning about being an enabler. I was responsible for helping the drug habit to continue by making sure Smokey didn't have to feel the consequences of his actions. I made sure bills were paid by working extra, instead of making Smokey give more of his paycheck to me. I took care of the home front, instead of giving him chores to help. I made sure Smokey had stability and whatever the cost, I paid the price. All of this allowed him to do his drug habit. Without my support, he would have to take responsibility for his life.

My familiar worries were back—the fear he would end up on the street, hungry, drugged, maybe even dead. *They tell me I have to learn to practice tough love, but it just breaks my heart to do that to him. I'm so much more of a softy. But, I have to overcome my role too, and mine is nowhere near as hard as drug addiction. Although, they say it is harder because I am addicted to love, which is more primal than drugs…hmmm.*

It was time for me to find a counselor.

Smokey was struggling with the group. Many attending were professionals who spent their earnings on cocaine. Smokey's inability to read put him in a different category, making him feel like he didn't belong. He finally found one man he bonded with, who became his advocate.

It was a very difficult period for us. We felt as though we existed on a bed of raw feelings and were defensive with one another.

Somehow, Smokey's boss, Ed Willis, found out about his problem and surprised both of us by encouraging him to get back in the reading program. Ed thought it would help him concentrate on something else, and ultimately help him in the long run. Smokey was overcome with appreciation for the support and decided to follow his advice.

I decided to tell Smokey about my decision to see a counselor. All his old insecurities came back—mainly, that a counselor would advise me to leave him. He was obviously worried about my decision but saw I was determined. He backed off. Staying firm with the decision made me feel better.

Summer heat was in full swing, adding to the strain. Smokey was learning to adapt to working in the heat but still suffered exhaustion from it. After work, I would drive to Barton Springs to jump in the cold water to refresh and visit with friends. Sometimes we would go to outdoor concerts or go camping at Lake Travis. We were attempting to get our rhythm back.

Smokey started jamming on weekends with The Mustangs, who were hot in the blues scene. They were family men with jobs and didn't allow cocaine use for group members. I hoped they would be a positive influence. Charles, the head of the band, took a special liking to Smokey and seemed to be a father figure for him. Charles wanted to see him succeed and beat the habit.

I started reading self-help books and found a small bookstore not far from home. One hot summer afternoon, as I strolled through the aisles, I noticed two women talking and overheard one say she was a counselor. The woman was middle-aged, with wavy black hair to her shoulders and bangs hanging to her big round red glasses. She wore an embroidered peasant top and dark knee-length skirt. For some reason, I couldn't help watching the women talk and was drawn to the one woman's energy and smile.

Usually, I would only see counselors recommended by someone. But something drove me to wait until the other woman left and I walked up to this woman and said, "I overheard you say you were a counselor …"

"Oh, hi, yes, I am. Do you need one?" I nodded. "Well, I have an opening, if you want to come see me on Tuesday. I work out of my house. My name is Barbara Sturgill." She smiled that broad grin which had drawn my attention.

"Oh, well, that would be great. My name is Eli. What is your charge?"

"I do sliding scale, so whatever you can afford is fine."

"I really can only afford twenty dollars a session …"

"That's fine. Oh, just so you know, I use art therapy with my clients. I'm an artist and have combined it with my therapy sessions. Is that okay?"

I was ecstatic. "Art therapy … that sounds even better."

We set an appointment and I took her card. I shook Barbara's hand and watched her buy a book and leave. Barbara had a faint limp as she exited the store. Suddenly, I felt my gypsy spirit pat me on the back for following my intuition. The vision disappeared in an instant.

What was that? A good omen, I'm sure of it.

Pondering

PART 3

Chapter 32

Following Frida

I felt nervous, but when I saw the cozy house where Ms. Sturgill lived, I was relieved. Obviously, this woman wasn't pretentious or arrogant; her place was so ... rustic and lived-in. Every part of the house was filled with either books or art, which included many, many masks of all shapes, sizes, and cultures. *I am going to like this woman, I can already tell. It is obvious she has an artist's soul.*

"Hi Eli, come on into my office." Ms. Sturgill gave me a big welcoming smile. "Tea?"

"No, thanks."

After getting situated, Ms. Sturgill asked me to tell her about myself by drawing a picture.

"Don't you want me to tell you the basics first?" *Hmmm, I thought the art would come later...*

"We'll get to all that. Just go to the shelves and find some materials that would best help you describe yourself to me. Whatever works for you."

I decided to start with paper and crayons. I felt frustrated and ended up scribbling color all over the page. I showed it to Ms. Sturgill and said, "This is me ... confused and scrambled."

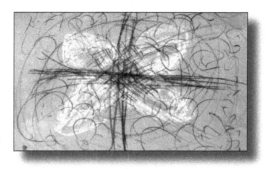

Total Confusion

Ms. Sturgill looked at the art as if it were a masterpiece. "Good. Now, let's talk. I'll introduce myself first. My name is Barbara Sturgill, but please call me Barbara. I'm originally from New Jersey and have been here for thirty years. Originally, I was a professional artist and found myself drawn to the counseling field. I found the arts were very compatible in this field, so I've been putting them together with much success. I am working on getting an Art Therapy license, but presently have a certificate and five years' experience in the Drug and Alcohol Abuse Program with the State of Texas. I have opened my own practice and see about twenty people presently. I use a Jungian approach to therapy and combine other eclectic practices with it. I am deeply spiritual, but don't have an organized religious affiliation. I consider myself Jewish, but that's more culturally than religiously, and I have a gypsy soul! Okay, your turn. Feel free to ask questions."

I was stunned at the introduction and how many points intersected with mine. "Wow! I think this is going to work out just fine. My name is Eli Weintraub, and yes, I am also Jewish, but feel just like you. I've always said I have a gypsy soul—it's amazing you even said that. My mom and dad are also from New Jersey, but I was raised in Los Alamos, New Mexico. I love art and am presently doing batik. The reason I'm here is that I am confused and need someone to help me work it through. I've been living with a man and we have been having trouble. Also, I have issues I need to look at, related to my parents. My brother just came out as being gay, so that's another complication with the family. I've been really depressed."

"What type of problems are you and your boyfriend having?"

"I haven't really talked about this to anyone, but … cocaine. He can't stay away from it."

"How long has this been going on?"

"Since before I met him, four or so years ago … in 1984." I felt as though I'd just betrayed Smokey, sharing this information with Barbara.

"Has he hurt you, physically?"

"No, never. It's emotional abuse, I think. That's what it feels like. Barbara, I feel terrible sharing this with you. Smokey, that's his name, thinks I'm here to get rid of him, but that's not the case. I love him more than anything and want to make this work. But, it seems impossible. Cocaine is his other woman."

We talked back and forth for a little while, getting acquainted, but I was filled with apprehension.

"Eli, we need to wrap up. Sounds like there is a lot of work to do, and don't worry, we will get things figured out. Next week same time works for you?"

"Yeah, sure." I exited the office feeling out-of-body and not sure I was doing the right thing. *What if Barbara does want me to leave Smokey … I won't, I can't … But, I like her. We have a lot in common, and she does know about drug abuse and working with it, so hopefully it will help us.*

As soon as I got home I delved into my batik and started a new piece, thinking about Barbara and Frida Kahlo. *Please guide me and bring my art forth.*

I was deep in the process when Smokey came in from work. I thought of not telling him I attended the first session, but I had to be honest. "I saw my counselor for the first time today, babe."

Smokey tensed up and looked at me. "Oh. How was it?"

"I really like her. She's an artist too. I want you to meet her; you'll like her."

"I don't want to meet her. I don't trust her."

Before I reacted to his comment, I took a deep breath and reminded myself of his insecurities. So, instead, I was more loving than ever, trying to convince Smokey of my allegiance. It worked, and the two of us had a stress-free evening together.

* * *

Over the course of the next month, I started to relax with Barbara and look forward to doing my weekly impromptu piece of art. Barbara was very insightful and saw things in the lines, forms and colors that eluded me, but once pointed out, I felt like a light came on. Barbara was adamant in following my lead and description of my own art.

"Eli, you know best what is going on with you, so I will never tell you what your own art means. You tell me first, and then we can discuss it. I might see things you don't, but will always offer it as an insight; it's up to you if you agree or not. The quality of line, color, texture and depth all represent something within you that's trying to have a voice. Respect and listen to what information it's portraying. If it's too scary, back off. Let the materials do the talking for you. Sometimes words just get in the way."

"It does feel scary ... and blurred. It's just a bunch of lines, scribbles and mess that comes out. Shouldn't I be able to be clearer?"

"It's a process, Eli. We are like onions with layers, and we have to pull them off one by one. Inside is the core which looks very different from the skin and all the protecting layers, just like us."

"I agree. Most of the time I feel like I'm living different lives, like I need the layers for protection of my real self. Then I get confused, and blank out."

"That's survival mode. Be patient. Even if you don't feel you are progressing, you are. It can be very subtle. You have to learn to trust yourself, which requires trust in your environment. It takes time to identify and feel secure in that. The psyche protects us from danger, even if it's from ourselves."

"Yeah, sometimes I think I'm my worst enemy with the choices I make ..."

"Tell me about these two drawings..." Barbara sat back to listen, as if I were the most important person in the world.

Under Attack   *Clue of the Dingle-Bobs*

"It feels like I'm under attack, but I'm protected within by keeping a pointy boundary of anger and confusion. Something is inside, but it's encased in grey numbness and yellow yuckiness.

The other one has an above and below going on. Something is trying to grow below, but there is a line ... one is blue ... maybe depression and the other is red, pain, and the yellow is hope ... or maybe it's the yellow yuckiness. Above are clouds and a mass of confusion, below it is the same, but more complicated, and trying to grow flowers, but is struggling. The black dingle-bobs over the red flower feel like something hanging over my head ... and heart. The dingle-bobs remind me of those buses in Mexico; they all have them lining the windshields ... I feel overwhelmed ... I'm getting queasy I can't think straight ..."

"That's enough for today, Eli. Close your eyes and rest ..."

Every time, leaving the office I felt out-of-body and needed to be alone afterward, to get settled. On my fifth visit, I started referring to the accident for the first time after doing my drawings. I suppose I had finally reached that layer of the onion.

"I have so much pain and loss from my accident ... I just want to hide all the time." My voice felt as if it was coming from someone else as I despondently explained my drawings.

Hidden Wound   *Hiding Distress*

"Accident? What accident ... what happened?" Barbara was surprised to hear the quick version and that I had waited so long to mention such a traumatic history. I was very vague, but said enough to raise a red flag with Barbara. "Eli, are you okay? You look pale."

"Uh, yeah, I'm dizzy. Let me close my eyes a minute." I closed my eyes, but couldn't shake off the out-of-body feeling and had to stop the session. "What happened? I feel very lightheaded."

"I'm going to teach you some techniques to stay grounded. I think we need to slow down. It's those layers of the onion. Don't worry." Barbara got a glimpse of the real me that day and approached the sessions much differently after that. More art was done and we allocated ten minutes before the end of each session to help me put things back in a 'safe place' before I left.

"You see, Eli, you need to learn how to mentally and emotionally put these issues away before you head out the door. If you don't, they are open wounds the world can put salt on and cause more damage."

I understood. This was the problem that had plagued me ever since my accident. That is why I hid it all away; the world abused my open-book approach to sharing my history.

* * *

Smokey began getting nervous when I stopped sharing what happened in my sessions. I tried to explain it was to protect my fragility in the world, but Smokey thought I was just hiding things from him.

"I'm not hiding things from you, Smokey. I promise!"

"I don't believe you. You are talking about how to get me out of your life ..."

"Smokey ... please, don't go there. How many times do I have to tell you I want you?"

"Marry me then ..."

"I will, when you are clean from cocaine for an entire year."

"I asked you to marry me a year ago and you still won't."

"Well, you did cocaine since then too, so the year doesn't count."

"What shit, what a bunch of shit ..." Smokey felt everything was futile. All his efforts cancelled by a few times falling off the wagon. It wasn't fair. "I think I'll go out ... see you later."

I said nothing; the writing was on the wall. That night when he didn't come home I did art all night, art which included teardrops mixed with the paper.

When Smokey came in the next morning to get his uniform for work, neither of us said a word to each other.

Both of our hearts were breaking and we didn't know how to fix things anymore. That day I felt like a walking zombie.

Maybe if I try to just take care of normal daily chores. Okay, let's see ... I need to pay bills. I need to get rent paid. I went to the closet where we kept the money and when I reached in, it was gone, all of it. I tore the closet apart to find the money and realized Smokey had taken it.

He came walking in after work, with the angry energy that accompanied a cocaine hangover, and stormed past me.

"Smokey, I can't believe you took our money—our rent money,

Smokey. Now we are both going to lose our home. How can you do this to me? I can't do this. It's not the way I want to live. I like having a roof over my head, I like knowing bills are paid. I can't believe you did this!"

"Fuck you, Eli. Fuck you."

He had never said that to me before, and it hit like a lance through the heart and soul. "Don't yell at me and be so ugly!"

Smokey screamed the obscenity again. He didn't even look like himself; he looked like he was filled with the devil.

That's it, no more. I deserve better. I've done nothing but help and try to be a good person and he comes at me saying that and taking our money.

"It's over, Smokey. I'm not doing this anymore. You have to move out. I can't live with someone who bites the hand that feeds him. OUT!"

Smokey was shocked and didn't believe me. His anger took over and he yelled and screamed a little while longer before striding out the front door. When he returned the next day, all his belongings were sitting on the porch.

"Eli, you can't do this to me. Please, I'm sorry. I'll make it up to you. My work buddies talked sense into me. I'll do right, I promise," he pleaded, from outside the front door.

I wanted to believe him, I wanted to continue loving him like I always had, but I couldn't. Something broke when he stole the money then cursed at me with such a cold stare.

I cried inside while Smokey circled the apartment yelling, crying, and begging for forgiveness. "Let me in, Eli, please. Let's work this out! I love you! I can't live without you … PLEASE!" But I couldn't. My heart was breaking, but his actions proved not even I was immune from his addiction.

"I have to be able to trust the man I love, Smokey. You stole our hard-earned money to sniff up your nose. We both work our butts off every day to keep a roof over our heads and food in our bellies. In one moment, you took all that and stomped it into the ground—and you say you care?"

"I need help, Eli, I need help! Help me …" He sat on the ground outside the bedroom window with his head in his hands and cried.

I listened and sobbed as it tore me up, but I couldn't do it this time. This went on for more than three hours, until I finally came up with something I would accept.

"Smokey, come on in here." He lifted his head with hope and gingerly entered and sat on the couch, looking at me with those sad eyes.

"This is the deal. You have to move out. That is the only way you will ever learn how to take responsibility for your own life. I will help you find an apartment, set up a budget, and teach you to maintain it. If you decide to do cocaine, it will be with your own money and risk. We will see how it goes. I don't know if I can continue seeing you. I love you still, but you hurt me to the core, Smokey, and you continue doing it. I will be happy to support any efforts toward getting clean, but not any that don't. That's it, take it or leave it all."

Smokey continued to beg for forgiveness and another chance. "Eli, I don't want to live on my own … I've never been good at it … I'll lose everything without you … Please, I love you and need you …"

I wouldn't budge. "That's the offer, Smokey; I won't live with you, wondering if you are stealing our rent money."

Smokey started seeing I wasn't going to give in. He got real quiet and finally nodded. "Okay, Eli. Can I stay until we find a place for me?"

I agreed to it and was actually glad, because I was going to have a real hard time learning how to live without this man I loved with all my heart and soul. "Why did you have to do this, Smokey, why? Trust is a hard thing to get back."

Not much was said as we curled up together, recognizing a new wind was in the air.

Smokey kept hoping I would change my mind as we looked for an apartment, but I didn't. When we finally found something affordable and in the same area, it wasn't available until the fall, so we put down a deposit to secure it. Already, finances were wrecked, but my landlord agreed to give me three months to get rent caught up. We saved every penny and I picked up a few more waitressing shifts on the weekends to pad the pocketbook for the upcoming expenses. Smokey played gigs with the Mustangs for extra cash. His check was minimal, and it would be a challenge for even a frugal person to make it on that amount.

I figured out a budget for Smokey to live on and started teaching him to manage his money, something I had always done for us. He would never have any extra, it was all necessary for bills and food. Garage sales helped fill the apartment and a cheap bike would be Smokey's transportation. He continued to hope for a change of heart, but I was committed to the change. The effort somehow renewed our relationship, but I could only enjoy his company by knowing he was moving out. I hoped trust could be regained, but presently, I remained constantly guarded.

* * *

Sessions with Barbara helped stem the tide of my anxiety during this period. Her background in drug abuse counseling helped me maintain perspective on the enabling role I played. "I just want to help him get set up. It's an impossible task for him to do it on his own and succeed, and more than anything I want him to succeed. Maybe if he does, we can hope for a future together. Once he's set up, I'll step back and let the cards fall where they must …"

"I think that's a good plan, Eli. I know how difficult this must be, but giving him assistance to make the change and then stepping back is healthy. Remember, you can't give a nickel if you only have three cents. Take care of yourself too."

"I'm glad to hear that. It's so different for him without reading skills and his history of childhood abuse; he's already got many risks against him. I don't want to enable, but I believe some people need extra care … like me too."

I did art about Smokey. Most were about the love that held our fragile hope together. It helped me as I tried to start letting go of the tie we'd established, living together. I knew we would spend time together at each other's apartment but deep down I knew this change would influence the bond.

Crushed   *Frozen Anger*

I shared some drawings with Barbara. "I feel like he stomped on my heart and broke it. It's raggedy and ripped … so sad and angry. We'd been growing so well, which is the surrounding green, but the black boot has taken over. The black moon and sun surrounded with dark blue is us. I'm cradled within his dark unknown and depression. The yellow … maybe that's hope."

I took a deep breath as I shifted my focus to the other drawing.

"This one portrays the spiritual core we have together and how the knife is trying to cut it with his ugliness, tears, and pain. We are drowning in deep blue depression. I was just scribbling color when I saw the word dog appear ... I feel like I'm being treated like a dog. You know what is funny ... it spells god backwards ... for some reason I like that."

"Why is the knife so big?" Barbara peered over her big red glasses at the drawing.

"It feels impossible to cut the core, so it would take one that big and cruel to do the job ... Him saying 'fuck you' to me the other day, cut me to my core."

"Is it necessary to cut the core? Sounds painful. Can you do it another way less hurtful?"

"I don't know. Whatever I try to do to disconnect my love from Smokey doesn't work. The bond is from my essential core to his. It's deep."

"Maybe we can do some visualization that is less harsh, gentler."

"I like that idea. Let's try it."

Barbara talked me through a meditation using color to change the dynamic and lessen the deep hurt in my core a little bit. I changed the knife to white energy and slowly eased apart our core bond of dysfunction. It became a routine tool for me, to manage the pain.

* * *

The winds of fall arrived, as did Smokey's move. It was a difficult affair for both of us but necessary for my emotional well-being. I was tired of enabling, knowing the inevitable fall was around any corner. My fragility demanded it.

The last item was moved and I helped unpack and cook the first dinner in the apartment. Initially, it felt like just another move together, but when it was time for me to go home, we both stood looking at each other, feeling lost and overcome with sadness.

"I'll come by after work tomorrow, Smokey. Maybe we can have dinner together again."

"I can't believe this is happening. I feel like I'm in a bad dream. Eli, why don't you stay with me tonight?"

I was determined to be strong, but my heart said, "Well, it *is* the first night—why not?" Smokey burst into a smile and hugged me long and passionately.

"Woman, I have to get it right. I want you in my life."

Months passed quickly. We spent most nights and time off together. I thought it was crazy I was doing this, but we had a long established routine together that wasn't going to disappear easily, especially when Smokey was in one of his up trends and on good behavior. It was almost fun to decide which apartment to stay at while we were establishing this new sequence.

Smokey was making progress learning how to budget his money and pay bills. I helped him with everything still, until he confidently could take over the processes. His illiteracy problem was like a sore thumb, now that I was trying to wean myself away from the responsibility. Smokey struggled with his emotional upset when he couldn't read a bill or remember the procedures, but my patience was the thread that tied it all together and helped him overcome his fear of basic responsibilities.

My sessions with Barbara focused on getting through the day-to-day during this difficult transition. My art expressions were soft pastel, simple with occasional boldness. The lines and forms were basic and unidentifiable with an undercurrent of something, something yet to be seen.

Frida stayed with me as I drew, but I was unable to reach real depth. I often got dizzy during the sessions and would stop until it passed. Barbara was very caring and insightful, but I still had a wall up and wouldn't trust.

Chapter 33

Bad News

"Hey Eli, this is Doug …"

"Hey bro, what a surprise." Without much small talk, Doug revealed the purpose of the call.

"We need to go visit Howard …"

I had a sinking feeling in my gut when I heard his tone. "What's going on?"

Doug's voice cracked. "Eli, Howard just called me … he has HIV."

HIV and AIDS were new on the scene, and I wasn't sure what that signified, but I knew it wasn't good. "Shit." Silence.

* * *

I was telling Smokey about the trip and, surprisingly, he didn't get angry. He was finally getting the picture of this family problem and didn't take my leaving personally. This would be the first time he would be on his own, in his own apartment, on a weekend.

Doug had been visiting Howard occasionally over the years, and he saw his twin transforming into someone he hardly knew anymore. Howard opened the door and I had to suppress a gasp, he was so thin and pale. His eyes had a look of knowing. Everyone felt awkward. The elephant in the room was pushed aside as we three siblings tried to reconnect.

"I don't want Mom and Dad to know. Maybe I can beat this. I don't want to put them through anything. Doug, Eli, if I do get AIDS I want you to promise me that you will not let them know where I am. I can't let them see me like this, I just can't. Dad has already sent me letters trying to 'cure' my gayness and when I wrote back, refusing his help, I got a letter saying he disowns me."

We tried to talk Howard into letting our parents see him, but he was adamant. With uncertainty and heavy hearts, both Doug and I agreed to the promise. We were in shock at what was occurring with Doug's twin. Poor Doug, he took it hard, very hard. We spent the remainder of the visit catching up and just being in each other's company.

* * *

I felt numb when I got back home. It was late Sunday evening, and I knew Smokey was always home at night to get ready for work the next day. I decided to pass by and tell him about the visit. I really needed his arms around me right now, but he wasn't home.

This was the first slap of reality, the firm reminder that we had our own lives now. Up to this point, we had maintained a mutual rhythm as he got settled into the new apartment. I wanted this, but now was feeling angry and lost at the change. *He has the right to do whatever he wants. We do have an understanding to be true for the time being, so I do trust him there, I think …*

Just as I was starting to fall apart, Smokey rolled up on his bike. "Babe!"

Relief filled my heart as I approached him and broke down sobbing. "Where were you?"

"There was a jam at the Hole in the Wall tonight, so since you weren't around, I thought I'd go … You look bad, girl. Come in and tell me about the visit." He was so caring and loving as I unraveled the story about the trip. *This is why I can't stop loving this guy, he knows me so well and can tend to pain with such tenderness.*

I fell asleep in his arms and awoke to his kiss as he left for work the next morning. "Just lock the door when you go. I'll come by after work … take care, Eli."

Chapter 34

Frida is in the House

Vibrant Loss

Barbara looked over her glasses at the new piece I'd just finished. Instead of being pale, vibrant colors blended together to create a blurred texture. I had shared the visit to Howard and cried heartily.

"I feel like glue inside, mucky, mucky glue. I want to disappear; life is too damn hard, and my heart can't take it anymore ..." Then I got dizzy and we had to stop the session.

"Eli, I want you to start working on creating a safe place. This is an internal place you can always go, wherever you are and whenever you get overwhelmed. It's going to take time and practice to get yourself there immediately, but you've got to do this before we can proceed. First I will lead you through a meditation where you visualize your safe place. It is totally up to you how you design it, and you write all the rules required for anyone to enter."

I closed my eyes and as Barbara spoke I started imagining my safe place. *I feel safe in nature, so instead of a room, it will be a space defined by big tall ponderosa pine trees. It will be high on a hill, overlooking the sea in one direction and mesas on the other. A fresh-water stream will go right through, and I can bathe and drink from it. My bed will be the softest moss, and furniture will be boulders and tree trunks, cozy and comfortable with natural fiber tapestries and beautiful works of art. Animals of all sorts will be my companions and protect me. Any person who wants in will have to request permission and honor my rules to be civil, trustworthy, and honest.*

"I like this place, Barbara. I feel better just creating it. I'll continue to add to it as time goes on."

"I also would like you to start doing safe drawings whenever you are feeling overwhelmed, and don't do any other type until you are centered in safe feelings."

Cloak of Safety

"This is my first 'safe' drawing. I feel like a tiny fetus or embryo … fragile, very fragile … it could die very easily. Then I decided to protect it with a cozy cloak. It has softness and room to protect its overwhelmed fears. It's like a baby blanket with a dingle-bob on the hood—there I go again with dingle-bobs—a coat of many colors, maybe spiritual protection like Jacob in the Bible."

"Eli, do you notice how simple, soft and pastel it is? I think that reflects the newness of it, like a new layer you are exploring. The others have started becoming more bold and colorful, which tells me you are delving into deeper psyche territory."

"I agree. The richer the texture and color, the more intense my feelings are … very interesting."

I was starting to trust Barbara more. Her observations and intuition were validating and helped me not feel so alone and crazy. Barbara seemed like the older sister I'd always wanted. She worried about me and took extra effort to show me I was cared about.

* * *

Smokey and I started getting into a new routine, staying together only on weekends. It was too hard to carry on a routine while going back and forth. By now, Smokey was getting to like his own apartment and saw that I wasn't abandoning him; I was continuing to help him learn the finances. He also got more serious about his reading classes and found a tutor he was comfortable with. Smokey only played special gigs with the Mustangs and occasionally went out to jam. He knew he was vulnerable to the temptations in the music scene.

I found a painting table at a garage sale and started drawing at home in the middle of the night, with Reggae and Brazilian music serenading me. After experimenting with watercolors, acrylic, collage, and chalk in my sessions with Barbara, I found color oil pastels were the medium I most liked.

The colors were rich, varied, and had a very smooth feeling to them as I pushed and pulled them across different types of paper. It was also interesting to go back and scrape off color and create design that way. I spent hours and hours playing and being surprised with what appeared on the page.

A trance-like state engulfed these sessions, and hours passed like minutes. Finally, around three in the morning, I would slide into bed. Barbara told me to keep my artwork visible around the house, so that I would see it in passing from one room to the next. Sometimes, I would stare at my work of the week and wait to see what evolved from it. Usually, one piece led to another to another to another; I felt like a faucet running wide open with creative juices. When something emerged that felt scary, I followed Barbara's instructions to do a safe piece, and usually I wouldn't go back to it until I was with Barbara.

When Smokey saw my art, he was curious and was an avid groupie of whatever I worked on, no matter how simple or complex it was. I had done a batik of Smokey with his long dreads, now down to his shoulders, playing the harps. I learned a way to frame it with an upholstery technique and gave it to him for his birthday.

Smokey's mouth hung ajar when he saw it. "Babe, this is incredible! Thank you so much. This is the best present I have ever gotten. I will cherish it forever. Would you sign it? Put the date on it too, June 19, 1990. This is an important occasion! We need to celebrate. Let's go out to eat, then go find some reggae and dance."

"That sounds perfect. I am very proud of you, Smokey." I leaned over and kissed him.

"Yeah, I'm proud of me too! I'm also proud of us, Eli. We have been together for seven years now, that's a first for me."

"Me too. We've been through a lot together." *I pray he stays on track …*

* * *

My work with Barbara had a breakthrough. I had been doing blurred color drawings for months. The colors were changing from soft pastels to intense and expressive, although still very abstract. One day, an image popped out during one of the sessions. In the last frame, it was a mother holding a baby.

"Tell me about this, Eli …" Barbara was as surprised as I.

Lost Motherhood

I couldn't talk and started crying. Once the initial energy was released, I looked at it. "It's the mother I'll never be and the baby I'll never have … I'm so angry … and sad … and empty … there's not much more to say … and I'm feeling foggy again … when is this ever going to stop?"

"Okay, I want you to take this home and keep it close to you. Let's see where this leads you. Good work, Eli. I think you've just had a breakthrough. Take care." Barbara smiled and embraced me as I departed.

After this drawing, a flood of images and art poured out of me. Texture and pattern were the basis of the artwork, but images starting popping out regularly. The impression would appear out of nowhere, and I wouldn't be content until I was at my drawing easel releasing it onto the paper. Frida continued to encourage me to get the pain out and allow the color and process change it into art.

Broken Puppet

•

"This is me, Barbara." I showed her a work that had emerged the previous week. "This is Nancy, and this is Eli. Nancy is the powerful, energized force in red and yellow that holds the body together, which is disconnected and half her brain is missing. She precariously connects to her historical world of family by her toe on the world and the burr is her heart; it doesn't feel much. She holds up Eli, who is weak, anemic and desperate—in empty, numb white and heavy blue—reaching in anguish. The white dove is a cloak of hope that carries them away. The hole is the void I live in, and the ladder is needed but can't be accessed."

"Wow, there are a lot of things going on here, Eli. This is the first time you've portrayed yourself as Nancy and Eli. Your identity is struggling to be seen."

"Lots of broken-ness and toil." *It's difficult to do these drawings, but at the same time I feel like I am finally connecting to the source of my problem. No words could ever explain what this image portrays. Even Barbara can understand me better now, seeing this image. Maybe it will help us both communicate better too. Words never seem to properly express my internal state. But art … it feels like I've finally found a voice in color, form and texture that expresses me more honestly than anything. Frida, I understand you so much better now. Thank you for showing me the way.*

I started to feel an internal fluidity I hadn't felt since before the accident. Something deep within was changing from immobile rock to molten lava—intimidating but *there*, as opposed to constant numbness. I couldn't wait to sit down to my easel late every night and let the musical rhythms pull images out of me. It was extremely daunting, but stirring.

Smokey was also very taken by the revealing imagery. Seeing the art helped him understand me better and get an idea of what was at the root of my distress. He also learned that he wasn't the topic, which relieved him. He saw how important the art was and he encouraged me to do it, whereas before, he would try to get me to spend time with him instead.

Smokey started doing more things on his own, allowing me the space to do art.

*

Chapter 35

The Straw That Broke the Camel's Back

I had just returned from Los Alamos, a family meeting about Howard, and was feeling sad. I walked up to the house in Austin, happy to see my pooches as they ran in circles. "Did Smokey take good care of you guys? I missed you ..."

I called Smokey, but didn't get an answer. It was Sunday night, and I figured he went to jam. "Maybe I'll go over there and wait for him. I could use some company ..." I sat in the truck for an hour, and finally someone dropped Smokey off at the apartment. Instantly, I could tell he was high, and I tensed up. *Maybe it's just beer* ... As I watched him approach the door then turn to see the truck, he dropped his head and pretended he didn't see me. He opened the door and went in.

I knocked on the door and he opened it, acting as if everything was normal. "Babe, when did you get in?" His eyes were dilated, and he had the aura of cocaine on him.

The blank stare said it all. "So, who hooked you up this time, Smokey?"

"What are you talking about?"

"No use, Smokey, I've known you long enough to recognize the cocaine high. I guess you've made your decision with us. I'll go home now ..."

Smokey proceeded to plead his innocence, but it didn't work. I was done. *This will never change with him. I guess his death wish is stronger than mine. I know if I'm not in his life he will hit bottom, and I guess I'll have to live with that because I can't do this anymore, I'm way too fragile.*

I got in the truck, ignoring everything Smokey tried in order to hook me in, and went home to cry enough tears to fill the salt sea. My heart was ripped in every direction—from self, family, and Smokey. *It's all about survival now.*

Every day Smokey came by to talk with me. He said the same things he always did, but I didn't respond the same way. I was too empty. He got more and more desperate and tried everything to get my attention, from not paying bills, to exhausting himself, to sickness. Still, the hooks didn't work anymore. My badly wounded heart was Teflon now.

"Smokey is in the hospital, Eli, he wants to see you." Rusty came to the door. "He tried to take himself out. Eli, you can make it better … he needs you." I refused to go to his rescue. I didn't even want to know what he had done. *This is exactly what I feared the most.* I knew this was his bottom, and it was up to him to get it together, if he survived.

I felt absolutely cold inside—numb. My attempts to help would be futile until he helped himself. His boss came by and talked to me. The court had ordered rehab for Smokey, and I was to stay clear of him. Once out of rehab, he would move into a group home. They didn't even want me to know where he would be or to contact him. I prayed that the support system would give him what he needed to get through.

Smokey, I will always love you … you touched my soul.

Chapter 36

Key Information

Sessions with Barbara became more difficult than ever. Between Smokey, Howard, and self, loss consumed me. Dizziness and nausea plagued my sessions, and the art that began to unravel was like a tsunami wave. Each week, I started to produce pieces that defined the numbness within me. Themes of mother/child, escape, loss, confusion, and death emerged.

Timeline of Chaos

"Very nice, Eli. Looks like a time line. Tell me about it." Barbara was fascinated with the developing art.

"Well, I started with the colored strips. I just wanted to feel like I was creating order. Then the numb horizontal person came in and out of ... time, yeah, it does feel like it's related to time, and the clock too, timelessness ... that's it ... timelessness, no sense of time. Next, the woman materialized, a strong woman with milk dripping from her breast. She's deep garnet red, the color of blood and loss. She has milk to feed a baby, but the baby is tucked in a tea cup … losing milk … feels like 'crying over spilled milk,' which is the baby … Then death appeared … watching over it all, lurking in the background. That last image is me, trying to escape it all. I was starting to feel unsafe and thought I better put some safe image in, so I put that charm of the guardian angel you gave me. Then lastly, there is a person with vines growing out of her, trying to grow and capture the fleeing image of me. It feels like I'm just trying to get some sense of clarity."

"Yes, it's as if you are defining the parameters of self. I think you are struggling with a lost identity problem."

"Definitely. I feel like a bundle of everything and everyone else but me. I don't even know who 'me' is …" Suddenly, the wave of nausea and dizziness descended and we ended the session.

"Eli, would you like to go to an art opening with me?" Barbara asked as I was ready to go.

I was honored to be invited and readily agreed.

"Eli, I know this is unconventional, but I meet with supervisors weekly to review my caseload and will discuss this with them. I like you and value our friendship. As an artist, you would enjoy this event. I think we can work together and be friends, don't you?"

"Actually Barbara, I think that is the only way I can trust enough to get through this. Your caring has given me the additional layer of support I've needed to face whatever lurks beneath it all. I thank you, because I feel the same way and if either of us starts to change, we can cross that bridge when we get to it." We nodded, hugged, and made plans for the art opening.

Barbara's friendship developed easily. Both of us worked to respect the boundary between therapy and friendship by never talking about my 'stuff' when we were outside the office. Barbara's supervisors were leery of the friendship but didn't outright oppose it.

One week, I walked into the office for my session and Barbara was very excited. "Eli, I think I've figured out what your diagnosis is. I've been looking in the official handbook of psychiatric problems, the DSM II R, and finally have found what matches. It's called Post Traumatic Stress Disorder, PTSD. My supervisors and I have been trying to figure it out, and they agree. Not many have heard of this before. It's mostly been attributed to war veterans, but the symptoms match yours. You have a classic case of it, and now I know how to go forward with your work.

First, I want you to read this copy I've made; it describes the symptoms; see if you agree. I'm so excited. I think we will start getting somewhere." I liked that there was a medical name attached to all my confusion. It gave me hope. That night, I read the information and realized Barbara had nailed it.

The criteria for PTSD:

A - Exposed to trauma. *I definitely have that* ... Trauma is a type of wounding of the body and/or psyche and influences emotions, spirit, will to live, beliefs about self and world, dignity and a sense of security. It can create depersonalization, feelings of vulnerability, loss of trust in self and society. *That's it, that's me!*

B- Re-experience the trauma. PTSD is a cycle of re-experiencing the trauma, followed by attempts to bury the memories and feelings associated. *I've definitely done that very completely* ... Dreams, nightmares, and flashbacks often occur. Feelings appear in other forms not related to any particular memory of trauma, i.e. anger, fearful, moody for no apparent reason. *OHHHHH, that makes so much sense* ...

C – Numbing and avoidance. *I completely live this one* ... PTSD's central features are the deadening and shutting off of emotion and psychic numbing. The feelings experienced in trauma shake the individual to the core (fear, sadness, guilt, anger). Shutting down helps to avoid the intensity but results in mood swings, out of control and crazy behavior. This is not easily understood and is often misinterpreted by others; the individual retreats mentally, socially, and physically to avoid the pain. *This is exactly my life!* ...Triggers in life can re-stimulate the trauma and avoidance of them can cause problems in jobs, relationships, and society. *So that's part of my not being able to watch anything related to death, blood, loud crunching metal ... this makes so much sense* ...

D – Hyper-arousal symptoms. Fight-or-flight and freeze reactions occur with PTSD triggers. Body chemistry of the adrenal glands can be altered by trauma which then become hypersensitive, resulting in increased heart rate, blood pressure, muscle tension, and blood sugar and can result in the fight-or-flight behavior. The opposite will cause the freeze reaction where thinking or moving happens in slow motion. *This explains so much of my past actions ... like when I blank out...*

E – Duration. Partial or severe PTSD is determined by how many criteria exist and how intense they are. If there are multiple traumas, the individual is more likely to exhibit disassociated behavior, self-destructiveness, and mood swings. *Well, meet Eli …*

I relate entirely. This has been the story of my life since the accident. I always want to flee and escape or I'm too frozen to act. Fight … not so much, that one scares me more. But flight … I'd make a great bird! After Dad called me a slut, I was filled with flight. Anytime things got tough, I moved or left. Then I isolated.

PTSD … having a name for it somehow it validates me and all my craziness. It gives me a place to start.

Barbara had given more information:

Biochemical changes: The central nervous system receives shocks when trauma happens and can disrupt the body's delicate balance. Some experience difficulties in clear thinking, memory loss, regulating emotions, relating to people, and sustaining hope for the future. *I have definitely lived with all of those …* Ignorance of this biochemical component can create a dynamic of feeling like a failure, due to the inability to control reactions. *I've been frustrated with this forever …*

Depression: Normal depression is an expression of grief related to an external loss, such as a loved one, a pet or valued object. Clinical depression is only partially conscious, or unconscious, and the grief expressed is over psychological or spiritual loss such as loss of innocence, beliefs once held, or loss of self-respect; it grows over time, whereas normal depression lessens. *I lost my innocence with the accident and nothing fit together anymore. I have been angry with myself because I can't seem to deal with it …* Self-hatred, fatigue, indecision, withdrawal, low concentration, overwhelmed feelings, and inability to function are symptoms. *Well … I am clinically depressed then …*

Feelings and thoughts: Coming to terms with overwhelming feelings is an important step to start healing PTSD. It takes great courage to identify and reconcile them, in order to reclaim this missing element of the personality. It can be very threatening and seem the whole world is going to dissolve when looking into these feelings. Time and patience is required. *I get dizzy just thinking about it …*

Common PTSD feelings:

- Loss of invulnerability; lost feelings of safety and trust in others and the world, a sense of doom for the future and fear the trauma will reoccur. *That's related to feeling I will not live long … death is around every corner.*

- Loss of an orderly world; "Why did this happen to me?" or "I thought if I was a good person things like this wouldn't happen." In conclusion, life becomes meaningless and incomprehensible, punishment is deserved, views of human decency and social justice, or spiritual and religious views become confused. *Since the accident I have always struggled with feelings that God doesn't exist …*

- Feel like a child; forget and have to relearn coping behavior and mechanisms. *I've always felt like a newborn after the accident …*

- Withdrawal; isolation results from difficulties with confusion, coping, and self-doubt. *So, the PTSD is at the root of this aspect of my life …*

- Extreme rage and anger; due to loss of control over life, misunderstanding, and feelings of being crazy. *I know my rage is somewhere, but I've hidden it well…*

- Being discounted; feelings are not taken seriously, the event is minimalized. *I've always felt like no one really wants to hear what I have to say …*

- Stigmatization; long-term symptoms are seen as a moral or mental deficiency. *I feel I am broken, which then makes me feel embarrassed …*

- Denial; personal problems are seen as a weakness, character flaw, or incompetence, so individual hides them. *I have always found peace in hiding …*

PTSD is like a machine with a bearing that is wearing out. The longer the bearing is ignored, the chances are increased to have an accident and destroy the machine. The bearing must be taken care of for the machine to run well. *I am flabbergasted. For the first time, I don't feel so alone. Someone out there understands, and what is even better is that it can be healed … Hallelujah!!!!!!!!!!!!!!*

It was late night when I finished reading the material, and I sat on the porch with the dogs for a while to let it sink in. Just knowing the information brightened and cleared my perspective on life. A new sense of purpose filled me, and therapy took on a whole new meaning. A falling star raced across the universe, and I knew that my gypsy spirit, along with Frida, was watching over me and directing my path.

Elana is a name I have felt unconsciously for a long time. It feels like a combining of Eli and Nancy. I'll name my gypsy spirit Elana … she's the drumbeat who has been with me all along and will direct my healing to become whole and peaceful again. Good night, Elana! Good night, Frida!

The next day I was a jumble of emotions and numbness. I decided to escape to a matinee movie called *Truly Madly Deeply* and was profoundly moved by the story. Afterward, I sat in the truck, digesting the movie about a woman who lost her husband. He came back to their home as a spirit, and seeing him brought comfort to his grieving wife. She welcomed him back and cherished his companionship, even though he was a spirit in limbo. She avoided her outside life, including other relationships, to stay home with her deceased husband's spirit. The deceased husband would invite other souls in limbo to stay at this home with him, and she would come home from work daily, finding more and more of these souls inhabiting her home. Finally, it was out of hand and she ordered everyone out, which resulted in her husband leaving too. With that, she went forth to join life again.

It hit me like a cannonball that I also had been making choices to take a path that led to living with dying and death instead of a path to choose life. I realized my every decision needed to be reviewed to determine if it led me on the path of death or path of life, and to make sure I chose the life path from there on out. Just like the clarity I felt 'to try' I would now make sure I made the decision 'to live.' The shift was immediate and powerful.

That night, I sat at my easel until dawn, creating a new piece.

"Eli, this is beautiful. Much more intense and defined than the others." Barbara was astounded with the artwork.

Vista

"The center portrait is who I want to become. The flower is a beautiful bloom in the mind and represents the soul opening to heal. I'm still in darkness, but I have a protector ... a lioness. I can trust her to keep me safe, no matter what. There are gems around my face ... they show my hidden value, yet to be recognized. Eli is blue ... depressed, birthed in the Mexican landscape with death rising over the mesa with the moon ... that feels very scary. Down on the right corner is the gluey depression I live in. Someone is reaching out to help me but I am crouched and cramped, trying to reach but it's very difficult. I really like this one. I want to make things clear so I can see what's there, even if it is scary."

As soon as Barbara wanted me to talk more about the moon-like skull rising over the mesa, I got dizzy and nauseous. It was enough for the day.

I thought and worried about Smokey all the time and hoped he was doing well. I decided to call his old boss to see what he could tell me. I was relieved to hear he was following the program at the group home and was working. Ed said he had a long way to go and was in a difficult period, but he was sticking to the rules at the group home and wanting to overcome the addiction.

"He talks about you every day, Eli. He knows he screwed up to lose 'the best thing that ever happened to me,' as he puts it. He'll make it; I feel it. He's a good guy who has to learn to take responsibility for his own actions. It's going to take time and patience. Luckily, he has a great support system to get him through … not that you weren't, but they understand addiction. Feel free to keep in touch with me. I'll let you know if you can contact him … it won't be for at least six months though …" I was greatly relieved to have the conversation with Ed, which enabled me to worry less about Smokey and try to focus even more on my own self-work. That night I did a tribute drawing to our lost love.

Goodbye

Chapter 37

Ashes to Ashes

I was working on a drawing when the phone rang. "Eli, it's Doug ..." I intuitively knew I was going to San Francisco. "Howard is bedridden and his time is close. Rick will travel with you to San Francisco, meet me, and then we'll go visit Howard. I was just up there and all the roommates agree, it's time for us to come."

A dark, heavy pressure pushed down on my heart, and I felt I was falling backwards into dark depression. *Please give me strength, please ...*

His roommates made dinner for everyone that night, and we discussed Howard's wishes. Howard had planned everything before he became too sick. He had saved funeral money to throw a party for all his friends. A yacht would cruise the San Francisco Bay and as it passed a certain spot, everyone would throw his ashes into the waters while friends and family spoke. It was *so* Howard; he always lived life with gusto.

Half the ashes would be saved and brought back to Los Alamos for a family funeral. Even in death, Howard did not want Mom and Dad to see his lifestyle or friends, but at least he considered their need for closure in their own way. Howard requested Doug and me to be on the yacht, not including Rick because of his family responsibilities. Everything was already paid for, including an airline ticket for me.

The visit was somber and very sad for everyone.

By the time I said goodbye to my brother of thirty-nine years, I was devastated. "Howard, I love you. Peace be with you ..." Tears ran down my cheeks.

"Do your art ..." Howard's voice cracked, and he gave me a soft smile. "Go now, I'll be fine ..."

It was late when I arrived home. After a gleeful welcoming from my dogs, which Ann had taken care of, I had to sit down at my easel. Frida watched over as I transferred my grief onto paper.

Farewell, Howard

"Well, Barbara, this is about losing Howard. I am sad and angry; that takes up most of the page. My hair is like a river of tears ... red, burgundy ... hurt and heartbroken. The eyes look off to the side, maybe looking back at all that has been, and not happy about it. The other side ... well, I am bidding farewell to Howard on a beach of numbness. He is being called by the grim reaper, a skeleton, on the sailboat into the sea, a blur of blue melding into the sky. The big full moon watches over, ready to help with the passage of his soul. He doesn't want to go, but must pay the consequences of his actions. Junior, my dog, accompanies him, howling with sorrow and farewell while Rosie looks back at me ... worried."

I started sobbing. The sadness rekindled all the losses of my life and paralyzed my heart. Barbara just let me cry and held me as I broke down. Finally, the tears stopped and I sat in a daze.

"Are you sure you are ready to go? If you want to stay here for a while that would be fine. In fact, why don't you stay and have lunch with me?" Barbara saw how fragile I was. I accepted because I felt out-of-body and vulnerable to the world.

Two weeks later, the call came; Howard had passed, November 4, 1991, at home in his own bed.

After returning from San Francisco for the friends and community funeral, we drove to Los Alamos with the remainder of the ashes, and then prepared for the family funeral. Only the family was present, and Dad's good friend from the synagogue led the service. The cemetery looked out toward the beautiful Jemez Mountains, covered in snow and surrounded by ponderosa pines and canyons. A raven circled above our little group as the eulogy was spoken and we all wept.

The family spent two days together, leaning on each other for support. Dad had a softer presence and was humbled to the core. He and I had taken one of our walks along the canyon and stopped to look out over the beautiful vista of red mesas.

"I made a mistake moving out here. No Jewish community or relatives to help us raise you guys. I needed more support. Where else did I go wrong? Now, Howard is gone … and I couldn't help him …" Dad started crying again. This was something I would never get used to seeing in my eternally stoic father.

"Dad, you aren't responsible for the peer group Howard chose. You did everything you could, but when we become adults, there is little you can influence anymore. Dad, you did a fine job. Your pioneering spirit created independent children, strong minded. I love you Dad … and I want to thank you from the bottom of my heart for all you have done for me. I know I, too, have disappointed you, and believe me, I am paying for my mistakes. I want to make you proud of me again, Dad."

"I am proud of you, Cheney … you have gone through a lot, and I hope life gets easier for you." Again, Dad began to cry.

Once he had composed himself and the two of us walked in silence for a bit, I asked, "Dad, I have been struggling with some spiritual issues. You had a strict Jewish upbringing, yet you are a scientist … how do you view religion?"

He thought for a few minutes. "Everyone on this planet needs to believe in something. Faith is necessary to survive this crazy world. People need to have faith to endure, and religion provides that."

"But what if you don't have faith anymore?"

"Then you need to create it, do anything to get it back in your heart. It doesn't really matter where it comes from, faith just needs to be there. It will help you survive this life." Dad looked directly in my eyes, convincingly.

That made sense to me. I didn't believe there was a god anymore, not after all I had been through, and I was angry at it even if there was one. So, this concept of the necessity of faith struck a chord inside me and convinced me to start trying to create faith within. *My faith will be rooted in nature. I will just start pretending I feel it, then maybe I can fool myself into believing it until it's really present …* The conversation started to quell my angst and gave me hope.

"It's nice to talk to you this way, Dad; we've never done it before. Can we do more of it?"

"I'd love that, Cheney. You know how special you are to me?"

"Yes, Dad. I know now. You are also very special to me." The two of us hugged and we both felt better.

That night the family shared a quiet meal together and then sat by the fireplace, each lost in thought as the flames flickered with warmth.

Mom was preparing to say goodbye to me one more time. "I love you, darling, and I want you to find peace. Barbara and your art seem to be making a difference so continue, please." "Did I tell you one of the last things Howard said to me … 'Do your art'." We looked at each other with teary eyes and embraced.

I looked out into the clouds as the airplane headed to Austin. *Whew, I need to do art. Frida, I am ready to get this pain out of me. Guide me and give me strength. It was good to be around the family; we share the same burden of hurt. I wonder how Smokey is … I miss him.*

Chapter 38

Turning Point

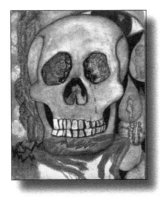

Death Unites

It makes me feel ill, just looking at this … it's about losing Howard and how we shared the common experience of meeting death. We hold hands in the eyes of death, acknowledging our bond. Howard is blue and black … his spirit only … Me, I'm crying blood tears for losing him and losing me. That's me at the bottom, almost in the jaws of death after my accident. Broken, ripped open, feeling dead, and hovering on a numb cloud. The broken body looks out toward the peaceful scenery of home in New Mexico … searching for a brighter day … the other side are my tears, losing my baby I could have had; I'm lost in this world like an infant, and broken. An eye overlooks it all, hiding behind death … her head blends into the mesas, which look like her hair … maybe trying to be grounded in the beauty of nature. Whew, I definitely feel dizzy and nauseous."

"Wow, Eli. This is amazing. We should start meeting twice a week. I think you need more support right now. You are becoming an amazing artist …"

I was trying to blink away the dizziness and white fog enveloping my mind; I just nodded before I closed my eyes to try and center myself.

"I want you to make sure you do safe drawings regularly now. If you need to contact me at any time, Eli, please do … anytime … okay?" Barbara saw something beginning to shift in me and knew losing Howard had thrown me back into a depression I had only just begun to lift out of.

"Okay, Barbara. I want this dizzy fog to lift permanently; I can't seem to get past it …"

"In your own time, Eli. Trust yourself, when you are ready it will happen. Your psyche protects you and will only give you what you can handle."

I sat on the porch after the session, contemplating life … and death. Suddenly, an image flashed through my mind and I went inside to get it down on paper. It was the moment of the bus wreck.

Moment of Impact

Gasp! Blackness, crunching, cracking, breaking of glass, bending of metal. Upside down landscape. Duck! Darkness. Pain. Crying, screaming, yelling, moaning, and groaning of people strewn all over. The smell of diesel. The bus driver stuck under the bus, then dead … paralyzed fear.

Frida, this is the first time I've remembered that moment of impact. It's time to examine the accident. I'm scared as hell, but I feel there is something waiting for me to find …

I knew I needed to do a safe drawing and took some time processing the last one. Dizziness and being nauseous was my constant companion throughout the day. I knew I was on the brink of something, but didn't know what. Grief consumed me, and I wanted to be alone most of the time and not have to expose my fragility to anyone.

Seeking Balance

I drew a Yin Yang to help center and create safety. The darkness held an all-knowing, protective wolf, and the light had a guardian angel watching over me, all securely rooted in nature and beauty.

My thoughts continually returned to Smokey. I missed him terribly but knew our paths were no longer parallel. Even if he did get clean, I knew how easy it was for him to backslide, and I didn't want to go there anymore. My struggle was to go forward and get healthy.

Paralyzed Grief

"It started out with the mixing of blue at the bottom of the page, and then the face emerged … that's my paralyzed grief and depression. It's at the root of everything, and it lurks hauntingly in my core. I hide it well though … the child lies on top of it all, naked, innocent, and unsure… looking out. The flowers are the bougainvillea of Mexico, beautifully surrounding and camouflaging the grief underneath and putting on a face of beauty to the world. Some are blue, related to the inner sadness and the others are pink, more related to heart … pain. And then a yellow aura surrounds them, keeping them protected from the world.

"New Mexico is in the distance … beauty, nature, the time when there was order in my life and the child looks out toward it wishing it was there. But again, the mesas are deep red and orange ... pain and the hurt of wanting something that is gone. The blue face really frightens me, it feels like it's killing me slowly, making my heart cold. Here I go again ... the dizziness and fog ..."

Barbara was getting accustomed to my reaction to the process and gave me time to get centered before we would discuss anything more. Once I was 'back' we discussed the grief, which led to tears and release, all of which helped my progress.

Every week I came in with a new drawing.

Death Has Her

"Barbara, it was crazy ... This drawing was *so* intense to do ... the blue from the last picture dove on to this week's piece ... see the blue woman diving? Then red flowed out of her arms, revealing the accident victim. I was in a pool of blood. I died, and those are flames of life leaving me from my opened belly ... and death appeared ... embracing me, surrounded in a tribute of red roses ... I died, Barbara ... I died ... blackness consumed me ... Then out of the darkness came flames, and then me, a sad angel rose out of the fire ... the flames of life, leaving the accident victim below turned into flowers, tulips, and from each tulip the souls of all the babies I might have had were released to the heavens ... Then from above, I watch and witness this with my dogs curled up and keeping me company and safe ... Whew, this one was the first time I met death. I died Barbara, I died ..."

"When you say 'I died,' who are you referring to, Eli?"

"Nancy. She's gone; she died in the accident. A new soul entered me then and became Eli."

"She's still there, Eli; we just have to connect to her."

"No, she's dead, Barbara. I know she's gone. I haven't felt her since I left Mexico. Nothing, *nada*. A new soul entered me. I have a new personality and feel completely different in my body ... in my body chemistry ... from all the transfusions, surgeries and drugs ... no she's gone ..."

"Well, let's give this time, Eli. I bet we can find her again."

I shook my head, not agreeing, but I had nothing more to say.

Once I got home, all I wanted to do was more art. Internal information was surging within me and it wanted out; it needed a voice through image. The process of mixing colors, creating textures, and feeling the soft oil pastels pull across the paper accessed a deeply hidden feeling. Words couldn't describe the complexity I felt, but playing with the colors did. I didn't know what would come out; it started with the colors and textures I craved. Then, through the process of blending and creating, the information presented itself, almost like a conduit to my unconscious. The image became my internal map, and once it was put on paper, I could see through the confusion and receive the message trapped within.

Once Barbara saw it, she understood me better. I began to not feel so alone. The process helped remove the fear from my soul, body, and mind and be less overwhelmed by the feelings. *Now, if I can just get through the dizziness and nausea.*

Runaway

"In this picture, I'm fleeing. I'm on a big black horse racing toward an image of my lost self. The person I'm seeking is only a mirrored reflection that will dissolve if reached. I'm galloping along a river of bluey grief and paralysis. Above me, the skeleton of death is surrounding and haunting me with jagged shock and fear. A windmill whips at my heels, slashing and pressing me forward. I turned the paper upside down to portray Mexico ... when my life went upside down ... the same horse and rider are skeletons ... Nancy died in Mexico but flees, clinging to Eli's shadow, and won't give me peace. Run, run, run ..."

"Eli, has anyone ever talked about death with you?" Barbara realized this might be why death had become so prominent in my drawings.

I hesitated and thought. "No, no one. It's almost as if it's a forbidden topic. Everyone is scared of it and just wants me to get on with life. Since the accident, my whole life has revolved around my having met death. It has changed my choices and entire perspective on how I see and live life. I know it's there at any moment, so all my actions come from a place where I am prepared to die.

"Thinking about the future is impossible, because what is the point? I may not make it there, so why create eggs in a basket that could break any time? I live for the here and now, but it's really hard in a world that requires thinking ahead ... I have absolutely no confidence in 'ahead.'

"I'm scared of dying, but at the same time, I know it well and will go with ease if the time comes ... I just don't want another accident full of surgeries, pain, infection, drugs ... pain and more pain ... let me die quickly and painlessly. Sometimes I feel I would welcome it just because I know how peaceful it will be ... much easier than struggling to survive ... but every single decision I make starts from my lessons about death and the fragility of mind, body and spirit.

"If I told everyone how I really feel, they would put me in a mental hospital. I mean, *no one* believes me when I say a new soul entered me when Nancy died. Actually, I don't even think you do ... but it happened. Maybe someone who has nearly died would understand me, but I haven't met anyone like that. I think we are all out there, hiding in our own confusion. There are so many mysteries of life and death, and often it's just easier to hold the thoughts to myself, knowing that only that end moment is when a person knows anything. Then again, the more I know ... the less I know ... see how confused I am?"

I retreated into the nauseous fogginess and was unable to proceed. It felt as if a core nerve had been hit. Every week a new drawing emerged.

"I wanted this to be a safe drawing because I've been pretty unsettled from the last one about death. It had its own agenda though. First the tree-like trunk opened into sort of an eruption. From the roots come my ancestors' souls passing through time and then released as my babies that I will never have, who then turn into angels in the heavens. The lost babies are like the limbs and leaves of the tree ... tree of life.

Ancestors and Angels

"The ancestors are surrounded in the burgundies, lavenders, and reds of love and loss ... I will never know them. Then the babies are encircled with blues of grief and depression and are white ... cold, empty, new, open and free.

"I sit on the base of the roots contemplating my tree of life, actually tree of loss. At my feet is an empty bag, open to being filled with ... something, I don't know what ... maybe answers to peace. Behind me a strong cheetah in fierce flames watches over me and protects me. So, I guess in the end it became a safe drawing. Then the other side is blurred ripples of unsettled confusion."

Today, All Day

"I sat outside by the river and sketched this in pencil. This is how I've felt every day since my accident. My eyes barely see out ... my brain is wiped clean like a slate ... missing. But somehow the rest of me functions like a regular, sort of, person. I call it *Today, All Day* because it describes my total existence ..."

"Another pencil drawing. For some reason the pencil made me feel more in control where things are black and white ... or gray, defined.

This is Elana."

"I've always felt there was a third persona I was waiting to become. It is the identity I would become when I found peace and serenity … my hoped-for persona. I call her Elana … a mix of Nancy and Eli. She is my gypsy spirit that survives eternally and is the real me.

"Her heart carries a baby that is a flower, breathing its soul into the world. Elana is the embodiment of intuition, beauty and art. The sun and moon show the way and watch over Elana within an ethereal atmosphere. Tears and texture fill her body and a shawl keeps her covered and protected. The hair is full and curled, with a scarf holding it, like an aura or halo of spirituality. Big, looped earrings of silver and a flower in her hair give her an expression of exotic depth. The eyes are soft and have seen things that make her humbled and knowing of life and death. She is at peace, maybe not happy, but at peace … This drawing gives me hope of something to become for my future. Definitely a safe drawing."

* * *

My life became a routine of work, art, and exercise. I swam in the cold waters of Barton Springs and walked along the river with my canine companions, Junior and Rosie. Occasionally, friends could entice me out for dinner or music, but mostly I wanted to be alone to protect my vulnerable art process. The loss of Howard and the loss of Smokey's love, the loss of babies … the memories hurt. Life hurt. But, I hid it well and, of my circle of friends, only Ann had a clue as to what was going on with my withdrawal from life.

One evening I was at home working on a new piece, lost in the creative process, when I heard Smokey's voice. Fear and joy filled my heart as I approached the door.

"Hey Eli! Damn, you look good!" Smokey had cut his dreads to a short afro and looked like the man I met in Oregon, but with a little weight on him.

"Smokey! Come in, how are you?" The last time I had seen him was well over nine months ago. My heart surged with love and caution. I knew I couldn't let my feelings take over and give him any inkling of hope for our relationship. It was over, and I did not want to go backward, no matter how much my heart yearned for his love. *I've worked so hard to heal and I'm too fragile. I can't handle anymore chaos in my life.*

"I can't stay long, but my group supervisor said I could contact you because I'm doing so well. Eli, you would really be proud of me. I actually want to stay in this program. I've been totally clean since I got out of the hospital and I'm learning my triggers that set off bad choices. I don't even go out and play music, other than an occasional gig for a wedding, but my supervisor goes with me. I want to stay clean … and guess what, I'm learning to read!"

"Wow! I am so proud of you, Smokey. I knew you could do it—that makes me so happy!" I drank in all he said.

"Eli, I want to be up front. I know I really messed up with us. I don't expect you to take me back. In fact, I want to get my act together, and I know it's going to take time. So, I know you can't wait for me, but I wanted to thank you for all you've done. You are the best thing that ever happened to me. Only because of you, I'm finally learning to stay on the right track. Unfortunately, I had to lose you as part of learning my lesson …"

I was astounded. I never expected him to say those things.

"I've learned so much, Eli." He told me about his group therapy, shared chores in the home, and a promotion at work. "I will always love you, Eli … tell me about you … how are the pooches?"

As happy as I was for Smokey, I felt a pang of anger, wishing the man he was becoming could be the one I could have. But, it was not to be.

I told him about Howard's passing and then showed him my artwork. Smokey was overcome with emotion as I shared the pictures with him.

"Eli, you have a gift … this art is amazing. Now, I understand you so much better. Tough stuff. I'm glad Barbara is there for you. Don't ever give up your art; it's your soul. Eli … I wish we could have made it together, girl …"

"Me too …" An awkward silence filled the space that used to vibrate with connection.

"Listen, would you like to see where I live? My group home supervisor, Tom, said I could bring you by."

I was hesitant because I knew my vulnerability would make me want to reconnect to him. "I would like to see it Smokey. I'm scared though, because we can't go back to what we had …"

"I know. I'm scared too. Maybe it's too soon."

"Maybe. Let me think about it, okay? Surely we can figure out how to stay friends, don't you think?"

"I don't know Eli. You are the woman I wanted to marry."

Reality was not fun. "Well, I would like to see where you live, your new life and friends. I can handle that."

Now Smokey hesitated. "I don't know Eli, maybe we should wait a while longer. I'm still really affected by you … I need to be stronger."

"Okay, that's fine Smokey. I'll talk to Barbara and you talk in your group, and let's see if there is a way for us to do this."

Smokey agreed, but we both were sad as we parted. We awkwardly hugged before he walked away with his familiar bouncing gait.

I plummeted into depression.

* * *

"I think it would be good to see his life, Eli. It would help with completion for both of you. He was yanked out of your life by his hospitalization, then went directly to the group home and was told he couldn't see you. Maybe he went on with life, but you were left abruptly. Take your time. You'll know when you are ready to see his life. Now, let's talk about you …" Barbara always knew what to do.

"I want to talk about the accident … my last thoughts." As I began to tell the story, from the moment I looked out the window of the bus, dizziness and fog encroached on my body. "I'm going into a white fog, Barbara …" I started to dry heave and almost fainted.

"Put your head between your knees, Eli … Can you hear me? ELI!" Barbara jumped up to keep me from falling off the couch and grabbed a towel for the heaving. "Eli! Eli!"

I entered into a deep white fog and felt suspended in time. I remained there, it seemed, for an eternity and heard nothing of Barbara's calling me. Ringing surged in my head and my stomach rolled over and over with heaves. Then the fog started to lift. It felt as if I was hovering over a body ... it was Nancy ... dead at the moment of impact at the accident. I gasped and reeled, seeing Nancy broken and dead ... and Nancy's spirit was angry, angry at me. Angry at Eli for running away and leaving Nancy neglected in this state for so long. Nancy needed comfort and to be put to rest.

I was trying to breathe when I finally heard in the far distance someone calling my name. I choked and tears burst forth. I felt as though I was hovering outside of my body and worked to return to be present. Barbara was talking, but I couldn't understand her. I lay back on the couch trying to regain composure and return from the white fog of numbness.

"I saw Nancy ... she was dead at the bus wreck. She was lying so limp and still ... so broken ... she's angry at me, Barbara. She's in a rage ... in a rage for me forgetting about her and leaving her desolate and broken ... I don't understand this. Nancy's spirit ... it must be her spirit left in limbo ... because she is dead ... I saw her ..." I was numb and overwhelmed.

Barbara didn't push the conversation and just let me ramble. Then I lay back on the couch and fell into a deep sleep. When I woke up, I was still very disoriented. I stayed for dinner with Barbara. We didn't talk about the event, but we both knew it was very significant.

"Are you sure you are okay to go home now?" Barbara was prepared to have me stay the night, if necessary.

"I think so. I just want to sleep. I have tomorrow off, so I'm going to just stay home. If I need you, I'll call. Maybe I can see you in a few days ... I'll let you know. Thanks, Barbara. Thanks for being here for me...."

"No problem, Eli. Call anytime, night or day. Come over if you want. You are always welcome."

I went home and stayed up most of the night, drawing. I needed to communicate with Nancy.

Nancy's Predicament

"This is how I found Nancy. She was bound and gagged over a bed of sad and angry flames. A black hand is trying to grasp her, but another hand, dripping blood, prevents it from getting her. She is surrounded by layers of hurt, loss, and numbness. Over her, death, disguised as a snake, hovers and is going to bite the hand, preventing the arm of darkness from getting Nancy. That's also Nancy hanging upside down in a void, powerless. On the other side, blood drips from the hand and becomes Eli's hair. Eli has her back turned away from Nancy and has her own tears of pain dripping from her eyes and down her back. The upper corner has the bougainvillea acting as a camouflage of protection.

"No wonder Nancy is so angry. She's being held prisoner in limbo. Eli has turned her back on her because she has her own pain to deal with. The only thing trying to get to her is a gripping blackness. Maybe it's a tunnel of darkness, which is the only access to her, but it's threatening. The arm and hand over Eli is trying to 'get a grip' on the darkness. Blood and pain drip from the fingers, drenching Eli … becoming her. I don't understand this. The arm is actually the viper of death."

"What would help Nancy, Eli?" Barbara was intrigued as she listened to me describe the picture.

I thought for a long time and then responded, "Love and care. She needs to be put to rest. I'm mad at her too, though. She's the one who was happy, had order in her life, and knew peace. My life has just been one trauma after another, and I'm angry and jealous of her."

"Eli, I think you need to work on resolving this relationship between Nancy and you. If you don't, peace will never be." I nodded and started to contemplate how to do it. Barbara led me through some dialogue between the two personas, which led to anger and tears, all of which helped get it out of my body and into the open to heal.

Making Amends   *Healing Home*

"I did another pencil drawing. Doing the detail and having total control over the lines helped to access the feelings and images. This is Eli, holding Nancy and caring about her as if she was her own child. The room and window portray a safe normal home environment to nurture love and care. It felt really good to do this, and it seems like the anger has dissipated. The other drawing shows a reconciliation of Nancy and Eli surrounded in a safe cozy home scene."

Rebirth

"This is a picture of celebration, of finding Nancy. The body in the middle is the accident victim who went through death, surgeries, pain, and physical loss but survived; the body carries a flower in the mouth of death. One leg is with Nancy and the other with Eli.

"Nancy is joyfully dancing, with sun and flowers, happy to be found. The baby crawling over the wall is escaping the darkness into a rebirth of freedom. The one blue flower has blue tears, because Nancy has lost her life, but lives rejoicing in spirit.

"Eli lives in blueness and it wraps her in a shawl of protection. She's turning to realize that Nancy has been found, and she looks toward the heart being given back to her from the arm of death and the accident. Eli still lives over fire—the hot seat—and from the red river of blood, a hand is reaching out to Eli, asking for help. I think it wants the heart to save it … to be cared about. Her flowers are black and of death, but there is hope."

The next few weeks were spent trying to blend the two personas through art.

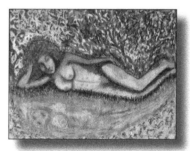
Reflection

Flow and Release

"In the first drawing, Nancy is above, looking at Eli's reflection below. Nancy is more 'real' looking and defined, just as her history is clear and known. Eli is more ethereal and abstract. Her colors portray more hurt and depression, whereas Nancy is more confident and sure, with more intense patterns and colors. For some reason, I really like this one. It feels as though the two have accepted each other as they are and have released the rage at one another.

"In the second one, I needed to draw myself as I exist now, without Nancy. I sit in a roiling wave of blue, trying to feel the flow of it. Eli is blue, literally and philosophically. She still has a lot to deal with, but she is more peaceful and looking out at the washing waters, wondering what is next. The two dancing African women represent Nancy, who has been released to the heavens to dance in joy and spiritual reconciliation. This drawing feels very releasing and peaceful."

* * *

Even though an element of peace was felt between the Nancy/Eli relationships, the focus now was just on me. The next layer of depression and fear started rising to the surface for me to examine. This layer, more than any of the others, was more overwhelming and frightening to look at. *Frida, help me through the next piece of terror I feel. I know loss is paramount....*

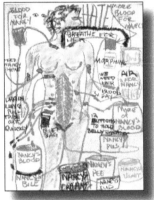

Poor Me

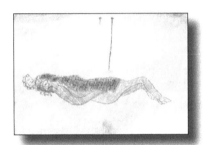

Pins and Needles

"I've needed to depict what I went through in the hospital. This shows every single tube, incision, infection, and surgery. Frida taught me that it's okay to show the pain, so here it is in graphic reality. I feel like I need to be truthful with what my body survived. It's at the root of my pain and shock.

The other picture shows how I felt most of the time, on a bed of needles poking through me. I was a human pin cushion. The skull is open exposing my green brain matter ... my lost mind. My face and torso are a mass of flesh, infection, and needles. UGH! I want it all to go away and disappear forever ..."

"Eli, all these years you have been trying to do just that and it hasn't worked. Your experience is something to be proud of surviving, Eli. Instead of running from it and wanting it to be different, your pain needs validation for all you've been through. Love it, respect it, own it. It is you and always will be. Don't turn from it, but embrace it as your true self. Only then will you be able to go forward."

I felt a shift upon hearing Barbara's statement. It was clear and powerful, similar to the day with the internist years ago when I decided 'to try.'

"I like that, Barbara. I've needed validation for so long and now I see, instead of running from the pain, I need to embrace and nurture it—it craves that validation. It is me and I've been such a warrior of survival, but I have never gotten that acknowledgement. I should be praising myself for all I've been through instead of feeling humiliated and embarrassed. I've touched a core wound and now know how to heal it. Thank you, Barbara, you are so intuitive and smart."

Once I realized the importance of giving a voice to my pain, images related to the hysterectomy consumed my creative expressions. This loss of female identity, babies, and motherhood were deeper than the other wounds. Those had physically healed and didn't carry the same emotional scarring as did the hysterectomy.

The Birth of Death

"Frida's permission to portray pain is the only way I could have done this drawing. It's even hard for me to look at, but this is what I feel. I've been carrying around a dead skeleton baby in my open and bloodied belly … I lie in a pool of blood, hiding from the hurt, humiliation and grief. I must release the baby … it's dead and harbors only death. The only way out for the baby skeleton is out the original wounds. I'm alone in nature, as the natives did, to birth the dead. A strong fierce cougar protects me while I am in this fragile state. So much sadness and loss …" I fought the fog as I shared with Barbara.

"Do you need to stop?"

"Not this time, Barbara … I need to talk and root this out. I feel so bad for her, Barbara … she's so alone with the loss …"

"Do you feel like drawing?"

"Sure."

Hurt and Lost

"That's me. My incision has closed and now I live with the rawness of the lost baby. I like these drawings, even if they are incredibly hard to do and show … they are the truth and validation I've needed, in order to face 'my' reality."

"Eli, these drawings help me to understand, too. The words can only go so far, but your images help me see the intensity and depth of your experience. Maybe that will help you to not feel so alone."

"I agree. I don't have to continue to try and explain something that has no words. Do these drawings bother you? I'm always worried others will freak out to see them, and then pull away from me at a time when I especially need understanding."

"I have no trouble viewing them. I do think some people will have issues when they see them, but it will be up to you, who to allow to see them. Once you get stronger, I don't think you will care as much, but until then, only show them to people you trust with the information."

I felt better having Barbara see and accept these hidden 'uglies.' It helped bring the therapy relationship closer. *I like being able to view my pain … it gets it outside of my body … it actually takes some of the energy with it so the intensity lessens but still confirms its existence.*

"I always get triggered by others who get to have children and lead normal lives. This picture depicts how I feel, fenced off in blackness with only myself and my dogs to have and to hold. Others can access the golden window of life, get children and head off toward their families' destiny. It hurts … and makes me feel so alone …"

"Many don't have children, Eli, and they still have productive lives." Barbara was trying to console me.

"I think the way it happened to me is the difference. I really wanted children and a family, and then suddenly it was taken, without my choice, knowledge or permission … only leaving scars, pain, and a loss of identity. This one I'm just going to have to learn to live with. I know perhaps I can adopt, but that's not related to the feelings of powerlessness and pain from having that possible destiny ripped away. People who have children always say to me, 'you're lucky because children can be so much trouble.' There is no way this can be lucky for me. Since childhood, I knew I wanted to be a mom and cherish that bond of love and the legacy of having a child … your own flesh and blood child, someone who loves you no matter what. Children give you purpose to live. For me, it just emphasizes my lack of continuity in life and makes it all feel so futile."

Fenced Out

"Eli, when one door closes, another opens. You have a different path now, which also has its gifts. Once you heal, those gifts will surface. Love yourself, Eli, don't hate yourself, or all you have been through won't be given the blessings you deserve."

I understood, but questioned whether I could be successful or not.

As I 'drew' out the core of pain, fear, and loss, a deep peace started emerging slowly.

Getting A Grip

"*Getting a Grip* is a reconciliation drawing. In the middle is Elana, the one I hope to be some day. On the left is Nancy, who died in the accident. The accident victim has a white lily in her mouth, representing the wish for peace and forgiveness, and it is surrounded in blue loss. On the right is Eli, somber, while a hand holds her face, as if it is trying to 'get a grip' on Eli and who she is. Darkness still touches Eli. This is definitely identity work, bringing together the disassociated personas. Each wears a red hat like shield on her head … they all know pain and hurt.

"Above them, a green fence separates and protects the unconscious process. Eli lies above, witnessing it all, curled up watching the beautiful bird carry the heart toward the personas below. She still has a huge hole where her heart should be and looks toward the heart, hoping she can have one someday. A circling whirl portrays a tunnel of confusion that still exists and threatens harmony. Over her, a quilt of colors keeps her comforted."

Reconcile

"This is another reconciliation drawing. Eli sits in the middle with me, myself, and I in her embrace. One is Eli, tired, lost and needing rest. The middle one is a baby, the one I can't have. And the last one is Nancy who is sad because she died. To the left is Father Time, taking away the dead Nancy to the place where all the released souls live. A strong horse ushers them to the other world. On the right, at the bottom, is my family, watching and witnessing. They are surrounded with pain and hurt, but together. The upper right shows growth of leaves and trees, which shade and provide life amidst the blue paralyzed depression, a sign of hope."

Chapter 39

The Next Door Opens

I was starting to feel again. Maybe the feelings were difficult, but they were not so numb. I began feeling more connected to the world. Doing the physical art process forced the disassociated parts to connect in the tangible world through materials and image. This process provided a sense of connection to my physical world, where I could see what was within and feel a sense of belonging. The art process became a sort of planning tool for me, to reconstruct and reinvent my life and who I wanted to be.

"Barbara, now that I've gotten to my core and have identified all the complications of pain and feelings, I'm more in control. It's as if a veil of fog has been lifting and I can finally see! Learning to give respect to my pain instead of running from it has changed my life course. I used to live in a hazy bubble, trying to connect and feel the world ... even trees, the air, flowers ... everything felt as though it was inaccessible and far away. Now, I'm in sync within and present in the moment. Relief and joy were once elusive, but now I experience it daily. I still fear it will disappear, but I have more confidence it won't. I've learned the power of the creative process to help identify, express, clarify, redress, reconcile and redefine myself."

"Eli, I am so proud of your progress. Not only has it been incredible to witness your process, but the artist you have become ... from scribbles to works of art! Would you be interested in sharing your story and pictures at a conference?" Barbara had finished her Master's in Art Therapy and had been asked to present at an annual psychology conference. Early in therapy, she had gotten permission from me to be part of her dissertation thesis; now she was excited to share it with her colleagues.

"Me?" I was in disbelief at the idea. "They all know so much more than I do …"

"Maybe in theory, but not from the perspective of a client. I think it would open the minds of many in this field to witness the process you went through. Your art is inspiring and could provide education in a very different format. I will honor your decision, but I think you are ready and definitely an expert in this awakening process."

After some convincing, I agreed to do it. The traditional approach of using only words had never worked well for me, and I wanted to give hope to others who struggled. I knew my story would help counselors understand the important healing tool that the creative process could provide their clients. It would also be a completion piece for me, after the five years I had worked with Barbara in putting my life back together and becoming a more functional person in society.

* * *

The lights dimmed in the auditorium filled with 200 psychology professionals. Barbara had completed the first half of her presentation. "Now I am proud to introduce Eli Weintraub, the inspiration for my master's thesis. Eli has been through a transformation these last five years. Her courage and perseverance has been incredible to witness, along with the art and artist she has become. Please sit back and celebrate with me as Eli shares some of her art and poetry."

Everyone watched me shyly approach the podium.

"Hi, everyone." I softly giggled, trying to control my anxiety. "I want to thank Barbara first and foremost. Her unconditional acceptance, warmth and intellect have helped me become whole again, after ten years of being lost. The other influence in this process was from Frida Kahlo whose example gave me permission to paint out the pain and turn it into beauty. The introduction of the arts as part of therapy was the game changer for me. All the years I've tried to use words to work my way back from the bottom; it was the creative process using color, texture and expression that finally touched my very numb and paralyzed soul. It became a map of my internal world to follow, explore, and reveal the lost and blocked emotions that kept me isolated and lost. They say a picture says a thousand words, and I am proof of that truth. Please sit back and witness my process of healing ..."

I started the slide show and narrated each image with poetry. Occasionally, the oohs and ahs from the audience punctuated the emotionally laden presentation. Several times I choked up at particularly powerful images, but was able to continue to the end.

Everyone gave me a standing ovation. Covered from head to toe with goose bumps, I took a bow and returned to my seat. Afterward, many came up and thanked me for the show and wished me the best of luck. Many said they would start learning about using art in their practices; they now understood the incredible tool they had at their disposal. They also encouraged me to continue sharing this process to help other lost souls.

I was elated and astonished at how well it went and was even happier that I remained 'in body' the whole time. Something shifted immediately after presenting, and I knew it was time to return to New Mexico, to be near family and go back to school for my Master's, hopefully in the Art Therapy Program at the University of New Mexico.

* * *

"Barbara, will you come visit me in New Mexico?"

"I would love to, Eli. Please keep in touch and if ever you need help, I'm a phone call away. Remember your art is a priority for you; it will help you when things get overwhelming. I love you, Eli. Take care, gypsy sister!"

We hugged, gave each other a heartfelt gaze, and I turned toward the next chapter of life.

One final step I needed to take before leaving Austin was to see Smokey.

"Well, babe, I wish you the best. I'll be here in Austin, probably living at this group home. One day I want to return to Oregon, but I need to make sure I have a job and can keep an apartment, and I'm not quite there yet. I will always love you. You saved my life, Eli. Really ... can I call?"

"Sure—once I get settled, I'll contact you. You did a lot for me too, Smokey. You understood and felt the depth of my pain, which helped me heal some of my brokenness and reconnect to my heart. Our love is very deep and special. I wish we could have figured it out, but our paths diverge here, Smokey. Peace be with you."

I leaned over, gave him a kiss and we parted ways. The pain and the hole were still there, but it didn't consume me the way it used to. Now, an excitement for the future took its place.

* * *

The little blue truck was loaded with only the most important things in my life, such as my art table and batik supplies. Rosie and Junior jumped into the truck bed, confused to see all the 'stuff' they had to share their space with, but they found their pillows and settled in before the topper was closed, securing them inside.

I turned to look at my apartment one last time and said a silent prayer for good things to come. *I'll take a long route home and begin to prepare to really live my life now … whole. Here I come, family!*

I started the truck and saw Austin recede in the mirror as I moved toward my future with Barbara, Frida, and my gypsy spirit guiding me.

Happy at last! Preparing to leave Austin with Rosie and Junior

Epilogue

I left Austin and moved to Albuquerque with hopes of joining the Art Therapy Program at the University of New Mexico but, much to my disappointment, learned the program was to be discontinued. Instead, I pursued my Master's degree and blended my interest in the arts with health. I met my future husband in this program and married at the end of my studies.

After graduating, I worked for UNM's Employee Health Promotion Program and successfully initiated the first Art for Health class for staff, an open art studio designed to reduce stress. At the same time, I worked as an artist in the Arts in Medicine Program at UNM's trauma hospital with nurses, therapists, and doctors to help support caretakers with the arts, music, and massage. After two years I became a manager in this program and helped the program grow in popularity.

Throughout my studies and work, I was my mother's and father's primary in-home caregiver for over 15 years; I was blessed to be able to witness a peaceful passing for both and to heal all past hurts.

I am now committed to sowing the seeds to inspire arts involvement of all styles as a therapeutic practice in our daily lives. It was a lifetime goal to write *Frida and Me* to encourage the use of art for healing trauma.

Having been raised in the mountains and mesas of New Mexico, Eli loves nature, its beauty and tranquility. She loves animals and is usually found walking on the beach or in the mountains with her dog, exploring all forms of life. She makes a delicious green chili stew with just the right amount of 'hot' and always has an art project in the making. Eli is committed to inspiring arts involvement of all styles as a therapeutic practice. She and her husband live in New Mexico and in Mexico.

Working professionally as Eli Weintraub Maurx, she can be contacted through her website at eliweintraubmaurx.com